HEALER OF HEARTS, HEALER OF MINDS

by

LAWRENCE F. CAREW

COMMUNITY OF THE CROSS PUBLICATIONS
13 EIGHTH AVENUE
DANBURY, CONNECTICUT 06810
(203) 748-4972

LIBRARY OF CONGRESS CATALOG CARD NUMBER 88-70965

INTERNATIONAL STANDARD BOOK NUMBER 0-943773-00-8

ACKNOWLEDGMENTS

The author is grateful for permission to quote from the following translations of the Sacred Scriptures:

The Revised Standard Version of the Bible, Copyrighted 1946, 1952, © 1971, 1973. (RSV)

HOLY BIBLE New International Version, Copyright ©, New York International Bible Society, 1978. Used by permission. (NIV)

Today's English Version Bible — Old Testament: © American Bible Society 1976, Deuterocanonicals/Apocrypha: © American Bible Society 1979, New Testament: © American Bible Society 1966, 1971, 1976. Used by permission. (TEV)

Special thanks for typing and word processing assistance to: Leona Tonchen, Carol Duncan, Clair Meyer, Patricia Behan, Karen Beck, Jill Kessler, Connie Kocot, Cliff Natoli, Brian Spaulding and Stephen Tonchen.

COVER PHOTOGRAPH: GLENN W. JOHNSON

COVER DESIGN: VINCENT ALBANO

This book is dedicated to those who made
it possible, especially my brothers and
sisters in the Community of the Cross.

TABLE OF CONTENTS

Introduction

Two basic convictions have inspired and guided the writing of this book. The first is a belief in the reality of what is called "inner healing." The other is a commitment to search out that healing which is able to occur when authentic wisdoms derived from Judeo-Christian spirituality and authentic wisdoms rooted in secular psychology, psychotherapy, or psychiatry are allowed to dialogue with each other, complement each other and even interpenetrate each other in the service of alleviating human hurt.

My cards are on the table, then. I believe in that inner healing which primarily comes through the agency of the prayer of faith. I likewise believe in that new wholeness which is able to be appropriated by individuals who take to heart the insights, self-realizations and interpersonal encounters made available through a counseling process unafraid to acknowledge or encounter human nature's spiritual dimension. This book has been written in hopes of exploring how both avenues of healing might be better brought together and better brought to bear upon those frustrations or nagging obstacles we all encounter as we fail now and again, or more often than not, in our attempts to be at one with ourselves, each other and even the God who loves us.

Perhaps, a brief autobiographical note on the author's part might not be inappropriate here. After five years' service in the Roman Catholic priesthood, I became involved in the Charismatic Renewal Movement in 1971. A conversion experience, entered into at that time, brought me into not only a far more personal relationship with Christ, but the gift of a far more whole-hearted devotion to the cause of His kingdom, as well. In time, I also discovered that this decision to place Jesus at the center of my heart and life had also been the occasion of profound changes occurring within my personality. Many of these changes could be characterized as new personality strengths. Others could best be described as the removal of pathological weaknesses. There was (and is now) no doubt in my mind that I'd come into deep inner healings not only of spirit but of attitudes and emotions, as well.

It also wasn't very long before I found myself involved in the founding of a Charismatic prayer group and Bible study, conceived as an outreach ministry to teenagers alienated from the ordinary avenues of involvement with the traditional churches. None of us knew, at that time, that we were really engaged in the laying of the foundation of what would eventually develop into an ecumenical Christian Community, known as The Community of the Cross.

The miracle of a true community of mutual commitment and brotherly-sisterly love in Christ, however, can only come about and be maintained if a lot of mental and emotional poison is drained from the human personality; only if that tendency towards a persistently selfish willfulness, so second nature to us, is radically reversed in the direction of caring compassionately about others. And so, most providentially, we soon found ourselves supplied with what could be called a crash-course on inner healing. God's Spirit, we believe, in His own mysterious ways unfolded to us one insight after another embedded in His inspired Word. We discovered that we'd been given intuitions, sometimes absorbed privately, sometimes ministered interpersonally, which actually allowed people to enter into real and deep and permanent healings of somewhat serious and even extremely serious personality impairments or character defects.

For a long time, it seemed to us that the only psychology we'd ever need was to be found in the Bible. It wasn't simply because the Scriptures were coming to be appreciated as a veritable goldmine of insights into how to gain greater self-understanding or how to unmess the mess of mind out of touch with the heart or the mess of both out of touch with God, either. We'd come to test every one of these perspectives on personality and found that they were valid. When people really wanted healings and sincerely prayed for them, they got them. Sometimes, slowly and somewhat painfully. Sometimes, suddenly and with relatively little awareness of discomfort. Sometimes, primarily as a result of lifting a hurt that one was aware of to God, privately, in prayer. Sometimes, as a result of having first been confronted by a brother and sister about a difficulty we hadn't wanted to own up to and then having consented to pray with them for the wholeness we knew we lacked.

Browsing occasionally through a local Christian bookstore led to my horizons eventually being broadened. On its shelves, you could find not only books which claimed that confronting un-Biblical behavior was the only valid and potentially successful therapy, but authors who felt free to take a considerably different position. God gave us the Bible, they argued, to apprise us most particularly of those things that we could never fully know, or would never come to realize, without His direct intervention. But He also gave us inquiring minds that longed to know more, and hearts that were able to hurt over other people's hurts. That combination of human curiosity and human empathy, (especially when brought into alignment with the Divine burden for the undoing of such human hurt) could lead to the uncovering of cures of bodily diseases hitherto thought incurable, not to mention the discovery of causes and remedies of mental or emotional ailments.

Writers in this second category were clearly not at all ignorant of the sometimes atheistic presuppositions of certain therapies, not to mention some psychotherapists' frequent tendencies to reduce the personality to its purely mental/emotional or physical dimensions; or the occasional attempts of some psychologists to equate our behavior with little more than mechanistic reactions to worldly stimuli. Nonetheless, these Christian psychologists, etc., still argued for a therapeutic approach which would integrate authentic spiritual principles with valid contributions from the world of secular psychotherapy.

Reading books that espoused such a position came as a real eye-opener to me. This was something rarely spoken of in Catholic intellectual circles, even ten years ago. Realizing that not all of the psychotherapeutic world was anti-religious in sentiment, we had generally arrived at the stage of acceptance which Bernard Tyrrell calls "the separate specialization approach."[1] This view sees the role of the secular psychotherapist or counselor as strictly specializing in the healing of mental or emotional illness, and role of the clergyman

7

as strictly focusing upon spiritual or moral problems. We priests, for instance, might be happy to occasionally confer with a psychiatrist, say, over a common client we both were attempting to assist, although at a different time and in a different place. We'd be talking about how to help such an individual who was simultaneously experiencing problems in his or her spiritual and psychological "compartments" — problems which *really* couldn't overlap since the compartments were allegedly air-tight. We obviously hadn't allowed ourselves to wonder where spirit ended and soul began; or where soul ended and body began. Even if we supposed that they somehow interpenetrated each other, these essential dimensions of human personality, certainly the problems of one sector couldn't extend into another. Or, if so, then only psycho-somatically, with sickness of the psyche disturbing one's physical well-being. We weren't about to take such thinking back, one step further.

Now, at long last, we in the Catholic tradition are beginning to catch up with some of our more adventuresome Protestant colleagues. Words like "Psychotheology" or "Christotherapy" and expressions such as "the spiritual-psychological synthetic approach" or "the Christian Love Treatment" are now becoming part of our vocabulary. The integration of these two spheres of therapeutic concern is now being insisted upon and defended, even as models of such integration are concretely being presented by Catholic scholars. Theoretical justifications of this position from a Catholic point of view are becoming increasingly numerous.[2]

This brings us to the place of *Healer of Hearts, Healer of Minds*. As already seen, this writer endorses the "integrationist" approach just described and will attempt to show how it may be complemented by that inner healing that is appropriated directly through prayer.

Inner healing seemed, at first, to be almost synonymous with "healing of memories". Lately, it has occurred to many that inner healing is a lot more than that. A glance at the chapter headings of this book will provide the reader with some immediate indication of how much wider, in our belief, this exciting concept is able to be extended.

The Bible, as Abraham Heschel never seemed to tire of repeating, is not primarily a book about God from man's perspective; it is a book about man from God's perspective.[3] It has long been treasured as an unparalleled source of wisdom.

From the Scriptural point of view, wisdom is more than correct knowledge, more than common sense; it is a knowing about the right way to live; a sorting out of what brings life from what only seems to; a grasping on to what makes for true humanness and a rejection of what only counterfeits it.

There are two seemingly contradictory wisdoms which confront us when we search the Scriptures. One is the wisdom of how disoriented we are when we don't know whom we are meant to be in God and fail to choose that. Bluntly, it is the wisdom that tells us how deluded we are when we try to live and plan and act in indifferent resistance to His presence and His call; how capable of entering into what is stupid, what is evil, and therefore deathly, when we don't want the life which comes from His Fathering, Brothering, or En-Spiriting. The second is the wisdom of how high we can soar and how great we can become when we accept His love, enter into our sonship and daughterhood and allow Him to empower us to cast off self-centeredness and self-sufficiency. The wisdom of living life, here and now, to the full, as Jesus envisioned it and promised to help us realize.

It is only by keeping these two wisdoms side by side that we are able to maintain true balance. The Savior from Sin is also the Bringer of Life More Abundant. As Walter Brueggeman has beautifully expressed it, we are called not only to confess Christ as true God whom we serve but as true man whose humanity we are now invited to share in and make visible.[4] Each day, by grace, we are enabled to live more closely to the way He lived. If so, then we are likewise empowered to enter into the wound-healing, relationship-building, injustice-undoing, community-creating humanity that He gave such perfect evidence of.

To put it simply and pointedly, much of this book focuses on the woundedness of human nature and our need (graced with the courage, hope and assurance of the gentle-hearted Christ) to fully face up to that. If only the final portion of these somewhat extensive considerations predominantly focuses upon what we are saved for or healed for, that doesn't mean that we mean to fall once again into Christianity's repeated tendency to so emphasize our proneness to the destructive and the animalistic that our potential for the creative and the holy is all but passed over.

Hopefully, I have been healed a bit of male chauvinism by attempting, as best I could, to enter into the new discipline (for me) of inclusive language. Without getting mathematical about it, I ordinarily attempted to address that challenge by alternating my use of the personal and possessive pronouns, rather than resorting to the more cumbersome "his and her," etc.

What a master therapist He was, Jesus of Nazareth. Who has been able to match His ability, as J. B. Phillips has suggested, to appeal to the true self in every person He met, so many of whom were so covered and defended by masks and poses?[5] In His resurrection, He was seen as One who could pass through walls and walk through bolted doors. He'd always been doing it, of course, penetrating the walls barricading closed minds and the doors sealing off wounded hearts. It was precisely because He persistently exuded such affectionate warmth and such knowing compassion in His personal bearing that those He touched physically were also touched spiritually; that those whom He stirred emotionally and psychologically were so often quickened with that love which called them into wholeness at the center of who they were. May you who read these pages come to see that He's still here; that He's still the Healer of hearts; that He's still the Healer of minds.

Chapter 1

The Diagnosis

What's wrong with us? Or, better yet, what's most wrong with us? Some of us think we know: especially those of us who have finally decided that the taking of a personality inventory could no longer be postponed if we were ever to get free of whatever it was that was hanging us up. That certainly could lead to our "hang-up" being identified and dealt with, or, at least, to the beginning of dealing with it. Others of us simply may have accepted as axiom that everybody must be "hung up" somewhere and "That's Life," and there is no point in poking around underneath the surface or in the past – coping is living.

The good news about what is wrong with us is that we, even the most ruthlessly self-analytical of us, are probably wrong if we think we know. The good news is that it is not what we would be inclined to suspect. It is something else. The good news begins with the bad news God sees fit to announce to us: that our hang-up is a spiritual problem before it is an emotional or psychological one; that it is a trauma suffered not just in our childhood, but in mankind's childhood; that we are not responsible for having sustained the wound, or for having caught the disease.

This good news then becomes even better news. He who sees fit to diagnose sees fit to heal, if only we would accept His diagnosis and submit to His therapy. Sometimes, however, sin prevents us from hearing this good news. Catechism answers, exacted under fear of parents' or pastor's discipline; theological jargon, and the hair-splitting distinctions that too often accompany it; the scholarly sophistication of biblical experts who sometimes distract us from the most elementary revelation of all – these or similar circumstances may have educated us into ignorance. This is one side of the sin of sophistication; namely,

11

we may not realize that the Divine Author and the human authors fully intended that the basic thrust of their writings (now called Sacred Scripture) be, essentially, understood by anyone gifted with simple speech and simple faith.

Yet, *we* have compounded the problem. Another side of the sin of sophistication is that many of us would rather go on parading the facade of one who carries with him or her that wisdom and knowledge so carefully culled from the schools of life and living. We cannot be on a perpetual quest for truth, if truth is ever able to be found, however.

Original Sin can be seen as a doctrine, a biblical theme, an article of a creed, or even a quaint mythological antique. It can also be seen as what God wants to tell me about what is wrong, most wrong, with me. It is a revelation which we were meant to appreciate personally and reflect upon privately. This is especially true at those moments when we feel most aware that there is something radically wrong, either with the way we find ourselves responding to life, or with whatever we have made of ourselves up to this moment.

We are indebted to the Protestant evangelical tradition for prophetically reminding the rest of us that there is such a thing as the *assurance* of salvation. After all, faith does bring with it a mysterious evidence of things unseen and allows us to taste the substance of things hoped for (Heb. 11:1). To experience the need of a savior to "bail me out" of this or that tragic mess of my own making, however is not necessarily to move into full admission that I need Him just as much when disaster had not struck. Somehow, grace can hit home to us how very much we are in need of Him beyond all the trials and stresses of life. We can even know that He saves us from nothingness, and know it from the gut.

God's inspired word shows us what is wrong with us, in the deepest "part" the most important dimension of who we are. It is so right to look at *that* first. Already, of course, we may be inclined towards impatience and annoyance: "I picked up this book in the hopes of finding a solution to this hurt or that heartache. Do I really need to be subjected to another discussion about Original Sin?"

FRANCISCAN PUBLISHERS
Pulaski, Wisconsin 54162

...CY

...osary beads

...ary — Creed

...offer You the
...ul and Divinity
...ved Son and our
...st in atonement
...d the sins of the

...s:

...ne sorrowful passion
...w mercy unto us and
...orld." (10 times)

...God, Holy Omnipotent,
...mortal, have mercy on
...mes)

...h Ecclesiastical Approbation

"O Blood and Water, which hath gushed forth from the Heart of Jesus as a font of Mercy for us, I trust in Thee."

"The rays on the picture represent the blood and water which gushed fo— from the depth of My Mercy whe— agonizing Heart was opened on t'— The pale rays symbolize the v— justifies the soul; and the red— sent the blood, which is the li— soul. These rays shield the soul the wrath of My Father. Fortunate — who lives in their brilliance, for — just hand of God will never reach him.— — Words of our Lord to Sister Faustina

PRAYER

Most compassionate God, Father of Mercy and Lord of all consolation, who dost not wish the damnation of him who believes and trusts in Thee; look down upon us, we beseech Thee, according to the multitude of Thy mercies and increase Thy Mercy, that even in the greatest trials of this life we may always faithfully comply with Thy will, which is Mercy itself. Through Thy Son and our Lord Jesus Christ, who liveth and reigneth with Thee for ever and ever. Amen.

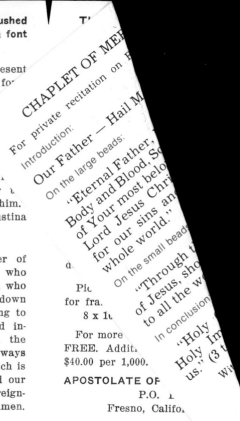

CHAPLET OF ME—

For private recitation on R—

Introduction:

Our Father — Hail M—

On the large beads:

"Eternal Father, Body and Blood, S— of Your most belo— Lord Jesus Chri— for our sins an— whole world."

On the small bead—

"Through t— of Jesus, sho— to all the w—

In conclusio—

"Holy Im— Holy Im— us." (3 t—

Pic— for fra.

8 x 1—

For more FREE. Addit— $40.00 per 1,000.

APOSTOLATE OF

P.O. —

Fresno, Califo—

Yet, that hurt, heartache, hang-up, or whatever — as much as it is truly rooted in a real circumstance which really happened to the real you in *this* life — happened to a person already wounded. That prior wound, in effect, doubles the stress caused by the secondary wound; it magnifies the painfulness far beyond what it would be if the original pain were not also there. That is why, if we deal with the deeper difficulty *first*, no matter how much another part of us may be clamoring for immediate attention, then that other part will experience speedy and significant relief even before it is faced up to and dealt with directly. Not only that, but as the pain of the secondary hurt also subsides, all those fears about its incurableness, all those anxieties about its having to remain a permanent fixture of our personality will begin to recede and we will start to breathe the fresh air of a new hope for a new us.

So it is right to begin in Eden; to go back with the eyes of faith to the Garden; to take another look at the doings of Adam and Eve, the Man and the Woman, to see whether or not we, while examining their plight, might simultaneously be confronting our own.

The Garden story is rich with symbolism. To say that any statement is symbolic, however, is not necessarily to say that it is only symbolic. Many realities can be both literally true and extremely symbolic at the same time. Symbolism, can even convey a literal truth more "literally" than a flat, declarative sentence.

One of the most exquisitely symbolic statements of this section of Genesis is the creation of Eve out of Adam's rib cage. It is a clear declaration that man and woman are to enjoy a reuniting. The rib is to return, but not as a rib. That special magnetism existing between the sexes, that urge to come together into a new and different kind of permanence is simply and symbolically stated to be of God, to be part of His deliberate and loving intent for mankind.

Another thing we see about ourselves in that simple story, not nearly as simplistic as we might suspect, is that the Man and the Woman were (or, we could say, the human personality was) originally created to know the presence of God instinctively. [1] The narrative, of course, is extremely compact, and we

13

have to let the Spirit show us what is between the lines as well as in the lines.

Envision the image of heartbroken God looking for the couple immediately after the Fall, for instance. The time is described as the "cool of the evening," as if in happier times Adam, Eve, and their Friend, God, strolled together through the Garden at that lovely hour, enjoying each other's company with light banter taking its place naturally beside romantic whisperings. Tonight, they are not at the trysting place and their Friend wonders why, and fears the worst.

One of the most surprising things about this section of Scripture, which describes the very first communications between Creator and creature (especially when we compare it with subsequent and similar encounters in the Old Testament), is that God does not reveal Himself *through* anything. He is just there. Elsewhere, we will witness God revealing Himself to humankind, or manifesting His presence through what are called "theophanies," such as a mysterious bush that keeps on burning, a massive pillar of fire or cloud, a roaring wind, or some kind of half-human, half-angelic apparition. In *Genesis* 2-3, however, He does not need to appeal to the couple through their senses as He will seem to be required to do later.

Spiritual realities are not easily perceived by most of us. The human personality, as we now know it, is not inclined towards the experience of the Divine Presence with anything even close to what we would call "ease." Many, if not most, people have great difficulty in communicating with God, even to the extent of wondering, occasionally, whether He actually exists or not. Humankind can certainly be considered to be "religious" from the viewpoint of social science (Millions of humans see fit to involve themselves in some form of religious activity.), but that is not at all to assert that those same people are able to say: "We just don't *believe in God*, we experience Him as a present reality."

So, Adam and Eve have sinned and they are hiding in the underbrush and they hear God calling for them. For the very first time, they are *afraid* of *Him*, and for the very first time, they feel naked. An uncomfortableness with Him is now humanity's experience of God's presence. That uncomfortableness is new.

Fear is now lurking somewhere in the depths of the human personality as it seeks to relate itself to the Divine. The couple jointly experiences a brand new awareness — a sense of nakedness. Even though they might be inclined to describe it as a strange feeling of embarrassment about not having clothes covering their bodies, we are certainly entitled to wonder if this nakedness might not symbolize something more than that. All in all, we are not overstating the case by saying that a radical change has occurred within the human personality.

One of the least debated assertions of modern psychologists is that love is a major source of personality strength: "I feel better about myself because you see fit to show me that you feel good about me... I feel more secure because of your interest in, attention towards, and affection for me." Children, for example, are more secure from the very beginning if they are held and embraced. They become increasingly insecure to the extent that the touch of love is denied. Babies who are fed, sheltered, but unheld will develop a physical disease which can lead to death, experts tell us.

Children, however, are not the only people in need of such affirming. Adolescents and adults continue to be its beneficiaries. When we develop to the stage when we are ready to experience romantic love, for instance, we simultaneously come to know a new dimension of feeling better about ourselves, a new dimension of deeper security.

Well, what about the Man and the Woman, then? If their original condition was to be able to communicate with Him and know Him as a friend, then that friendship surely brought with it the same thing which human friendships do, even if in a more profound and more spiritual way. It had to have bestowed personality strength and inner security. It must have brought what we perhaps could call a "covering."

The embrace is a "covering." So, too, the blanket is a universal symbol of security, for it keeps our bodies warm and protected, just as love keeps our hearts "warm" and secure. We might say of Adam and Eve, then, that they had experienced the covering, the sense of security which came from

15

knowing that God had "embraced" them and loved them in a ongoing way. Their spirits knew the love-touch of a God who was Spirit. The deepest core of their personalities was made to feel strong and protected because of that care, concern, and respect which flowed over them and into them so freely.

Adam and Eve were dependent on that love. It was so easy and right to choose to need it. It hardly seemed like a choice until the day came when it was suggested to them that such a dependence was demeaning and might be robbing them of that independence,self-reliance, and autonomy which brings TRUE HAPPINESS. So they chose *not* to depend, *not* to lean. They chose not to have to rely on the Love. They chose to choose without reliance upon the Guidance. They chose to provide for themselves and ignore the Providence.

By their choice, the Man and the Woman really choose fear. What they really choose is confusion. What they really choose is a sickening sense of insecurity. What they really choose is to know evil along with the illusion that to know evil, instead of only knowing good, is to become, thereby, twice as knowledgeable. The covering is gone. They have cast off the Love, and the nakedness they feel is not just physical.

Now, if the first thing you had ever sensed about yourself was your spiritual side and if, therefore, your spirit was the dominant dimension of who you were, then you would probably know spiritual things prior to knowing the physical, or you would know the physical in the light of the spiritual. If suddenly things are all topsy-turvy, however, and, without even knowing it, you sense physical things more readily than the spiritual,then you might well be suffering confusion about where your true nakedness lies. Without denying the possibility of a similar disorder in the sexual dimension of the personality occurring at that moment, it does not seem brash to suggest that Adam and Eve's experience of physical nakedness was likewise symbolic of their having stripped themselves of the security of God's love.

"Why are you hiding?" God asks them, in effect, and they feebly offer the excuse that they feel naked. It is easy to hear God replying: "You are naked, all right, because you had My friendship and you chose not to have it anymore. You presumed on the personality strength and inner security which My friendship brought you. *You* thought it was exclusively your own."

If someone who had been close to me suddenly rejected my friendship and said: "I don't want you any more," then the chances are that, beyond the pain and humiliation of such a disappointment, there would be the experience of deflated personality strength. The strength of my ego would be significantly diminished and then I might see that such security was not simply based in self-regard, my own feeling good about myself independently of the opinions of others. That strength had been intimately related to the fact that "I feel good about myself because others do." The Man and the Woman must have felt a similar draining of a similar security taken too much for granted.

Adam and Eve were Humankind. Humankind chose a path of no longer leaning on the Love, living in the Love, being guided by the Love. Why that ancient decision should flaw my humanity, as well as theirs, and leave me suffering from the same wound is in God's hands. If I choose, I may ponder the theories and arguments of the theologians as to the rightness of God's having permitted this. On the other hand, knowing that a solution has been provided, I may simply accept an inner assurance from Him that here, as elsewhere, He only acts and allows, out of His perfect Wisdom and Love.

We flee His presence and find communication with Him distasteful. We all have trembled with insecurity in a place we would not have thought existed, it is so deep. "Covering up" is second nature to us. Blaming anyone or anything else but ourselves seems to be the one universal talent or instinctive skill, along with the ability to communicate. That ever-gnawing, ever-present realization that it ought not to be this way is not just the experience of some. It is the experience of all. Our desperate need to be always right before the eyes of our fellows betrays the presence of a deeper suspicion that we are not even right with ourselves, let alone with Someone Else.

Besides the new feeling of nakedness, then, there is the freshly-found ease in lying. Adam insists that it was Eve's fault. Eve insists that it is the snake's fault. Blame-shifting, that deceptive talent we all seem to instinctively find within ourselves

17

to exonerate ourselves of an indictment we truly deserve, even as we piously try to pin on somebody else the responsibility for our sin, makes its first appearance. I say "piously" because at the exact moment we look around for a scapegoat, and find one, and start to accuse, we already half-believe that it *is* their fault and they *should* be punished. In time it will be quite possible for us to come to *fully* believe that *they really did it* and we had no part whatever in that misdeed. This is no curious hypothesis, by the way, that stands in any need of defense. If you deny that phenomenon as being in no way consonant with your own past experience you simply prove that you are a hopeless victim of disease. Not hopeless, really, for no one is more sympathetic with our malady than our Creator-Redeemer, and no one is more ready to help us deal with it.

Through the prophet Jeremiah, God describes Himself as the One who searches the mind and tests the heart, namely, the One who is accurately able to diagnose our condition. He speaks there in reference to the condition not of some but of all in one of the most important passages of all Scripture in terms of what is revealed about human personality: "More deceitful than all else is the human heart and desperately wicked. . ." (17:9, KJV), or, to barely paraphrase: the desperate wickedness of the human heart lies in its instinctive ability to deceive. . . .

Jesus quotes more than once, and Paul repeatedly focuses upon a similar passage from Isaiah, making it perhaps the most quoted passage in all Scripture and, accordingly, most worthy of our scrutiny:

> Be ever hearing, but never understanding; be ever seeing, but never perceiving. Make the heart of this people calloused; make their ears dull and close their eyes. Otherwise they might see with their eyes, understand with their hearts, and turn and be healed. (6:9, NIV) (also see 29:9-10; Ez. 12:2.)

The Psalmist refers to the self-blinded heart as "thick and gross" (119:70) just as the writer of Deuteronomy before him had referred to the people's need to have their hearts circumcised, that is, purged of a layer of useless spiritual tissue which prevented them from seeing that they were casually offering

Yahweh lip-service rather than loving Him with all their heart and soul (30:6).

It would seem clear from a close scrutiny of these and all other similarly pointed passages in both Testaments that God goes beyond simply reminding us again and again how prone to dishonesty we are (and, therefore, in need of deliverance from such a widespread compulsion and persistent bondage). He also takes great pains to show us that we are *particularly prone to the habit of deceiving ourselves.* This tendency is not simply the sin of some, like adultery or jealousy, it is the condition of all. It is a disease infecting the human heart.

Such an assertion proves itself in a sad but embarrassing way. We all know that we can do it, that we have done it — lie to ourselves, that is; lie (and even get ourselves to believe the lie) without its bothering us all that much. We are not all that threatened by such an easy inclination so ready to be reactivated at a second's notice. At worst, it is only a foible or peccadillo of ours that is not likely to cause us much of a problem.

We have deceived ourselves into believing that a frighteningly destructive tendency, an ability to be more comfortable with a lie than the truth, to have a greater affection for blindness than sight, for deafness than hearing — a lie, a blindness and a deafness which has the real potentiality of destroying our earthly happiness and depriving us eternally of the enjoyment of God — is nothing much to be bothered about. There are hundreds of other things far more worthy of our attention and concern, we think, and so are not only wrong in embracing such an attitude but downright deceived — self-deceived, that is. Even now we may be impatiently shifting in our chair resentful of this much space having been spent on something so trivial: "When is he going to get to my problem?"

St. Paul in his *Letter to the Romans* comments on the Isaiah 29:10 passage we quoted above. In speaking of the hardened hearts of his people, he uses a verb whose literal meaning comes from the Greek noun for callus. The imagery here is that of a callus-like substance growing on man's heart. Just as the callus on the body has little or none of the feeling which the healthy skin it replaces possessed, so the sinful heart is afflicted with an insensitivity to the very things it was created

19

to be sensitive to: an aliveness to goodness, truth, and the very presence of God Himself.

A body of water is a universal symbol in world literature for the spiritual side of human nature. Isaiah latches onto this imagery as he simply but graphically describes the process of self-deception: "But the wicked are like the troubled sea, when it cannot rest, whose waters cast up mire and dirt" (57:20, KJV).

When the surface of the water remains smooth, one may peer into the depths and see what is there. If the waters are my spirit, and unsettling realizations are contained there, I may not want to see them (or have *you* see any evidence of their presence, for that matter). Therefore, I choose to cast up "mire and dirt," a slimy film which will float on the surface of my spirit and conceal from consciousness that which lurks beneath.

The Jewish sage who wrote the *The Wisdom of Solomon* (about 100 B.C.) was profoundly interested in the inner workings of the human personality. While focusing on the dishonesty of the "unrighteousness" he comments:

> For while they supposed to lie hid on their secret sins, they were scattered under a dark veil of forgetfulness, being horribly astonished and troubled with strange apparitions. For neither might the cover that held them keep them from fear; but noises (as of waters) falling down sounded about them. . . . (17:3-4, KJV)

A "dark veil of forgetfulness," a black pall of oblivion is the image used by the wise man to describe the "cover" which the sinful individual wants to place on top of his own spirit's consciousness of sin. He opts, in effect, for a split-consciousness and he somehow accomplishes this through a *will* to "forget" that which he chooses not to have in conscious remembrance. Two thousand years before Freud, the phenomenon of repression—man's attempt to bury unwanted guilt-awareness in the unconscious—another Jewish doctor of the soul had already described the same thing! (Conversely, Jung sounds more like the prophet than the psychiatrist when he labels extremes of this phenomenon "malicious stupidity").

Split-consciousness, however, was not the way it was originally meant to be. Yet we all "suffer" from it. Everybody has a conscious part to his or her personality and an unconscious part, as well. There is also a mysterious line of demarcation dividing the two, that so often impenetrable curtain separating the conscious self not only from the awareness of sin (which is able to lodge itself in the spirit), but simultaneously cutting it off from the awareness of God's "voice" which that spirit was originally created to be able to respond to with ease.

While there are many in the field of psychology today who refuse to talk about the Unconscious, since it cannot be seen or measured but only known by its effects, it clearly seems pointless to deny its existence. Of those who do admit to its existence and seek to understand better the "laws" of its workings, some are now refusing to see the Unconscious as simply a murky dumping-ground for unwanted memories, or the cellar in which to hide embarrassing desires. More and more, it is being seen as also the place of man's religious instincts and spiritual hungerings. [2]

The author of the Wisdom of Solomon has blessed us with a penetrating spiritual perspective on our motives in secretly wanting the power to repress what we choose not to see:

> For wickedness is a cowardly thing; condemned by its own testimony; distressed by conscience, it has always exaggerated the difficulties. For fear is nothing but the surrender of helps that come from reason; and the inner expectation of help, being weak prefers ignorance of what causes the torment. (17:11-13, RSV)

Besides finding the denial of unpleasant truths so easy, beyond the instinctive dishonesty problem, we are also afflicted with a deeply-rooted anxiety or fear—fear of looking at the malady head-on; a fear, that it is even worse than we suspect; a fear that it is incurable; a fear that others will come to know this too; a fear that they will reject us on account of our being marked with this terrible blight; a fear which only spurs us on to even more profound self-dishonesty. Thus, the human spirit has, since the Garden's rebellion, tended towards the will to oblivion, forgetfulness of our widespread guilts and untamed lusts, oblivion even of that God whom we fear to be on the verge of condemning us precisely because of such things, or at least ready to reject us on account of our imagined unloveableness.

A "heart" needing to be circumcised of spiritual fat; a condition of spiritual drunkenness; self-blindness and self-deafness of the spirit; the waters of the spirit covered with slime; the dark veil of oblivion — all these images proclaim the same diagnosis. We *want* the ability to deceive ourselves, we *want* the refuge of a clouded consciousness — the unconscious divorced from consciousness, the power not to remember, not to know. That is what is wrong with us, too, God says, even as He offers to remedy the problem.

If, thus far, we have been able to see that Original Sin has somehow wounded our heart with the wound of self-rejection and has confused our consciousness with the wound of self-deception, we still need to focus upon one more aspect of our malady which we may call the wound of self-reliance, or self-sufficiency.

"You shall be as gods..." the serpent promised in the Temptation, and ironically, he was right, after a fashion. From that time on, apart from the merciful intervention of God, such is exactly what you and I would tend to think we were in one way or another. We want our own way, always tending to be manipulating our environment so that in one way or other it ends up being our own little world where we have the final say and get to call the shots, our way. We believe that we are Number One and no one is going to look out for Old Number One unless we do, or at least better than we can. These are the functions of World-Ruler, Creator, Savior. As Earl Jabay has pointed out, to have on one's moral code "as long as I feel it's right, *I* am free to do it" is making one's own point of view the ultimate norm of morality and setting oneself up as the Supreme Lawgiver.[3] God is sometimes defined as the All-knowing One, and we do not easily let go of the conviction that "I know what's best for me, better than anyone else," which means we have pretensions in the direction of that Divine attribute, too.

Let us look a little more closely at God's diagnosis of this side of our personality:

We all, like sheep, have gone astray,
each of us has turned to his own way;

22

and the Lord has laid on him the
iniquity of us all. (Is. 53:6, NIV)

Through the prophet we are told that we all are like the dumb
sheep; namely, that we are afflicted with a radical willfulness,
comfortable only with having our own way—a relentless insistence on our having the final word with respect to our being
guided. But only the shepherded sheep is safe and free; the
loose, straying sheep is perilously grazing along the borders of
death. Our "iniquity" is that we resent guidance, flee it, and
demand the "freedom" of self-guidance. It is because of that
iniquity, we are told, that stubborn iniquity in all of us, that
the Messiah will have to suffer and die. The Cross is to happen
for people who think that they will not be happy, cannot be
themselves without unconditionally having their own way. This
is so similar to the viewpoint of the Apostle Paul who pleaded
with the Corinthians to see that Christ "died for all, that those
who live might live *no longer for themselves* but for him..."
(2 Cor. 5:15, RSV, italics ours).

Jeremiah realized, too, that only in the opposite of willful
self-reliance could the real truth be found:

I know, O Lord, that the way of man
is not in himself,
that it is not in man who walks
to direct his steps....
(10:23,RSV)

Isaiah had similarly referred to those who were "proud
and lofty...high and lifted up" (2:12,NEB). We use the term
"inflated ego" today to describe the same phenomenon: power
giving somebody a false sense of superiority, the bogus identity
of being sovereign, the illusion of being in control. The prophet's call is to keep reminding the straying believer that this
is at the very heart of what is wrong with him or her, and
therefore, society as well.

Perhaps the prophet Habakkuk said it most simply and
most devastatingly when he cried out against "guilty men whose
might is their own god." (1:11) Your favorite idol can be yourself.

No one was apparently more self-possessed than Jesus, no one was apparently more independent, on one ever was able to give the impression, as much as He, that He was His own person. The fact of the matter was that He was *God-possessed.* His independence from custom and tribalism was based upon an incredible dependence upon the Father's love and will. He was the individual, *par excellence,* who lived completely in harmony with heavenly strategies, so often acceded to at the price of giving up His own. Yes, He stood on his own two feet, but he came to show us that those two "feet" were planted squarely on top of the Rock who was Yahweh.

Surrender and dependence are dirty words in much of contemporary psychology today. If we let Jesus teach us their true meaning, we will not only be enabled to find our true selves, but we will come to see people (mistakenly) call us independent, self-sufficient, autonomous — as was Jesus. We will *know* better, however.

Chapter 2

Healing of Self-Rejection

In his refreshing little book, *The Gospel According to Peanuts*, author Robert Short relays the story of a dizzy, mod, yet church-involved woman. After someone explains to her the doctrine of Original Sin, she remarks half in horror, half in disbelief, and fully flustered by such a revelation, "Well, if we're really all that messed up, then God help us!"[1]

But that's exactly the point. Only He can. The best part of God's Good News for us is that He wants to help us. Already, however, we may sense a restless stirring deep within us, either because we've been baptized as a baby, accepted Jesus Christ as our personal Savior as an adult, or have experienced some combination of the two. We *still*, however, feel very hurt, very hung-up, or very confused — perhaps even frustrated or annoyed, by now: "Here comes another salvation rap or evangelistic come-on — the old Cinderella story, except that Jesus takes the place of the fairy godmother and I'm Cinderella. And no twelve midnight riches-to-rags interval, either. One zap and right into 'happily ever after.' '

For people of a Catholic background, it was often some invisible blight scarring the heart, evident only to a God who wanted it washed off the soul of a baby no later than a month or so after its birth. For an individual of Protestant background, his total or close to total "depravity" was removed or divinely camouflaged at the moment of salvation, when the sinner "gave his life to Christ."

A predominant weakness in both views has to do with *receiving*. If the baby becoming child, becoming teen, becoming adult does not move progressively into the fullness of an experienced relationship with the Father through Christ in the Holy Spirit; if her baptism is not ultimately accompanied by on-going conversion, it runs the risk of being little more than a ceremony whose significance was never grasped, whose meaning was never responded to properly. Likewise, if the "born-again" believer does not allow the *event* of receiving Jesus' saving grace to become a *process* of growth in that grace, he remains an immature Christian whose personality and lifestyle gives far more witness to what grace has *not* been able to change than what it *has* been able to change.

Either way, even if we remain believers, faith for many focuses too much on what Grace did or is still doing down there, deep inside our hearts. In such cases, faith never gets strong enough to expect that what is happening to the inner person ought to become increasingly visible in the outer person, *evidenced* by permanently attractive and unusually consistent personality traits, that is, the fruits of the Spirit's indwelling (cf. Gal.5:22). Grace is meant to create beautiful people. If it does not, then either it is not there, or it is being perilously neglected.

The impression that the call to Salvation has left us with, whether we are Catholic or Protestant, is more often than we know, "God finds you repulsive": Get the baby baptized immediately, for God finds its condition repulsive. Sinner, get saved immediately — God finds your depravity repulsive. Get rid of the repulsiveness, and you can be God's friend, here and hereafter.

No wonder we still think (no matter how carefully our theology walls itself off from heresy) that Salvation is there primarily to help *God* be happy. Once you're "saved," God can take his finger off his nose — you don't stink anymore. We clergy, for instance, *say*, "God so loved the world that He sent his only begotten son . . .", but we so frequently *convey*, "God so hated the sight of sin that He sent His only begotten son . . ."

We throw in verses like that to cover ourselves, but the message relentlessly comes out the same: God wants to do *Himself* a favor by getting rid of an eyesore, by depolluting the "atmosphere," etc. We say, "God created the Sabbath for man," but almost invariably twist it into, "God created man for the Sabbath." By and large, Christian religion is still seen as something there to keep God happy, not there to make *us* happy (another word for "blessed," or "graced," by the way).

None of the evangelists record that when Jesus healed a leper, He held His nose and contorted His face. First of all, He loved the leper. Secondly, He touched him. Then came the healing. But what's that got to do with God, me, and salvation? Who am I to the Lord, before I accept His salvation?

He looks right past my sin and gazes lovingly at me. He may even be talking to me about that sin, but, strangely, I do not feel at all put down. My heart beats with hope, and any discomfort about the matter I feel is overshadowed by a sensation of relief. He is appealing to me as if I were someone who could hardly be satisfied with anything less than love — no, LOVE. He refers to the fact that it is sin that stands between us — as if that sin, that blockage, that condition of not having what ought to be there is something added to, or rather subtracted from the *real me*, the me He loves, who will never be able to fully appreciate that love unless sin goes.

At that moment, something deep within me shrinks back in shock. Simply and clearly, the appeal is to let go of the self-loathing; the self-manipulation of that which is in me, ugly and there to be faced, into that which no longer needs to be acknowledged since it can no longer be seen; the self-inflation of the outer me, leaving the whole person with no more substance than a big, bright balloon.

"But I can't *live* without these things," something tells me, something rooted, something insistent, something stubborn. "I can't give that up!" I stammer, knowing that my hesitation shields something bolder than I want to know.

He smiles at me with the same smile a close friend flashes at me when he needs to say to me, "Are you *crazy*? You've *got* to be kidding! You mean you *want* that junk; the self put-down in place of a serene acceptance of a healed, God-given uniqueness; a foolish burying of past hurt instead of a true deliverance from its power once and for all; a sick, illusory sense of superiority instead of a true unity with all your brothers and sisters in the family of my Father?"

I now begin to see that I don't have to change myself or prove myself before He'll accept me. *I'm already accepted.* I just need to accept my acceptance. I just need to accept the One who has already accepted me. As I accept Him, I hand over my helplessness as well; my helplessness to help myself; my helplessness to free myself of sin. I don't have to repent, then, in order to attract His love. I don't have to change myself in order to insure His forgiveness.

He is already reading the thoughts of my heart, because, as He speaks, He answers a doubt that hasn't even had time to form itself into words: "Child, when my Father looks at you, He hurts. 'It's a sin,' He says, 'for any of my children to suffer from such an emptiness. Those things and relationships with which they try to fill it can never satisfy a place reserved for the Infinite God. It is even more of a sin when they refuse to recognize this and throw themselves ever more frantically into new variations of that tired, hopeless theme. I hurt all the more for them as they make themselves even more helpless.' Child, your sins — using good things and good relationships to substitute for God's love, or relating to people and things in a twisted way — are attempts at self-happiness, self-salvation. The sins are symptoms of Sin. You can't envision yourself living without the security of being able to fall back on the sins, the ways you compensate for the emptiness and unhappiness of your deepest heart. The more you come to accept the love, the more you will come to see how you no longer need to sin . . .

"Just take my love. It will empower you to fully turn to me and the way of life I call you to. It will give you the strength to live on in my love instead of propelling yourself out of the energy of pride and self-promotion (Jn.15). It will ultimately undermine every remnant of what is selfish, base, and unworthy in all your attitudes and actions if you let it. That's what is meant by repenting; that's what it means to accept the gift of repentance. You can see that it's far more than the removal of what is wrong — it is the implanting and then the flourishing, and yes, finally the blossoming of everything that is right!"

The motive for turning to God through and with His Son is *love*, not fear. The immediate object of this call is not mankind or its sins, but *me* — not my sins. When attention is secondarily and eventually drawn to what is wrong with me, the main focus is upon not my behavior, but the wound in my heart. Salvation calls me first of all, just to be and not to do, to accept and not to talk or correct. To make myself available for loving, healing, cleansing. When it does become time to draw attention to my actions and their moral quality, I am reminded that I am expected to do no ethical thing in my own strength — only in and out of His strength in me. Only then am I to accept His call to *do* — things that are increasingly more loving and less selfish because I am coming to increasingly realize that "I can do all things in Him who strengthens me" (with His Love) (Phil.4:13,RSV).

Whatever Sin and sins do to the inner me and eventually the outer me before I accept His Salvation — that doesn't stop God from finding me lovable. Even then, "God shows His Love for us in that while we were yet sinners, Christ died for us" (Rom.5:8,RSV). However deformed I might appear to His sight, however inwardly scarred, He still finds something left of His image and likeness there, even if it is barely recognizable.

While perhaps the majority of contemporary authors in the field of psychology have avoided the word "love" "like the plague," certain psychologists are now beginning to stress the need for a healthy self-love as being at the very heart of emotional health and the well-being of the personality. Many Christian writers are picking up on this, and, perhaps not with the most careful scholarship, have promoted the pursuit of this kind of self-love as truly in the spirit of Gospels. On the other hand, a growing number of Christian theologians and scholars have seen fit to challenge this as nearly or wholly heretical, namely, a distortion of God's revelation. For that reason, we must apologize for placing what might seem to be undue emphasis in defending the rightness of loving yourself in a manner consonant with the counsel of the Scriptures. Some readers otherwise may end up intimidated by pastors, speakers, or writers, and thus back off from the very things they most need to see and absorb.

'Teacher, which is the great commandment in the Law?' And He said to him, ' "You shall love the Lord your God with all your heart, and with all your soul, and with all your mind." This is the great and first commandment. And a second is like it: "You shall love your neighbor as yourself." On these two commandments depend all the laws and the prophets.' (Mt. 22:37-40, RSV)

When Jesus answered His questioner that day, the newness of what He said came from putting the "old" together in a fresh way. He took a verse from Leviticus and a verse from Deuteronomy, and demonstrated in that starkness and brevity how clearly and simply God's law came from a heart summoning other hearts into a life of loving. Let's try to see what it meant literally and then go on from there, for it is the Scripture verse that those who promote Christian self-love often use to underline their position.

A look at the literal Hebrew, where it is first found in Leviticus (the second part of the command to love one's neighbor as oneself) shows us that the call was not to love someone but to love *to* (or towards) someone. One is called to exhibit an attitude of benevolence or care *towards* someone else: "Take that instinct you have for self-preservation, self-care, and your ongoing well-being and direct it toward your neighbor with corresponding force. Strike an equal balance between seeking your own good and your neighbor's good."

The Gospels or Leviticus, then, do not call me immediately to the love of affection either for my neighbor or myself. Does that mean, nevertheless, that self-affection is thereby excluded from such a call, or alien to it?

Before answering that question, however, a few added notes may be of help. First of all, the vocabulary of Christian literature is not always scientific, nor should it be. Sometimes, it uses the not-so-careful language of ordinary conversation, sometimes the extravagant language of love and devotion. Even Jesus proclaimed that a person cannot serve Him or follow Him without "hating himself," but He was hardly counseling self-hate. He was counseling the firm and complete rejection of self-centeredness or selfishness. That has not always been seen so clearly, however, and good Christian folks often come to think that anything human or attractive, or fulfilling was a distraction from God and the life He called us to lead. Thus, nothing connected with self-interest was acceptable. No form of self-consideration was seen to be reconcilable with living in God's love.

A (too human) idea of living sacrificially was viewed as a commitment to live without fulfillment. Thus, even Jesus was (wrongly) seen to be a martyr who gave up earthly happiness so that He could secure heavenly happiness for the rest of us. But a person who marveled at the beauty of nature and enjoyed banquets and the companionship of intimates, not to mention the presence of His Father, was hardly a man alien to the need for and the experience of fulfillment. The man who promised "abundant living" to His disciples was not just talking about the life to come. Self-rejection, nonetheless, came to be seen as the perfect counterpart to God-promotion, hatred of self, the surest way to come to the love of God.

On the other hand, love of self became the sin of sins. We have an expression today, "he or she really loves himself," a sarcastic turn of phase applied to people who conceitedly parade their talents, virtues, gifts, etc. People who have decided to "flaunt it" because they think they've "got it." That's the sense in which Christian literature, medieval right up to the present, (particularly Catholic and Calvinist) has castigated self-love. Self-love is equated with pride — the pride of taking an outstanding quality of mine (imagined or real) and magnifying its significance, even as it *covers over* some sensed inferiority or perception of failure. All of this is accomplished, of course, in the interests of making *me* thereby look better than *you*. (Some secular psychologies of self-esteem and self-assertiveness are really nothing else, by the way, than jargonized justifications for this kind of prideful behavior.)

But, on the other hand, might there be a *good* self-love, even a necessary self-love? Might there also be a *bad* self-rejection, a self-rejection that needs to be rejected? Would God ever be interested in helping me love myself? Would He likewise want to help me to rid myself of self-hate?

Jesus was not merely restating Leviticus. He was announcing a New Covenant's breaking through the limits of the Old; a deeper working of God's grace into and out of the human heart than ever before; a profounder opportunity to love with the power of that Love which cannot hold itself back at the

31

boundaries of benevolence and say, "for some, no affection will be shown or offered." Only in the New Covenant could all men and women be called into a loving which could be made increasingly free from the taint of self-promotion.

There is, perhaps, a bit of Divine sarcasm coloring the Old Covenant call: *Take some of that self-interest that serves you so well and turn it on your neighbor; her fortunes will surely improve.* Jesus certainly restates the original summons in order to show that this call was at the center of God's original self-revelation and Covenant-invitation to His people. He never intended to replace any of its ethical challenge, but rather to charge it with a whole new force, matched by a totally fresh opportunity for all peoples (now free to become God's people) to tap into the power of His love.

No true follower of Jesus can say to a "neighbor," "Since I have shown you the compassion of that Savior who dwells in my heart, I have done my duty. I do not have to go on to be open to the possibility of loving you with affection as well!" The Gospels surely imply that the more submitted we become to Jesus, the nearer we come to love as He loved and loves — namely with that shocking, undeserved affection which was there for anyone who wanted it and which continually embarrassed those who didn't.

God loves Himself unselfishly and invites me to love Him by somehow enabling me to enter into *His very act of loving Himself.* He loves me with the love of affection and offers me ever-increasing opportunities to love others with His love of affection. Furthermore, He not only permits me to love myself with the love of benevolence but expects me to. If that is the case, wouldn't He also want to enable me to love myself with the love of affection — His affection?

To love someone is to acknowledge their presence, to acknowledge to them the goodness of their presence, to acknowledge to them that the goodness of their presence fills us with delight: "It's good that you're here. It's good that you're you. I'm glad that you're here. I'm glad that you're you."

When we accept such a statement as being true — namely, that another has acknowledged our being there as good, that they've acknowledged our uniqueness as good, worthy of acknowledgment, and worthy of rejoicing over — then, and only then, can we authentically accept our own goodness, rejoice over our own uniqueness, and be glad that we are ourselves and nobody else. That joying in one's goodness and specialness is to love oneself "affectionately." It is something akin to rejoicing over another's presence, goodness, and specialness — the affectionate love we express to another.

It is important to realize, however, that self-love of this sort is the result of accepting another's love and accepting it as true. When somebody else loves me, especially when they show it to me as a spontaneous response to my being there, and do so consistently, I am then able to trust in the truthfulness of that expression. I am given *a reason* for believing in my own goodness or loveableness.

To simply tell yourself that you are good or loveable in the absence of anyone else's affirmation of that fact is to attempt loving yourself without having first found a basis in truth for such a belief. Such self-affirmation is doomed to be eventually undermined by doubt or fears that you only lied to yourself, namely told yourself what you wanted to hear in order to feel better. Loving yourself only because a self-help book told you that you ought to is not enough. You need to hear it from somebody else, somebody who really knows you. Even if, somehow, you could beat off the doubts or fears just mentioned, your attempts at self-love would only end up perverted by that icy isolationism which asserts that you only need yourself.

God has built us in such a way that it is impossible to love ourselves authentically without leaning in love on another. Furthermore, He's never lost that determination of His to bring us all together in love.[2]

If God can love Himself unselfishly, why can't He enable me to be conformed to His image by loving myself unselfishly? If God's self-love doesn't hang Him up in Himself, but forms the perfect "platform" for His reaching out beyond Himself for me, why can't I be blessed with that self-appreciation which can make me feel good about offering someone whom I know to be truly loveable and worthwhile to others in service and/or affection? Conversely, to demean, to doubt, or to "be down" on myself as I give myself to others surely is to devalue what I give detract from and the way I give it.

"Jesus, help me to love myself properly. Help me to love myself as you love me, in the way you love me, free from the taint of anything prideful. Amen."

Now, let us flip the coin over and focus for a while on self-hate or self-rejection. Once again, a Jewish sage of the Old Testament era, Jesus Sirach counsels us with a wisdom generally thought to be strictly contemporary:

> Son, keep your self-respect, but remain modest. Value yourself at your true worth. There is no excuse for a man to run himself down. No one respects a person who has no respect for himself. (Sirach 10:28-29, TEV)

The opening line of this passage may also be translated: "with humility cling to self-esteem." Either way, the impact of these lines favors a self-love which is seen to be not only allowable (when it is balanced by a spirit of humility), but necessary. The wise man then immediately bears down upon an evil kind of self-rejection, the disparagement or discrediting of oneself, which is becoming one's own enemy (perhaps the most common way we have of describing self-rejection).

Being "down" on yourself for *who* you are inevitably leads to a being "down" on yourself for *what* you are (what you fail to accomplish). The first part of verse 29 may also be translated: "who will grant acquittal to the man who passes a sentence of condemnation on himself?" Self-rejection is the father of self-condemnation. To the extent that we are unable to love ourselves for who we are, to that extent we will be unable to forgive ourselves for what we've failed to become, not to mention any past sin or misdeed.

We often hear that someone has a "poor self-image" or "low self-esteem." Self-esteem is a better word in this case because self-image or self-concept is basically an *idea* we have about ourselves, whereas self-esteem includes the notion of how we *react* to that idea — in this case, negatively. Thus, getting straightened out goes beyond replacing one kind of idea with another. It must include the replacement of attitudes which imply the notion of judgment ("I am no good, or close to it") and the notion of dislike ("I don't like who I am").

In order for this change to take place, however, two things need to happen: I need to see that I have accepted an inaccurate idea of myself' and then, that I have reacted wrongly to it. In other words, I need to see that I was misled into believing that I was inwardly ugly, worthless, etc., and that I have never stopped not liking myself for being that way.

We have already seen how the deepest part of the inner self was created to enjoy the embrace of God. We examined what intervened to disrupt the flow of that love into me and back towards the One who gives it. The biggest reason for feeling inwardly defective, we believe, rests in this: *I don't know* (by way of ongoing experience) *that God finds me loveable.*

There is, of course, another reason. The fact that the love of our parents for us, as well as the approval they gave us (along with that of other authority figures, like teachers and clergy) has often been highly conditional. We have also felt a sense of something not being there which ought to have been when they showed us love and/or approval. Some of it had something to do with their personal hang-ups, but we couldn't see that.

The child can only feel the difference between what he's experiencing and what he's meant to experience. He is primed to receive the perfect amount of love, for instance, coming to him from mother and father, and always in the tranquil climate which is created out of their ongoing affection for each other. On days that they were hurting (for one reason or another) that hurt would often end up placing itself as a blockage, hindering the flow of their love to him and also to one another. Somehow, he would know that he wasn't being accepted as much as he needed to be. What else could he do but interpret it as non-acceptance; feel it as rejection? There must be something *in him* that they don't find acceptable or loveable. Self-dislike of this supposed situation of defectiveness starts to implant itself and grow.

If that isn't bad enough, something else starts to happen. As soon as the child is old enough to walk, to understand,

and to do, the parents begin to set goals for him which hopefully are right and reasonable but which, unfortunately, sometimes aren't. But even when they are, a new and destructive experience often accompanies it. If in the past, the parents' love represented a holding back and thus was less than unconditional due to (often unconscious) personal weakness, now it becomes clearly conditional by decision. Love becomes the reward the parent gives the child for his perfect or near-perfect fulfillment of the task they have assigned him. When he fails, he suddenly finds himself to all extents and purposes — unloved. The chill of withdrawn affection greets him in the face of inadequacy or disobedience. He soon sees himself loved only in terms of successful accomplishment and unquestioning compliance, for when he is punished, his parents have not tried to impress upon him that it is *out of love* that they punish. Even when such is the motive, they often conceal it from him. This sort of love-manipulation can only increase feelings of self-annoyance and self-inadequacy. Experiences of failure and what it brings, more non-love, just provides the child with additional reasons to dislike and castigate himself.

If this is the case, love can only become increasingly identified with something which is earned or deserved. As John Powell (quoting Erich Fromm) notes, experiences of this nature can only leave a bitterness towards life and a cynicism about love itself in its train. The discovery that you are not loved for yourself but *only because you please* is, after all, nothing else but the realization that to be loved is to be used.[3]

Each negative experience with conditional love of this sort adds another "layer" to ever-thickening inner walls of self-hate and self-protectiveness against any more hurt of this kind. No wonder that we frequently find it so hard to accept love from others, accept it from God, and even are so uncomfortable when we decide that it is right in a particular instance to give our love to someone. No wonder we tend to feel we can't accept God's love and forgiveness until we've proven ourselves or healed ourselves first. No wonder we regularly quiver inwardly in fear, when it is time to offer or receive love. We are so afraid that the lover (or Lover) is going to detect our inner unloveableness and reject us on that account.

John wrote, "There is no fear in love, but perfect love casts out fear." (1 Jn. 4:8 RSV) Now, perhaps, we can see what that verse refers to: our fear of being rejected on account of the inner disfigurement that sin has brought us (including the sin of self-uncharitableness); our fear of being unable to please the impossible requirements of *the* authority figure of authority figures. God himself.

Perfect Love (that is, God) needs to "cast out" before "It" can be put in. Such casting out includes not only the fear of our unloveableness but the very thing which has caused it to be there in the first place: the fact that we chose to believe the lie that we were unloveable and then chose to hate ourselves on that account. We need a deliverance from something that has been rooting itself within us with increasing insidiousness for years. We need to pray for that deliverance with persistent faith and be patient with ourselves (and with God) until the full victory has been appropriated.

This, by the way, is probably the chief reason why so many people are unable to *experience* God's love. Too much of their inner heart is still locked into self-dislike. The same thing they do with the human love that has been offered them, they do with God's. They devalue its currency. They only see a comparatively small part of their inner person as loveable and accordingly reduce the "quantity" of the love which is bestowed on them, to the "size" which will "cover" the loveable "part." The rest they throw away, like a man who has been given a gift of ten dollars and then throws nine of them away, saying, "That person would never give me more than a dollar. That's all I'm worth to him. The remainder has to be counterfeit!"

We need also to see that hate is not always accompanied by passionately intense emotion. If someone hates me, she need not get violent with me by deed or word. She may well ignore me, look through me as though I weren't there; display an apathetic indifference to my presence. We often feel nothing for people we really hate because we didn't want to admit the original hate-emotion to them or to ourselves at earlier moments of provocation and just buried it. (More troubled marriages today reach a "cold war" than "hot war" climax, in this counselor's experience.)

Similarly, self-hate and self-condemnation can often take the form of self-apathy, that is, a deep inner numbness or deadness to love of self which can only reflect itself in the inability to "feel" the love of others. An excuse like, "I just don't get emotional about loving," is often given to justify this widespread condition. Those who have given their lives to Christ (even in the way we earlier counseled) and still have come to know little or nothing of the experience of His closeness and affection are generally people, in this writer's estimation, who, without fully realizing it, are still holding on to a significant residue of self-resentment or the self-apathy numbness we just mentioned. When such inner hurt is acknowledged and handed over to Him, we are able to appreciate that a true and deeply personal experience of our Lord's affection on this earth is meant for all of us, not just some of us.

Dr. Conrad Baars, in his brief but beautiful book, "*Born Only Once,*" shows so simply that when someone finds delight in me, *I am revealed to myself as good* and in that sense I receive from the other who I am. How much more so when the other happens to be The Other?"[4]

Carl Jung, commenting on Jesus' summons to clothe the naked, feed the hungry, and forgive the one who has insulted us, asks with ironic poignancy: *What do I do if I discover that the beggar, that the naked man, that the enemy, is inside of myself?* The answer is clear. We must tend to the beggar within, we must clothe the naked one within, we must embrace the enemy who is ourself.[5]

Chapter 3

Healing of Self-Deception

The Son of Man has come to search out and save what is lost (Lk. 19:10), and we have lost part of ourselves. Part of that part is our spiritual dimension. The proof of such an assertion can perhaps best be found in the way you choose to answer the following questions: *Do you know that you have a spirit? Have you experienced the spiritual side of you, or is it merely something someone told you is there, and, if so, do you believe them or not?* Even if you say that you believe in the spiritual part of you because it is a doctrine of your faith, you are still saying, "I don't know it for myself."

Then, too, there's the question of our unconscious; not understanding why we do the things we do when we consciously intend to do the opposite:

> I do not understand my own actions. For I do not do what I want to do but the very thing I hate. Now if I do what I do not want, I agree that the law is good. So then it is no longer I that do it, but sin which dwells within me. For I know that nothing good dwells within me, that is, in my flesh. I can will what is right, but I cannot do it. For I do not do the good I want, but the evil I do not want is what I do. Now if I do what I do not want, it is no longer I that do it, but sin which dwells within me. So I find it to be a law that when I want to do right, evil lies close at hand. For I delight in the law of God in my innermost self, but I see in my members another law at war with the law of my mind and making me captive to the law of sin which dwells in my members... So then I of myself serve the law of God with my mind, but with my flesh I serve the law of sin. (Rom. 7:15-23, 25 b,RSV)

Scripture scholars and theologians will argue about this passage till the end of time. Does it refer to the condition of Paul or a man like Paul, a pious Jew examining his spiritual problems prior to his conversion to Christ? Or is it Paul's personalizing of the plight of the recently reborn Christian, wondering why he isn't completely healed? Sidestepping that controversy, we still are left with Paul's teaching that apart from Grace, fully submitted to, we are afflicted with an inner division which is ultimately unnatural.

Something in me that I am not directly conscious of thwarts my stated intention to do the right thing, the moral thing. An urge to do evil, hidden from immediate view, challenges and overrules the conscious decision to do the opposite. This camouflaged counter-force, an irresistible impulse to do evil, the Apostle sees as something alien; something which ought not to be there; something which is a part of him but not the person he sees himself to be (or wants to be) "...it is no longer I that do it, but sin which dwells within me." (Rom. 7:17, RSV) Sin, Paul says, that power which prompts me to commit sins, lurks somewhere within me (my members) where I am not conscious of its presence.

Sin is a spiritual sickness before it is anything else—before it twists the emotions, clouds the intellect or ulcerates the stomach, Christian tradition has never stopped reminding us. It is a "sickness of the spirit" (which, like cancer, is not something we are easily or instantly able to be conscious of). To be human is to suffer the affliction of a spirit which was created to be conscious, but is now unconscious, at least in that "part" of it which is sin-impaired.

A simple but inspired poem of unknown authorship describes the same phenomenon from a slightly different perspective:

"Within my earthly temple there's a crowd: There's one of us that's humble, one that's proud. There's one that's broken-hearted for his sins, and one that unrepentant sits and grins. There's one that loves his neighbor as himself, And one that cares for naught but fame and self. From much perplexing care I would be free If I could once determine which is me!" [1]

Paul's passage and the little poem speak so familiarly to us. We see ourselves in both. While the apostle's terminology might be not always our own, his experience certainly is: *My self, the conscious me, who reasons what is best and then chooses to do what is best, is embarrassingly contradicted by something else.* That "something else" comes from underneath what I would prefer to think of as the total me. It rises up from "underneath" my intellect and my will (my conscious personal identity), even as it overrules its thinking and its willing. I am forced to admit, thereby, that there's more to me than meets the eye, (my own "eye" included).

Split personality, then, is not simply an affliction of severely disturbed mental patients. I've got one too. My conscious personality is split-off from another aspect of me, not very conscious, if conscious at all.

If that "horizontal" kind of split weren't bad enough, I'm further split "vertically" into a "good-bad" kind of split. That "something else" down there assumes the identity of a "someone else," because when it gets me to do an evil thing I didn't plan on doing or speak an evil sentence I hadn't planned on speaking, "someone" had to have done that or said that.

"Where are You?" God asks Adam. And Adam replies, "I hid myself." Now, God knows where Adam is. His question then, can only be meant to help Adam see what he has done to himself, and how he is failing to remedy his self-inflicted wound.

Adam might better have said: "I am now more comfortable *not* being with You than being with You, because I fear Your rejection. I am also *hiding from myself* because I can't bear taking responsibility for what I freely chose to do, and would prefer to blame it all on Eve. Finally, I am hiding a part of myself from her, not just a bodily part, but that part of me which cannot fully expose itself to her, since it is also ashamed at just trying to pin all the blame on her. . ."[2]

Adam's want to lose all of his God-awareness, some of his self-awareness and to curtail significantly Eve's former easy access to his inner self was the new defense system he felt he needed to establish when God was no longer able to be his protector. He now almost instinctively wills to live behind these barriers to self-transparency, these walls hiding his heart from other hearts, these "places" where now he is even able to hide out from himself.

The root meaning of rejection is to "cast behind" or "throw back"; in this case to cast behind (or beyond) our conscious recognition, or to throw back into a place where it will be out of sight. The unwanted elements of the self are buried. Their very existence is denied.

Self-deception, then, is a form of self-rejection. Just like Adam, we all have experienced an "instinct" to deny as quickly as we can that which we don't want to see; to deny it so powerfully, in fact, that even we don't remember what we buried or *that* we buried it.

Instantaneous self-deception is what psychologists call *repression*. They classify it as a "mechanism" of defense, namely something by which a person acts mechanically, to protect himself or herself automatically, with unnatural compulsiveness. They likewise tell us that it is the most widespread of the mechanisms and "universally employed" (which apparently means that *everybody* does it). It is generally held that this process is an unconscious one; and, to a great degree, it is. The fact, however, that many people are able to come to realize that they are repress-ors, struggle against the tendency and progressively eliminate significant aspects of it from their lives as a result of outside help, both divine and human, seems to indicate that they were able to bring to surface something they had known all along at a deeper level; that they had somehow *willed* to avail themselves of the "benefits" of repression.

Grace, on the other hand, in this writer's personal experience (and in the experience of some of his counselees) often has the effect of a slow motion instant replay. You watch yourself being "caught in the act" of trying to force down out of conscious awareness an unpleasant self-revelation. When we feel we are ready to get healed of what Keith Miller calls our "mental slight of hand tricks," then undoubtedly it will be given to us to "witness" our expertise. [3]

It is in childhood, when we are most aware of our smallness and helplessness, that in the face of threat and hurt, we first harness our pretending power in the service of no longer "seeing" what was just there a minute ago. We soon learn that if we can summon imaginary friends to our side and fantasize ourselves as being in the midst of exciting adventures, then we can do exactly the opposite when real people and real situations become too "heavy" to handle. We pretend to ourselves that these threats no longer exist.

Yet, even then, in all our innocence, we were initiating one of the most perverse patterns imaginable. Without realizing it, we were already *sinning against ourselves.* Any temporary benefit which this "forgetting" might accomplish would come to be more than outweighed by its pernicious effects in the long run. Proficient, progressively swift and ever more powerful self-liars we had become, and still are — apart from God's merciful intervention.

We automatically try to defend ourselves when something inwardly inconsistent with the way we want to appear to ourselves and others threatens to show itself on the surface. We don't like feeling anxious and we don't want any unpleasant revelations, either. Little wonder, then, that other defense mechanisms, other instinctive dishonesties in our personality, which aren't quite as camouflaged as repression seem to automatically flow from our determination to protect ourselves through denial. Eugene Kennedy uses the apt illustration of a self-sealing tire. Our defenses work like that. When something punctures our idealized self-picture and threatens to lower our self-esteem we patch it up with the inner sealant. [4]

Rationalization, for instance, whereby we attempt to justify our behavior by refusing to face our real motives for doing, feeling or thinking something and propose more acceptable ones to ourselves and others.

Projection, when we blame our failures on someone or something else. (Adam employed these two mechanisms together when he attempted to absolve himself of blame by trying to put it all on Eve. When he refers to her as "the woman *you* gave me" he also betrays, most likely, his resentment at God for somehow being to blame by giving him both a wife and freedom, as well.) In its extreme form (quite common!) people actually come to believe that they, for instance, are actually victims of other people's hate, jealousy or inconsideration when actually they are the ones who initiated and nurtured that negative attitude. They are attempting to deal with their own hang-ups by seeing them in others and striking out at those inconsistencies, scapegoat-wise in those individuals. When Jesus asked: "Why do you look at the speck of sawdust in your brother's eye, and pay no attention to the plank in your eye? How can you say to your brother, 'Let me take the speck out of your eye,' when all the time there is a plank in your own eye?" (Mt. 7:3-4, NIV) He was inviting folks to rid themselves of this devastatingly destructive defense.

Reaction formation, when we cover over our real feelings about a person or situation by expressing on the surface exactly the opposite. (Judas kissing Christ at the moment of betrayal is probably a good example of this, since he most likely was telling himself that it was only for "Jesus' own good" that he was handing Him over to the corrective custody of the ecclesiastical authorities). Excessive emotion towards, or devotion to parents, authority figures, or even the church often masks deep-seated hostility towards the *object of our alleged affection*. "Coming on too strong" is often a clue to the presence of this defense.

Idealization, whereby we attribute to others qualities they don't actually have, and correspondingly refuse to acknowledge their foibles. This is one of the areas where human love shows itself to be radically and consistently different from Divine love. Without submission to that love, almost invariably we will find ourselves blinded to the faults of those closest to us. God's love, as already suggested, accepts the faults of the loved one with a view to their being transformed through healing. Many, if not most, love relationships are partially based in an (often unspoken) agreement upon mutual idealization: "I will never 'see' or mention certain of your faults, if you will overlook and never mention certain of mine." (True relationships in Christ are based in the opposite: "I trust you and count on the Christ in you to tell me what I need to hear and show me what I need to see about what's not right in my life," and vice-versa). Christians, by the way, sometimes even resort to this mechanism in reference to their relationship with God. When in a time of trial, for instance, it seems as if God "let them down" they deny to themselves that they feel betrayed by the One in whom they trusted and praise "His wonders" all the more. This undoubtedly accounts for many of the "plastic smiles" which

44

believers often flash unconvincingly at each other and at "unbelievers."

To behave this way habitually in one or more of these areas just mentioned is to stand in need of being healed of our defensiveness. We all stand in massive need of being delivered from the instinct to want to fool ourselves and even an *affection* for "snowing" ourselves. The dishonesty God needs to save us *all* from is not the dishonesty of calumny, slander, embezzlement, burglary, shoplifting or bank robbery, shady business practice, or other kinds of malicious lying. We can be innocent of all these things or even healed-in-repentance of all these things and yet in God's eyes still be seen as desperately dishonest.

Such a source of suffering for ourselves and others, Jesus would surely long to heal us of. If Salvation is what we need, then this is surely what we need to be saved from — self-salvation via the lie. Little wonder, then, that the Crucified One pours out his blood and cries out from indescribable torment and out of unfathomable compassion for those who " . . . don't know what they are doing." (Luke 23:34, TEV)

If the conscious self finds itself under attack from impulses and energies coming from a place somewhere hidden underneath the self, then knowledge about these forces, their nature and dynamics is clearly essential. We have already briefly considered Paul's description of this phenomenon. Some have wondered whether it is essentially the same thing Freud described when he described how the Ego can become swamped by demands from the Id or Superego. While these three components of personality in his theory are hardly unassailable "facts," they represented on his part an attempt to "get behind" human behavior, to see what prompts us to do the things we do. Insofar as he was doing *that* he was doing something which Jesus was trying to get his disciples and prospective disciples to do — search out honest self-understanding, while never being satisfied with things the way they simply appear to be. Jesus is the Son of the God who "searches hearts and minds." He searches, not out of morbid curiosity or a mean spirit of fault-finding. He searches out so that He may heal.

How can you say good things when you are evil? For the mouth speaks what the heart is full of. A good person brings good things out of his treasure of good things... (Mt. 12:34-35, TEV) ...Listen and understand: It is not what goes into a person's mouth that makes him ritually unclean; rather what comes out of it makes him unclean... Don't you understand? Anything that goes into a person's mouth goes into his stomach and then on out of his body. But the things that come out of the mouth come from the heart, and these are the things that make a man ritually unclean. For from his heart come the evil ideas which lead him to kill, commit adultery, and do other immoral things; to rob, lie, and slander others. These are the things that make a person unclean. But to eat without washing your hands as they say you should — this doesn't make a person unclean. (Mt. 15:10, 11, 17-20, TEV)

I don't believe we are adding to or subtracting from the meaning of these last verses, if we paraphrase them this way: "There's no point in simply looking at your behavior in its sinfulness as if *that* were the problem. That evil behavior is but a symptom of a wounded heart..." (This woundedness of the heart that Jesus refers to here can be readily reduced, by the way, into three components: unbridled lust, the will to violence and dishonesty.)

Now let's look at the earlier passage. This quote was directed at certain Pharisees, men of scriptural scholarship and churchly accomplishment. We may similarly resort to paraphrase again, without distorting its basic meaning, with the following: "Your words may be the right words formed out of thoughts floating across the 'top' of your conscious mind. The problem is, however, that they may actually represent the exact opposite of what you really intend from the heart, even if you don't allow yourself to see that. 'Loving' words often mask intentions of hate; 'pious' words often mask an attitude of prideful superiority..."

Jesus does not fault, in this instance, their external demeanor. As in the Parable of the Pharisee and the Publican (Lk. 18:9-14), he doesn't insinuate that their letter-perfect behavior according to law and tradition necessarily had to be hiding secret violations of that law and tradition (even though He didn't hesitate to suggest that such was part of the problem for some of them, elsewhere (Mt. 23:23; Mk. 10:7).

Because he felt that he had accomplished this "righteousness" by means of his own will power, this kind of Pharisee felt superior to those who were unable or unwilling to match his religious and ethical prowess. It sadly left him with an arrogant superiority and a cool aloofness towards those who were weaker, the very people the Old Testament God managed to have so much compassion for and tenderness towards. Harshness in judging others became a vehicle for ego-inflation for him and the very many more that he represented, so prone to the practice of (what Jesus called) "exalting" oneself at the expense of others.

This brings us back to Freud and his model of personality structure. It remains still theory, a pioneering hypothesis about what makes a person "tick" at the deepest level. While rightly criticized for its deterministic and pessimistic view of humanity, it presented, nonetheless, a helpful tool for evaluating so much of what troubles so many. As Rollo May points out, even among scholars and experts there has been, in addition to legitimate attempts at challenging, criticizing and correcting his assumptions, a not insignificant over-reaction. By suggesting how instinctively inclined towards self-delusion we tend to be; how much our motives are clouded by the thirst for power and pleasure and how much our virtue is very often little more than the fruit of fear and compulsiveness, Freud has hit a very raw nerve indeed, robbing man of "the luxury of being hypocritical and dishonest," not to mention petty and selfish. [5] Under this aspect, he is a victim of the same kind of criticism and rejection Jesus encountered and for the same basic reason. Each said that there's a whole lot more to the person than meets the eye; that the personality contains much more depth than people realize or want to know. Each also said that an individual can hide from this depth and the ugliness which may lurk there. While the Master disclosed that salvation could only come when what was hidden in the darkness was brought into the light, the doctor maintained, in a similar vein that personality healing could only happen by replacing the unconscious with the conscious. But what Freud considered to be natural in man Jesus saw to be unnatural, namely his impulse towards, and his bondage to lust and violence.

Jesus never used the word "unconscious" but he did suggest that people could hide their deepest motives not only from others but even from themselves. Freud said the same thing, but he called that hiding process "*repression*" and the "place" where unwanted things got hidden, the "unconscious." He furthermore saw two forces operating from that place—the "Id" and the "Superego." Out of how the conscious personality, the "Ego," reacts to these forces and absorbs their influence comes human behavior healthy or unhealthy, social or anti-social, balanced or unbalanced. These forces, then, can work out a compromise or can be very much in conflict with each other. If they are in conflict they will deepen the barrier between the conscious and the unconscious and that barrier will hide an even more profound splitting of motive or desire down below.

Id represents the inner world of subjective experience with no direct knowledge of the outer world of objective reality. Id fulfills its needs by creating a restlessness which signals the conscious mind that it is there and is hungry (for food, sexual expression or power).

The *Ego* is the conscious part of man who must respond to the tension caused by the Id. He is able to be aware of not only what is going on within the "house" of self to a greater degree but also what is going on outside the "house." He is the executive of the body and his job is to find out whether there is in the real world that which will satisfy the need which has been signaled to him from below. He is the "reality principle" who decides whether the requests of the "pleasure principle" are reasonable, whether, the "I want it now" of the Id (which is indifferent to consequences) may need to be postponed, modified or even denied.

The *Superego* is like a cross between a clergyman and a judge, the personalization of the rules laid down by the parents for the child who up to about the age of five or so was unable to judge for itself what was harmful or safe, good or bad, right or wrong! For that reason, by using tactics of approval or disapproval, praise and blame, reward and punishment, the parents act as a *substitute conscience* for the child who, gradually, to a greater or lesser degree, makes their commands and prohibitions its own by way of compliance, out of hope for reward or out of fear of punishment.

Because of the child's relative ignorance and smallness in the face of its parents' seeming all knowingness and size, Superego becomes programmed with the tone of infallible absoluteness in its commands, the call for perfection in the fulfillment of its requirements, and a lack of forgiveness in the face of failure. Just as the parent served as a watchdog over what it judged excessive in terms of the child's demands for gratification of various sorts, rewarding its willingness to exercise restraint, while punishing the opposite; so Superego tends to exercise a similar function in supervision of the Ego when it seems to give too much play to the Id, as well as a punishing function when it judges that Ego has been too lenient in giving into its demands.

What if Id, then, says to Ego, "I want pleasure now" and Superego says, "No decent human being would ever want to have pleasure, for pleasure's sake"? Ego has to resolve that conflict. Often he resolves it through dishonesty. A married man, for instance, who wants to seduce his secretary may initiate a conversation with her about how "over-worked" she seems; and would she like to go out for drinks, after work to unwind...? Ego thereby represses his motive of seduction (the Superego's complaint about his immoral intentions). Ego gets himself to believe that all he wants to do is reward the tired girl's devotion, etc... All kinds of defense mechanisms of course, can be employed in this way so that people can satisfy their desires without the Superego's complaint.

Such an "inside" view of personality also helps to explain the source of otherwise unexplainable anxiety which attacks so many, so often. A sensual or violent impulse becomes so strong that the Ego has a very difficult time keeping it buried or repressed and is *afraid* that it will be forced to consciously acknowledge its existence.[6]

Our purpose here is not to endorse Freud's theories, in anything close to an all-embracing way. But when he said, in effect, that man's primary motivation is self-gratification via the pursuit of pleasure or power (whose extremes are promiscuity and violence); and when he argued that these "baser" drives dishonestly dress themselves up in the guise of innocence, unselfishness or kindness, was he really saying anything radically different from what Jesus is reported to have said in Matthew 15, when he declared that messed-up behavior is rooted in a hurting heart inclined towards promiscuity, violence and dishonesty?

Freud's solution to this problem was honesty (admitting your true motivation to yourself) followed by a re-education of the Superego (accepting the fact that you are essentially a selfish being) so that the Ego can realistically gratify that selfishness in a socially acceptable manner.

Jesus' solution (like Freud's) is based on an honest self-admission of the selfishness and dishonesty of one's motives: "But that's not your true self," He effectively cries out to us, contradicting Freud: "That's, rather, what you cannot help but being apart from my Father's love..."

The Christian psychologist, Lawrence Crabb, has I believe, convincingly suggested that the two drives at our personality's center which Freud saw to be based in the need for pleasure and power are what invariably result from the absence of God's loving presence. If my truest needs are to live in the conscious ongoing awareness of God's affection and under His guidance into the kind of purposeful life which He has uniquely provided for the unique me, then my deepest needs are really for *security* and *significance.* To the extent that security needs of the "inner me" are frustrated, I will compensate through self-gratification of the "outer me" in sensual and selfish pursuits; to the extent that I am unable to sense my inner uniqueness and my specialness lived out through the roles God has provided for me, I will compensate through the pursuit of power and possession.[7]

The restoration of God's love to my inner core, then, is designed to replace Id-based instincts ("...the sin which dwells within me") with love-directed impulses, if I will accept the fullness of what He has to offer. I will first need, however, to acknowledge that formerly acceptable motives of the past were far murkier than I originally deemed them to be.

There is another parallel between the teachings of Jesus and Freud which we need to reflect on here, before moving on to other things. The hypocritical Superego and the self-righteous Pharisee would seem to have a lot in common. Even if Freud is right about the existence of a Superego moderating the instinctive desires of the child through fear of punishment or disapproval and inclining it to the performance of its duties out of the hope of reward or approval, what does that have to do with the adult? When she acts morally, doesn't she operate now out of conscience, out of a reasoned consideration of alternatives based on ethical standards or spiritual convictions she has now made her own? Or could it be that a refined, educated person, socially and intellectually mature is still responding automatically, reflexively or rotely out of the disapproval fears and approval 'needs' of a child within who has never grown up? If an otherwise mature adult can give evidence of consistent, incongruous immaturity in a certain area of her personality, doesn't that mean that something earlier in her life prevented her from *ever growing up* in that one affected area? That isn't difficult for most of us to see. Nor should it be all that difficult to see that the same thing could happen to freeze the child-conscience at four or five, so that what appears to be respect for the meaning of sexuality or the right to personal possessions may still be nothing more (or nothing much more) than a sense of guilt or fear building a dam between instinct and its expression. In the same vein, apparently unselfish acts and ostensibly considerate gestures may be nothing more (or little more) than an attempt to gain that prestige or approval which merely takes the place of the lollipop or cookie.

Transactional Analysis, a current approach to emotional healing, helps, I believe, to throw a bit of light on why such a situation might exist. It sees the conscious personality as ordinarily reflecting one of three "ego states," the Parent, Adult and Child. The Parental ego state is heavily influenced by the Superego, as is the Adult by the Ego and the Child by the Id. The present state of mind likewise, seems to be influenced by the "playback" of past events, which included not only encounters with real people and situations but *the feelings* and *deep inner reactions* which may have been part of our response to these at the time.

It would appear that transactionalists like Eric Berne and Thomas Harris have something important to say about the formation of the "Parent."[8] In addition to what Freud suggested about the formation of the Superego, the T.A. proponents also focus upon the *way* the child was presented with the "do's" and "don'ts" at that important formation period. The child does not simply understand the command and internalize it out of motives of fear or approval. It also records its reactions to the *way* these commands were given. They weren't always given in a firm and reasonable manner, with affection and concern framing the way they were issued. They were sometimes issued with looks of horror or of vindictiveness, spoken in tones of disgust and condemnation. At times they could communicate not mere correction, but carried the suggestion how stupid the child must have been to have violated its parent's admonition even that this blunder might have happened as a result of the child's ongoing stupidity.

Or perhaps the instructions of the parent were issued with an unnecessarily stern intensity and were needlessly dramatized. When words like "never," "always" and "never forget that" were employed to specify the importance or all-inclusiveness of the parent's edict they, similarly, may have been over-used or over-emphasized. Then, of course, there's the situation of "do as I say, but not as I do," an inconsistency between what the parent commands and what the parent does, himself or herself.

The Transactionalists' conclusion, then, is that early moments of Superego formation are able to be genuinely traumatic. If there were a pattern of being *wrongly* instructed or corrected from an emotional point of view, it may merely have been localized to a particular kind of life-situation. On the other hand, such an unhealthy influence upon formation might have been implemented always and everywhere, or nearly so.

Around inner decisions to comply with my parents' demands can collect *my reactions* to those demands. A legitimate request, presented violently, can be internalized with exaggerated fear. A reasonable correction, overstated, can leave the child scarred with inner shame. An unreasonable edict can leave the inner personality seething with anger, frustration, or rebellion. A sound instruction reasonably presented can still inject confusion into the child's pre-conscience, if the parent rarely if ever personally follows the counsel he or she imparts so readily. The greater the frequency of this destructive parental influence, of course, the more damage done.

We also should probably mention here, briefly, a bit of the other side of the coin. Over-rewarding and over-praising can leave the child excessively dependent on stroking. He may end up unwilling to ever take initiative in the direction of responsibility without the prospect of clear and promised reward. Too much repetition of "oughts" and "don'ts" even when given benevolently, can leave the child robbed of a sense of strength and freedom, convinced in later life that he can't make decisions on his own, especially the ethical ones, or that someone else will have to act as his conscience at moments of demanding moral choices.

Situations which put us in the position of having to make value judgements and decisions of right or wrong very often bear a real similarity to parallel events in childhood. Somehow, we unconsciously sense the connection, and if we are not healed of the fear, confusion, shame or whatever, these repressed hurts will strongly influence and even control mechanically our apparently free and moral choices. What may have appeared to us and others as a mature act of conscience may in reality be little more than the childish reflex of Superego.

When true conscience is formed, an individual recognizes in law and obligation those factors which actually promote the strength and freedom of her personality. Conscience and consciousness are derived from the same root. The person of conscience is the person of consciousness; she is conscious of herself in a healthy way, of her inner pluses and minuses, of what in her will promote her true development and what in her is able to impede that development. She is conscious, as well, of the needs and rights of others and has come to see how law and duty are able to help her to rightly relate herself to society. It is because she sees that certain things are right for her and others, while other things are harmful that "oughts" and "shouldn'ts" operate powerfully within her as catalysts of motivation.

We have not mentioned *consciousness of God* up until now, because what has been described immediately above is also able to be applied to the non-believer or humanist who may decide to live by a code equivalent to the Ten Commandments. In the biblical viewpoint on life, however, there is offered to humankind the possibility of God-consciousness. To be conscious of a God who is Love is to become conscious of being loved by Him. It is also to become conscious of loving out of His love. As one grows in his awareness of the presence, the dynamic presence of this kind of a God who dwells in the human heart (when invited to do so), he simultaneously becomes aware of the possibilities of merging the flow of his heart with the flow of God's heart. He begins to be able to relate to everyone and everything out of the love-consciousness of God with increasing effectiveness. In this case, conscience includes the increased ability to distinguish between what promotes or what hinders that flow. Since one now lives in and for God, the Other, the motive of conscience is not so much self-development anymore, as living for God; for to the extent that we refuse to be for that Other we also refuse to be for ourselves.

Over a hundred years before Christ, the Pharisee movement was initiated in Judaism as a legitimate attempt to recover spiritual perspectives and re-instigate deeper devotion to God. Even in Jesus' time there were those who had remained true to the original spirit of this endeavor.(cf Acts 5:33-39) The Pharisee we are talking about here, then, is someone who ended up accomplishing the opposite of what he had originally started out to do, namely, become more authentically spiritual. *But, he couldn't see it.* As far as he was concerned, he was righteous on the way to becoming more righteous, if that were possible. He did all kinds of "spiritual" things. He showed an extraordinary dedication to high moral standards. And yet, in the eyes of Jesus, he was dreadfully deceived, "blind" and hypocritical.[9]

To employ some of the terminology we introduced earlier, we could say, I believe, that he was a victim of a traumatically internalized Superego; that is, he was significantly wounded in his moral and religious upbringing by parents or other authority figures and was never able to shake free of that destructive influence.

The child is naturally curious, disarmingly spontaneous, expectantly positive. When the parental hand of restraint and correction presses down too heavily, the woundedness which results leads to: a fear or hatred of the new replacing its curiosity; an affection for a mechanical repetitiveness in place of its former spontaneity; a negative insistence on sameness drowning out its positiveness and expectancy.

This might help us to see, perhaps, why so many of the Pharisees were so rigidly locked into an extreme traditionalism; why they tended to over-ritualize every aspect of Jewish life; and why they had such a "hellfire-and-damnation" approach to humankind's obligation to respond to God and His (alleged) will. Underneath it all, these cultured, highly educated men were still frightened, angry little boys, living more by the blind instinct of Superego rather than the considered enlightenment of conscience.

They were obsessively focused upon externals and, conversely, remarkably unconcerned about inwardness. Because the inner person was tormented by fears of unloveableness, they unlovingly preached a gospel of the untainted outer person, whose words and deeds were to be letter-perfect, according to law and tradition.

Because they were so locked-in by childhood hurt to the need for approval-reward, they couldn't help but evidence an unhealthy lust for external recognition and praise: "...You are those who justify yourselves before men...[who love]...the praise of men more than the praise of God." (Lk. 16:15 and Jn. 12:43, RSV)

Because they had the same feelings of inferiority as everybody else, but had achieved high social prominence, they arrogantly tended to view themselves as superior human beings, especially, in the spiritual realms: "...this crowd who do not know the law are cursed." (Jn. 7:49, RSV).

Because they were so unwilling to deal with disturbing attitudes and desires which they denied to themselves ever having had, they needed to busy themselves to reform everybody else's behavior!

Because they couldn't enjoy the true security which issues forth from a heart whose hurts have been acknowledged and healed they had to find their security in rule-making, inhibitions and repression.

Because they alleged themselves to be custodians of a living faith in a living God they had to compensate for the lack of real life in their relationship with Yahweh by creating new laws and new traditions, a counterfeit flexibility contrived to cover the deadness of it all.

Because they carried so much heaviness within, such a sadness-burden issuing forth from unhealed hurt, such a fear of being corrected any further in a negative or put-down kind of way, they were never able to laugh at themselves. They could only transfer that heaviness instead to the situations they found themselves in or onto the people they encountered: *God is sombre and heavy-handed, so his representatives must honor Him by being dour and pompous.*

They didn't really need a Savior because they had nothing to be saved from. They didn't need a healer either because they had nothing to be healed of. They hated Jesus because He saw their hidden fears and hates and offered to help. He confronted, in effect, their affection for repression and the other defense mechanisms. Dishonesty was far more a friend to them than God was.

It was Winston Churchill, I believe, who coined the expression "bodyguard of lies" to describe an allied intelligence operation in World War II, perhaps paraphrasing Isaiah who characterized sinners as those who "have made lies...[their] refuge and in falsehood...have taken...[their] shelter." (Is. 28: 15, RSV). Such Pharisees were men protected by a bodyguard of lies. That bodyguard was the only protector they felt they needed, the only messiah many of them ever wanted.

Why so much time spent on the Superego and the Pharisees? Because underneath our "veil of forgetfulness" may lurk remnants of pre-conscience, pockets of Pharisaism. Without fully realizing it, we may be hanging desperately onto the hurts that came at that crucial formation period. We may need to see that in certain areas we've been reacting out of fear rather than acting out of love: rebounding out of the unconscious rather than choosing out of consciousness; loving the lie a lot more than loving the Lord.

But He is still there to help us find what is lost: "...to bring good tidings to the afflicted, ...to bind up the brokenhearted, to proclaim liberty to the captives and the opening of the prison to those who are bound." (Is. 61:1, RSV)

Chapter 4

Healing of Self-Sufficiency

Did you ever hear the proverb: "Pray as if everything depended on God and work as if everything depended on you?" It's a bad one.[1] It seems at first glance to strike the proper contrast between matters spiritual and matters pertaining to the world. It can't, however, because the man who works as if everything depends on him doesn't really believe that God is going to be all that much help, if any at all.

If it all ultimately depends on God and I can truly depend on Him, as I do what I am supposed to do, then I'm *just not going to have to work as hard.* The burden of it stays with Him. I'll be glad to help, of course, but He's the One who's really got to do it.

Let's talk to believers first. Many of us were taught that there were certain facts that we needed to know about God. They could be found in the Bible, creeds or church doctrines,etc. Depending on which denomination you were raised in, you discovered that it was necessary to accept some of these facts as a prerequisite to Salvation. Many of these facts could not be proven. They had to be taken on faith. Faith for so many, then, ended up being (instead of the channel through which God's favor flowed into you) the favor you did for God. The thing you did to keep Him on your side. Belief in facts, rather than belief in a Person, was the way it often tended to come across—holding on, as J.B. Phillips says, to "good ideas, tenaciously."[2]

But even if you *do* believe in a person, namely, that He exists—that isn't the same thing as trusting him. I believe (at the moment this pen moves across this page, in 1980) that the Ayatollah Khomeini exists. I don't trust him, however. If I had anything to say about it, I certainly wouldn't entrust my welfare or safety into the hands of anyone like him. Belief and trust, then, can mean the same thing, but *they don't have to*. I can believe in you without trusting you — even if you're God.

We were, a lot of us, introduced to God (or His Son) by way of explanation or description; we were told we needed to believe in Him. Some of us decided to. Then we were also informed that He had given us a code of ethics, the Ten Commandments, and that He expected us to keep them. The way this was to be done was by the exertion of will-power, assisted (when necessary) by a transfusion of grace.

Faith and morality, as these things were presented to us, came across as activities which we could instigate through strength of will. Such feats of will-flexing often left us feeling rather pleased with ourselves: "I am a good person because I believe the right things and perform the appointed things." For that reason, the very elements which were meant to deliver us of pride and self-reliance became vehicles, so often, for reinforcing what Original Sin left us prone to: thinking that we could go it alone; thinking that we could do it all by ourselves; thinking that we were just fine spiritually and morally, when as a matter of fact we were a mess on the way to getting worse.

The good news here is that, if you were indoctrinated with some version of the above, you never really heard the Good News. You only *thought* you did. That's why what's wrong with you, deep down, can still be something grace can heal, and love can make whole — even though you've given the (Christian) religion route the old college try and therefore *know* that it doesn't work. It was the *caricature* that didn't work — you may have yet to try the real thing!

So much of the good news Jesus came to show us is that we are victims of caricatures. Caricatures of God and caricatures of ourselves. To borrow again from J. B. Phillips and Morton Kelsey as well, we may summarize the teachings of Jesus this way: Before He unfolded the wonders and glories of the New Covenant which (fulfilled and surpassed the promises of the Old), our Lord needed to demonstrate that most people had managed to miss the point of what had been laid out for them to spiritually prepare them for that unparalleled moment of

Grace. He first had to correct the caricatures. He first proclaimed that their "God was too small"; and then, that their "man was too small."[3]

Their God was too small. The religious leaders of Jesus' day for the most part were not heretics. They adhered to and taught the official doctrine. They transmitted with careful fidelity the traditions which spoke of God's having formed a covenant with their forefathers, among whom were numbered kings, prophets and saints. They did not cast doubt on those stories which told about a personal Lord choosing individuals to lead His people into a covenant community (or *back* into what was supposed to be an environment of faith and justice when they were straying from that.) But when they taught that God is a living God, it generally came across as "God *was* a living God." If they happened to say: "Listen to what God says," it more often than not came across as: "Listen to what God *said*." Should they happen to proclaim that God was faithful and compassionate, it was spoken in such tones of coldness and aloofness, that the message said one thing but conveyed another. When they said, in effect: "God gave us the Law so that we could live happier and more fulfilled lives," it invariably came across as "God will only be made happy by your keeping of his (many) laws, even if that makes your already burdened life even more burdensome..."

That's why, as we noted earlier, Jesus shouted out with marvelous simplicity and exciting directness "...the Sabbath was made for man, not man for the Sabbath" (Mk. 2:27). Religion was made for the benefit of the people; and so, humankind was not created for the sake of populating and supporting spiritual institutions: "The wisdom of your fathers has been handed on to you to make life easier, not harder; to lift burdens, not impose them. You have made God a distant God when He is so wonderfully close. You have made Him to be relentlessly vindictive when He is so persistently compassionate. You have made faith in what God did once with your grandfathers more important than believing in what He is doing now with you. You have made the written letter of what He said or did more important than the Spirit who makes those words more real and relevant than ever before by applying them in freshness and newness to the here and now..."

"Salvation is something you accept to get God to be pleased with you. Prayer is something you do to keep him happy. Moral living is something you've got to strive for to avoid His emnity or insure His continued benevolence..." *Duty, obligation, burden* — that's the way, so very often the Gospel came or still comes across to us. And we secretly wonder whether it's ultimately any more to our benefit than the bulk of our taxes. We view it so often as little more than a necessary evil.

God has been grossly misrepresented. That's what Jesus said to his contemporaries about their religious upbringing. How would He be able to say anything else but the same to us, today? Every misrepresentation that the Pharisees promoted in reference to the God we now call "Father," Christian teachers have repeatedly duplicated with respect to the Son and the Holy Spirit as well. Ever so careful to avoid distorting doctrine, they end up distorting the Person, instead.

Their man was too small. When Jesus (cf.Jn.3) met with that secretive seeker after truth, Nicodemus, a prominent religious leader of his day, He showed that learned man that he had fallen prey to the pitfall of calling the part the whole. Nicodemus had equated knowing about God, with knowing him personally. He'd mistaken head-knowledge for heart-knowledge. He'd made words directed at God the equivalent of prayer. He stood in need of being shown, therefore, that praying is supposed to include the communication of *oneself*, not simply one's ideas or desires.

Jesus must introduce Nicodemus to his need for rebirth, if he is ever to come to experience this new accessibility to God's presence and power, namely, the Kingdom. As He does, He mildly chides the inquisitive Pharisee for not knowing what he ought to have already known, as a mature and learned son of Abraham. Matthew twice records that Jesus had directed the attention of the Pharisees to Hosea 6:6, indicating that the Savior had not only viewed the verse as a key summary passage, crystallizing the heart of Old Testament thinking; but that He saw it containing a crucial point which they were constantly missing:

62

For I desire steadfast love and not sacrifice, the knowledge of
God rather than burnt offerings. (RSV)

Hosea was a prophet, who approximately 800 years before
Christ announced to his contemporaries that there was no
knowledge of God in the land (4:1,5:4). He wasn't bemoaning
ignorance of ceremony, tradition or doctrine, however. The
noun he used when speaking of such knowledge was *daath*,
and the verb, *yada*. It was the same word the Hebrew scriptures use when they speak of Adam "knowing" Eve, when she
conceived and bore Cain. This kind of knowing is an act which
goes far beyond mental activity or the acquiring of new ideas.
It involves emotional and spiritual activity as well. It signifies
activity implying inner attachment to, dedication to, or compassion for another person. When Hosea spoke of not knowing
God, he was talking about not having an inner attachment
to God; about not being spiritually and emotionally involved
with Him; about not being loyally committed to Him, as a
faithful bride to her husband. As Rabbi Heschel points out,
it even included the notion of sympathy with and for God,
identifying with His passion to be loved and His sadness in
having to suffer that love's rejection and betrayal. It involved
an openness to empathize with the Unrequited Lover.[4]
It is easy to think that reflections about God or the things
of God is something which is, in effect, the equivalent of the
heart reaching out for Him, pumping with full force. For that
reason, Jesus essentially declares to Nicodemus and the rest of
his contemporaries, "You hardly realize that you have a heart.
You may acknowledge its presence but you rarely, if ever use
it or even begin to examine its incredible potentialities. You
are afraid of intimacy. You are uncomfortable with communion. You vastly underplay the necessity of love having first
place in your lives. You may weigh and ponder my teachings,
but you rarely, if ever, learn of *Me* and examine the recesses
of my heart as I have invited you to do." (cf.Mt.11:29)
Jesus came to tell us all that we *all* contain unfathomable
depths; that we all can come to taste ways of knowing that
we do not yet know; ways of loving that we've rarely, if ever

experienced; capabilities for closeness to God and to one another that we wouldn't have dreamed possible.

Jesus comes not only to correct the caricatures we may have of God being anything less than a passionate lover but also our caricatures of ourselves. God isn't God if He isn't seen to be a passionate lover. And we are not ourselves yet, and hardly in His image and likeness, unless we want to be as full of that fiery affection as we are able to be.

The paradox of our age is that we are, by and large, a people who are downright desperate for guidance. Yet more often than not, our search for direction is unconsciously sabotaged by a pre-programmed demand that the one who gives us that guidance will teach us how to become guidance-free. No one seems to get a greater following today than the person who promises to show us how to take "total charge" of our lives. We want to be our own guides.

"I am the chief guide, protector and savior of me. I'm having a little difficulty right now directing myself as effectively as I might. I know that if I could get a better slant on how to do it, I'll finally be "home free" to do and get the things which will make me permanently happy."

The above statement (or something like it) is one which most of us live by. It is an act of affirming to oneself who one is and what he or she can do. Many, if not most Christians, (including many considering themselves "born-again") would have no problem with such a creed after having given lip service to their belief in, or commitments to, "God," "Jesus," "the Lord," "My Savior" or whatever. If so, they are caught in an amazing contradiction, for they are saying that they are their own god and savior and God is their god and savior at one and the same time. As long as you acknowledge "Him" as the real boss, then you are free to take care of everything else your own way, with proper deference, of course, given to the keeping of His (ten) rules, they apparently believe.

When the Hebrews received the Torah from the hand of Moses and as a people ratified it as the word of God to them and the law of God for them, they accepted it in this sense: God was a living God who would keep on speaking to them. The Torah was His *guidance* and *instruction* given to them in the context of an ongoing dialogue. It was not simply a code of laws or "the" Law. It meant, in the final analysis, that they were re-accepting for themselves what had been rejected in the Garden: *to be human is to always stand in need of guidance from God.*

Their experience in the wilderness after the Exodus was that of a people always on the move, guided by that God who was somehow hidden in the pillar of cloud by day and the pillar of fire by night. When the cloud lifted and moved, that was their cue to pack up and move on. Such was intended to be the most graphic of lessons for them, one that was ever meant to stay with them, even after the Guidance had led them safely into the Promised Land where they were allowed to settle. They might not always need the Pillar but they would always need the Guidance. Yet, the new opportunities and the new freedoms of the "land of milk and honey" only served to convince them repeatedly that they needed Him less and less. The Torah became "their" Torah, the Law which had been given to them they came to view as their own possession. It became a God-substitute, in place of the direction given in dialogue. At times, that Law could be cynically manipulated, when it wasn't ignored, outright. Even when it was kept, it could be kept, some thought, apart from the surrender of the individual to that Person who was God and apart from trust in His compassionate protectiveness — the very trap to which so many of the Pharisees of Jesus' time fell prey.

When Jesus came, He proclaimed a whole new closeness of God breaking in; a radically fresh availability of the Presence and therefore of the Guidance. He described Himself as someone who was in constant contact with His Father, never saying anything unless that Father would have Him say it, never doing anything unless the Father would have Him do it (Jn. 5:19, 8:29, 12:49-50). He even declared that His disciples would be empowered to live in the very same way, out of the very same kind of dependence upon the living Guidance. (Jn.14)

The Pillar and the Tablets "without" in the Old Covenant would give way in the New to a Torah written on the hearts of individuals by the Spirit of God dwelling *within* them. What Ezekiel and Jeremiah had foreseen in the dim future (Jer. 31:

31-34; Ez.36:26) Paul would characterize as prophecy fulfilled: now the "sons of God" are those not simply indwelt by God's Spirit but *"led" by Him* — as well (Gal.5:18,5:25, Rom.8:15). God was now "around" more than ever before, to reveal His presence and will to those who sought that presence and wanted that will.

The Church of the New Testament encouraged its members to seek Him within, to lean on Him within, to listen to Him within and so to be "led" from within, where the Spirit of God really had come to dwell. Just about every church since, (Catholic, Orthodox or Protestant) has, with rare periodic exceptions, preached "look to the written Word" or "Look to the leaders" almost exclusively, as if either were ever meant by the Founder to stand as a substitute for an absent or incommunicative Indweller. In doing so, *at best*, they preached only *part* of the Gospel, while implying that it was the whole.

Apart from God, the personality is saddled with a directionless heart or core, whose impulses tug, turn and twist it in many directions, often contradictory, and always short of where it really needs to go. Without being directed in the direction of God and without taking its direction from Him, once properly aligned, human nature will always be the victim of such impulses.

The above-mentioned "alignment" is a turning of the self so that it may be placed in proper relationship with God. That relationship is a lot more than: "I believe in you and will try to keep the Ten Commandments or "I'll take your salvation into my heart, if that's what you really want..." *Turn* is at the root of the word conversion, and we are talking here about conversion. The New Testament Greek word *metanoia*, conveys the notion of turning from sin, turning towards God, especially by a complete change of outlook and attitude. The focus is on a transformed heart and mind.

The Hebrew word *teshuvah* is perhaps even more concrete and clear. It refers to the turning of the whole person towards God: *I am turning completely towards One whom I was either truly ignorant of, or aware of but in a somewhat distracted way, before. I turn squarely towards One who loves me unreservedly, and I face Him. I see that He is someone whom*

66

I can trust completely. More than that, I know that I can entrust my very self into His hands.

The counsel of King Jehosophat of Juda to his troops may be literally translated: "...trust yourselves to the Lord your God and you will remain entrusted" (2 Chron.20:20). That is what we must do personally and individually with our Lord: *entrust ourselves into His hands.* Like little children wounded and unhappy, we go up to our Father who is God and ask to be picked up, held, comforted, healed and loved – *forever.* This is rebirth. This is being born again from above. This is allowing ourselves to become like little children again.

We admit that deep down we had been turned in on ourselves, turned-off to being guided, turned away from real loving. Something in us which, if left unchecked would ensure our emergence as outrageous, arrogant, self-centered, spoiled-brat "adults" is still somehow hanging on. It is still there lurking beneath the surface and hiding behind pleasant smiles and softly spoken words. A radical wilfulness. A "I-must-have-my own-way-at-all-costs." A "I-know-what's-best-for-me-better-than-anybody-else-and-I'll-get-it-too." How very reminiscent of Isaiah's comment: "All we like sheep have gone astray; we have turned every one to his own way..." (53:6,RSV)

We said earlier that an entering into God-dependence would be particularly offensive to non-or ex-believers. Actually, for the most part, dependence is just as offensive to believers. Otherwise, they would be known for their surrenderedness; their docility to the living God who still guides; their affection for imitating their Master's habit of never doing or saying anything without attempting to consult and consciously lean upon the One who dwells within.

The Old Testament counsel from Chronicles is reminiscent of Paul's advice to the jailer at Philippi which may be freely but accurately translated from the Greek: "...remove yourself from your own keeping and entrust yourself into Jesus' keeping and you...will be saved." (Acts 16:31). It helps here to take one more look at the second part of the original counsel from Chronicles: "...entrust yourself...and *remain entrusted.*"

The Deuteronomist came to experience the foreshadowing of what was meant to be the ongoing experience of all, all of the time, when he said, "The eternal God is your dwelling place and underneath are the everlasting arms." (Dt.33:27,RSV). That's a poetic way of saying: "my security ("underneath") is, above all, derived from God's love-embrace ("arms") which is not on-again off-again, but utterly free of inconsistency ("everlasting").

It isn't such a terrible demand, this call to dependency, this summons to surrender, when viewed in this way—or is it? We are automatically so suspicious of it and so instinctively skeptical of it. The Scriptures seem to indicate that we would be, anyway; even if we'd never had bad experiences with authority figures of various sorts attempting to manipulate us into a passivity which would be to their advantage. But, perhaps now is the time to look a little more closely at what we may have already suffered in this way. For most of us "unsurrendered types," it is at least part of our present problem: we are inclined to be extra self-protective because people are always trying to get us to do things we don't want to do, or to be people we don't want to be.

The most common source of unfair pressure of this sort ordinarily comes from the home. When the child is born, he is totally dependent upon his parents for all his needs, physical and emotional as well. As he becomes older and can do more for himself he gradually becomes less dependent, up to the day when he strikes out on his own, providing for his own material well-being apart from home and seeking new-love-securities, usually from romantic relationships. He is now free, of course, to maintain a close love-relationship with his parents, but the dependency of that love will be: "I choose to keep on *needing* you as friend and companion," even though I no longer need you as a provider of food, shelter and guidance.

This, of course, is the ideal situation, when the parents allow the child to move into increased independence at the "right" time with a view to complete emancipation. Wise parents somehow know that in gradually letting go of the reins of control they are not letting go of a person they love, but are actually fostering the basis for new closeness to their children which ought to characterize their relationship when the kids become social equals.

So very many parents refuse to take that risk, however. A minority, I would suspect, through intimidation and threat so emasculate their child psychologically that he is close to being permanently fearful (without therapy) of undertaking anything or going anywhere, without their implied or expressed bidding. But the majority would seem to be "bribed" into a sick dependency by the "favors" of parents (in this counselor's experience): more often mothers with sons, and fathers with daughters) into sticking around for these bribe-favors and going along with their wishes in hopes of even greater "kickbacks." Very often this produces a deeply seated conviction on the part of the "victim" that he or she cannot cope in life without the hovering presence of parents or parent-substitutes, even though this unfortunate identity-component might be buried deep in the subconscious.

A similar temptation is for the Church's shepherds to become conscience-substitutes for these susceptible types, so very willing so often to go along uncomplainingly with whatever Father or Pastor says. Instead of helping people to form their own consciences, to assume more and more confidence in their ability to hear God speaking and guiding from within, echoing and applying the spirit of God's written word to the situations of life, such clergy discourage, in one way or another, the formation of a true conscience.

These are two big reasons why a lot of us hate words like dependence, submission, or surrender. Too sophisticated for Peoples' Temple or the Moonies we may be particularly susceptible, nonetheless to being taken in by the slick soft-sell of folks like Wayne "Your Erroneous Zones" Dyer. This successful author/psychologist (besides providing helpful advice and practical insights) plays on fears bred in us over the years (through such draining experiences). He counsels us, therefore, that we will only be happy when we are *totally independent*.[5]

Such independence, according to the doctor, means that we are finally free to be ourselves and do our own thing, especially because we have decided to make our choices without allowing any relationship-ties of ours exercise any claim upon the moderation of our desires. To be psychologically independent is to come to the place where you no longer need others (which isn't the same as wanting others, he hastens to reassure us). You don't help your children, for instance, grow in self-confidence, then, by putting their needs ahead of your own desires. That would be setting bad example. You show them how happy you are gratifying your own desires, even when your kids apparently require of you a bit of self-sacrifice on your part, if their present needs are to be effectively met. That way you give them what they really need most: the example they need so that they eventually can become as aggressively self-centered and exploitatively successful as you are.

Given the need that countless people have to free themselves of sickly dependencies, it's no wonder folks like Dyer are able to garner such lucrative followings. We do, after all, bear the spiritual image and likeness of the folks who originally got suckered on: "You'll only be happy and free if you become your own god and run your own garden." In addition, there are so many of us who find ourselves inwardly braced against the ploys of parent-figure manipulators ordering us to go along with them, or to keep leaning on them and so find our identity in being the proverbial clinging vine.

A parable offered by this writer in another book seems appropriate to include here as well:

There once was a man who was an expert camper and hunter. He would periodically go deep into the wilderness for months at a time, and only return after he'd fulfilled his desired quota of game. One day, far from civilization, being the only human for miles around, he accidentally slipped and badly broke his leg. After much struggle and in extreme pain, he set the leg himself and bound it with makeshift splints. Many weeks later, he walked back into town and announced to his friends how he had single-handedly and successfully doctored himself, in such confining circumstances, against such overwhelming odds... The slight twinge of pain he felt every time he walked never went away, however, and it was only be carefully controlling his reactions that he could shield this pain from the observation of others. He increasingly realized that his leg had not set properly and would probably have to be broken by a doctor and reset. But he hesitated and delayed and continued to tell his attentive associates how all alone in the wilderness he had successfully set his own broken leg... [6]

Deep down we know that we really haven't done all that great a job of doctoring ourselves, of healing ourselves inwardly, "getting our heads on straight" or our "acts together." Captains of the ship of self, we have frequently been unable to steer that vessel safely away from dangerous shoals, and so protect it from springing leaks or lost propellers. So often she has nearly sunk or at least run indefinitely aground. Deep gashes and rusty patches scar so much of her underside, which lies hidden beneath the sea's surface, while we've slapped bright paint over her corroding and creaky hull and polished her decks and cabins. The Skipper stands straight and handles the wheel so smartly, as his charge sails proudly onward and outward into the uncharted seas of life ahead: *we've made it safely this far; we're sure to maintain our perfect record.*

But yesterday's charts are no good and the fancy ship is more like a creaky rustbucket. The Captain needs to admit that he doesn't know the way and that the vessel needs a complete overhaul, just as the self-doctored woodsman should have confessed that his makeshift setting and splinting was little more than amateurish and temporary. Yet, something within us counsels us that it is better to doctor ourselves through self-quackery than to go to the real physician. Something from deep within nearly compels us to consider as foolish and humiliating any admission that we might need tie up at the Deity's dry dock; that we might need to look at the Master Shipbuilder's original plans; the Master Mapmaker's latest charts.

To get the self off its own hands and into His; to take the pressure off the self so that it no longer needs to be its own final answer, its own ultimate support, its own unchallenged source of affirmation, guidance and protection unto itself — that is the favor God wants to do for us. That is the grace He offers. And there is no ultimate understanding of why we would want to play the role of the woodsman and want to be the chartless pilot of an unseaworthy vessel, but we do. Deep, deep within lies the mysterious root of pride that is downright dumb and insanely irrational, even as it generates the air of cool control, the aura of indomitable courage, the knowing smile of someone always in the right.

71

A diseased, wounded, frightened, fragmented, directionless self, passing itself off as healthy, whole, secure, "together" and intelligently purposeful in terms of reaching out for what is most importantly and ultimately meaningful is what God sees when he looks at you and me not taking advantage of what He offers. It's the hurting self that I need to surrender. Only so that He could give it back to me, freed of whatever made it hurt in the first place.

I am self-centered because I am hurt, deep down there. I only keep thinking about my teeth when I'm bothered by a cavity, otherwise once they're brushed, I give them no further thought. I think constantly about my thumb many minutes of every hour, on one particular day-only because of a big sore hangnail. Otherwise, to know that it's there and working well is enough. I think constantly about me with undue and constant introspection because the self is somehow afflicted and paining; but because it has *always* been that way and I've learned to live with the pain, I have come to view my self-preoccupation as normal.

To paraphrase E. Stanley Jones, we become angry and lose our temper because someone has dared to thwart the hurting self; we are impure because the self which feels deprived is convinced that pleasure's comfort is its immediate due. We are jealous and needlessly competitive because someone is apparently getting ahead of the self saddled with feelings of inferiority; we lie to others because the self (feeling itself "unjustly" deprived of something it wants) claims the right to the advantage it will gain over the one whom it has deceived; we become withdrawn and self-pitying because the self claims the right to regale itself with the full array of sympathy which no one else could possibly offer it.[7]

Viewed from this perspective the violent tantrums, the crass sensuality, the enviousness, the deceptiveness, the self-pity are ultimately symptoms of deeper difficulty rather than being simply personal problems in their own right. They are symptoms of the unsurrendered self. Such a state of rebellious unsurrenderedness, of I-don't-need-to-lean-on-anyone-else-but-me-ness is a sickness in itself, a disease in its own right, spawning secondary infections, feeding and spreading surface contagions from underneath.

For St. Paul, to be saved, was to be *justified*. To experience salvation was to be a beneficiary of God's *justification*. The original meaning of that expression in Hebrew was derived from the vocabulary of law, meaning that to be justified is to be declared innocent or acquitted (by a court). In the time between the Testaments it had taken on the added meaning of "finding favor" in God's eyes (cf. 2 Esdras 12:7). This was the sense in which Jesus used the word in Luke's Gospel (chapter 18) when he declared that the publican went home "justified," for his humble prayer crying out for mercy had been accepted by God as honest and worthy and was thereby answered.

St. Paul uses the word in both the legal and non-legal sense. In the legal, when he says things like: "Who will accuse God's chosen people? God himself declares them not guilty . . ." (literally: "It is God who justifies") (Rom. 8:33, TEV). In the non-legal when, for instance, in Romans 4 he talks about Abraham, who is still our model for walking by faith in the Christian dispensation, as being justified by faith, and not by his works. That Old Testament saint found favor with God by trusting Him and maintained that favor by ongoing confidence in God's goodness to him, and fidelity towards him, the Apostle declares.

Even though we are guilty of sin, Christ's death wins for us much more than a complete pardon. God's attitude towards us (should we accept that forgiveness) is like that of the Prodigal Son's father: "as far as I am concerned, it is as if *you'd never sinned*."

It goes even beyond that, however. To be granted God's justice is to be invested with a living power which overcomes selfishness and sin. Even more incredibly, it brings the power to live as Jesus lived, in pureness of love, sensitivity and self-giving. We get to have God's righteousness dwelling within us as a dynamic force enabling us to be sons of God after the spirit of and in the image of the Son.

The problem is that this justifying power, this energy to make us inwardly right with God, ourselves and each other

73

is offered to people who have already known so much of the power of another kind of "justification."

I can arrange my inner impulses by only allowing myself to hear that "inner voice" which only tells me what I want to hear and even temporarily feel at peace with myself as a result. I am able to dismiss my own sins, or view my acts of selfishness as if they were nothing, or as if I had never done them-by a mere act of the will. I find a freedom to focus my attention beyond myself onto desirable objects, situations or even persons and attempt to invest them,too, with the power to make me feel secure, whole, affirmed, "ok" or "together," in the inner self. At the same time I say of them that *they* are my deepest needs so that when I have them, I have *everything*. Whatever, then, is within or without which will temporarily kill our hungering for God (and with it our need to accept His help and healing) we may well find ourselves willing to make our "god."

We refer here, of course, not just to unbelievers but to those believers who, when push comes to shove, when things are at their tightest, look to husband, wife, legitimate pleasures and satisfactions, bank account, reputation, success, car, boat or house etc, as that which will restore and maintain the feeling of security or o.k.-ness.

Good things and fine relationships in themselves become tainted as a result of our spiritual misuse of them in our ongoing attempt to justify ourselves, to prove ourselves, to make ourselves secure in the illusion of rightness and wholeness. We make them "idols" in the scriptural sense of the word, as we take what God intended for us as means and helps for us along the way to our ultimate end, and make them ends in themselves, substitutes for the only One who can satisfy our profoundest yearnings.

An idol is anything we worship instead of God or value more than Him. An idol is also an image made by "human hands." I want the image or appearance of rightness and wholeness. I may use these things (or even you) to maintain this image. The ultimate idol is, therefore, myself. But not really myself. It's a false self, in addition to being a false god. The self I would like to be (but could never make myself by

74

my own efforts) I will still try to get you to think I am, anyway. And if you believe it...maybe I will too.

Hosea had counseled his wayward countrymen that they should pray a prayer which included this promise to God: "We will never more say 'our gods' to what our own hands have made..." (14:3 NIV). We, too, will not know the full healing of God's salvation without wholeheartedly entering into the sentiments of such a prayer ourselves.

The work of our hands onto which we had projected our own powers or desired powers (which has the appearance of God) is still a "thing." I "surrender" to that thing because I know I can control things. Mysteriously and ironically, that thing-god ends up controlling me, offering me the salvation of sameness (which is really deterioration) and the security of self-sufficiency, whereas in reality I am over-mortgaged to other things and other selves used as things in such a way that I never find my true self. Only a real God can give us a true relationship with ourselves, make us want genuine relationship with others and bring us to welcome sincerity of relationship with Him.[8]

Richard Rohr calls Original Sin "that sin by which we were sinned against."[9] It's the trauma carried by all of us. A trauma which originated at the dawn of mankind's history and which still mysteriously affects us all, as flawed love and the mistrust it spawns passes on down from generation to generation.

We have looked at this reality from many different points of view and yet we have still really spoken only of one wound, one malady, one defect. It may seem by now, that we have been talking about many different things wrong with us. But that isn't really the case. To reject self is to hate self, but it is also to bury what I hate; and to bury what I hate is to deceive self; and to deceive self is to try to provide the illusion of being whole; and to provide the illusion of being whole for yourself is to look to yourself for salvation. It's all the same sickly process simply seen from various vantage points for the sake, hopefully, of clearer perspective. A certain amount of overlapping, then, is unavoidable. Let us look at this process from just one more "angle."

Besides having a desperate need to be always right, I also have a desperate need to be in control. "Desperate" was not an adjective chosen lightly. We don't simply have a need to be justifying our present pose. It is a desperate need. If God isn't there to do it for me — make me right, that is — then invariably I'll do it for myself. Who can bear to live with the feeling that she's wrong? Such a suspicion is inevitably dealt with immediately, if not sooner. So, too, with the need to be in control. In control of what? Everything.

I have a desperate need to be in control of everything. To somehow be "on top of" everything I experience. Such an "instinct," fueled as it is by the fires of desperation, would seem to indicate that, somehow, at the deepest core of me. I am very much aware of being out of control, of being off-center, of not having a firm grip on something I *need* to have a grip on. I compensate by trying to bring everything and everyone I touch under my power.

Somehow anything not subordinate to me is immediately perceived as a threat, for, to the extent that I don't have God to hold on to deep within me, I need to be "God" for myself. And so, for instance, I will *have* to own a piece of land (lien-free). I will *have* to have my own house (mortgage-free). I will *have* to have more capital than I can spend. I will *have* to have a job where I am free not only to do what most fulfills me but where I can be boss to more and more subordinates. I will *have* to have a wife whose role will only galvanize my drive for more and more success and who will find her chief happiness in seeing me happy in that pursuit. I will *have* to have children whom I will teach to become increasingly pliable to my suggestions; who will need to become what I think they should become, transitionally and ultimately, (e.g., an athlete, just like Dad, on the way to becoming just as socially prominent or financially successful, if not more so . . .)

That isn't everybody, of course, The above examples are those of a typical middle-class American male. But it does, nonetheless, come pretty close to being *Everyman*. For if we juggle the secondary characteristics, desires, and qualities enough, we can apply that little autobiography to almost any man or woman of any culture. To be human is to need to possess.

To be human (in the sense of "post-Eden" human) is to be possessed by a desperate need to possess, to be in control.

Adam the Steward, when fallen, is almost invariably deformed into Adam the Exploiter. The world which was given to humanity to be reverently cared for, is simply seen as that which needs to be plundered in order that I may be enriched. The need to possess that we must briefly focus upon here, however, is the need to *possess* people. Other aspects of pathological control will be touched upon in our treatment of healing of emotions.

Instinctively, we need to possess people as things. We were originally created to be able to enter into intimacy with God and with each other. Because of the Fall, however, the need we have to touch and embrace tends to degenerate into the need to grip and manipulate. We know we need to love and be loved, but something deep and nearly compulsive flaws our reaching out for that in both intent and execution, so that we end up turning the one we "love" into someone we "use" as a stimulus to the self-love of self-gratification.

Only a minority of us are capable of any real intimacy beyond the physical. Superficial and selfish use of the one allegedly loved is what our attempts at real closeness so frequently wind down to, even when apparently and originally well-launched in the right direction. So few seem ever to discover the spiritual dimension of human relationship, where heart truly touches heart, where deepening trust allows ever more profound sharing.

What is so expectant of closeness yet to be experienced, is tragically overruled in large numbers of us by something else deep within, which tells us not to trust the other, not to lean on the other, not to share secrets with the other, not to let ourself go in vulnerability and confidence into the arms of the other, but rather to only *pretend* to trust to share secrets with the other, *pretend* vulnerability while you practice pseudo-intimacy, etc. A *loving deceit* all in the service, of course, propping me up at your expense; of gratifying me inwardly while I pretend to give *back* to you; while all the time I really (or mainly) just care about me.

So very many of us dare not take the risk of opening ourselves up in a deeper place to the other; of respecting with all reverence their right never to be manipulated or deceitfully used; of admitting our need for them as lovers and their ongoing closeness; of approaching the other with no intent of controlling them, but only in the spirit of wanting to enter into a purer pact of mutual interdependence. At least not with any consistency.

And what is true of the other is just as true of the Other — God, our Father, Savior and Sanctifier. The original decision not to trust the Love struck such a blow at the want for intimacy with Him, at the desire for communion with Him, at the rightness of the impulse to lean on Him as our Lover, that we frequently find ourselves helpless to do little else than sin out of that Sin, react selfishly and blindly out of that woundedness.

If we don't reject (as worthy of our time and consideration) the thought of a love-pact-surrender to Him, then we are sorely tempted to only enter into the same kind of relationship with Him as we do with each other: one that leaves us in control; one that leaves us calling the shots, never losing the upper hand; one that lives out of the head, while using words of the heart; one that pretends to lean even as we lean upon the only one we could ever trust — ourselves.

Why has so much of Christianity ended up being little more than a dry, dusty head-trip, hung-up in codes and creeds, bible verses and doctrines — memorized, categorized or promulgated with such mathematical precision and unapologetic dreariness? Because people needed to be in control.

Words, even sacred or inspired ones, as well as the laws, ceremonies, institutions, etc. of the Church (even where any or all these things prove to be right and relevant) are all elements some of us are all too able to be comfortable with, because all of them are manipulable; all of them can be brought into submission to our purposes; all of them can be brought under our control. And to the extent that we are unwilling or unable to love the Person they are meant to lead us to, we end up "loving" them instead.

Any romance which starts out with good intentions and the right words, but in which the lover or the beloved or both refuse to give up control, can only end up being a drab frustrating matter of empty words, faded memories, mechanical love-making and artificial intimacy.

"Christianity" is, with tragic frequency, very much the same thing. I leave the reader to draw out the parallels here, which seem to be nearly perfect.

The Biblical word, "justification," is sometimes paraphrased as: "just as if you'd never sinned." It may also be paraphrased as: "I long to re-make you so that you will be 'just as if you were never sinned against.' "

But to be that way is to be no longer afraid of union, no longer fearful of intimacy, no longer distrustful of the dependency of the lover upon the beloved. Human justice means that what you have taken away from me you must restore to me. God's justice is: *what has been taken away from us through our "parents' " fault and with our belated approval, He wants to restore:* "I *do* justice to Myself, to My limitless compassion and affection by restoring you to your original heritage which you have no right to, and could never earn . . . I want you to have restored to you your forfeited legacy of on-going dependence on Me, your Beloved. If you want to enter into the romance of heart-secrets being mutually exchanged every day; if you desire a whole new freedom to love others the same way, then I give it to you, now . . ."

God-justified or self-justified, God-sufficient or self-sufficient, God-leaning or self-leaning, God-"saviored" or self-"saviored," God-guided or self-guided, being basically "into" myself or ever reaching outwards in love — the choice is ours, thanks to the One who gives us both ". . . to will and to do of His good pleasure." (Phil.2:13)

Chapter 5

Healing Prayer (I)

If the essence of the Fall was somehow caught up in: "God, we don't want you around...", then for that sentiment to be reversed, or for its effect to be undone, one will not be able to avoid saying: "I don't go along with that. I want you to be around."

If we are in need of being saved, then we will have to be saved from not only not having Him around but saved from not wanting to have Him around.

Nothing proved more clearly how little humankind really wanted God around than the Crucifixion. When Jesus allowed *human flesh*, human traits, human words, human personality to become flawless vessels, unspoiled conveyances, matchless conductors for godliness to flow through; when the earth-born Son revealed Himself to be the perfect reflection in human form of what His Heavenly Father was like, the typical reaction to all that was:

> He had no form or comeliness that we should look at Him and no beauty that we should desire Him. He was despised and rejected by men ... as one from whom men hide their faces. He was despised and we esteemed Him not... (Is. 53:2-3, RSV)

Isaiah described Jesus "in advance" (in a passage our Lord would later refer to as prophetic of Himself) as one without form or beauty. He meant, of course, that the beauty of the Servant's holiness, the purity of the way He imaged the Father, contradicted humankind's idea of what is attractive, beautiful or even charismatic. It wasn't sex-appeal, animal magnetism, a carefully cultivated image, or "charisma" which constituted His attractiveness.

Humility, approachability, warmth, mingling with an unwillingness to tolerate hypocrisy, pomposity, manipulativeness, not to mention a low tolerance for the phony was an unpalatable combination for most, it would appear.

The author of The Wisdom of Solomon (about 100 B.C.) penned a similarly prophetic passage, long believed to likewise have special applicability to the life of Jesus (cf. 2:12-20). The way of life of the "righteous man" is particularly disturbing element to His contemporaries and is in such contradiction to their own. His very presence is a rebuke to their thoughts, plans and lifestyle. His familiarity with God is *particularly* offensive.

We should not attempt to fancy ourselves as being all that different from them. For those of us who don't know whether God exists or not, few of that number choose to launch themselves on anything close to what could be described as a spiritual pilgrimage or a quest for the Ultimate. For those who do acknowledge themselves to be believers, an hour-long diet of a weekly sermon, hymns, or occasional sacrament interspersed with a few assorted prayers seems to be quite sufficient. Even for the so-called committed, the idea of living in the presence of God; that this is the normal christian life is not so much dismissed as impossible as conveniently admired (from afar) as being a "wonderful thing"; a "special gift" given to the rare saint or mystic...

If we knew that He loved us and were *there*, then we wouldn't have to castigate ourselves for feelings of inadequacy or inferiority, for they would surely be dissolving progressively by the day. In the face of threat and opposition we wouldn't have to retreat into self-delusion, either. We could turn to Him and find *Him* to be our refuge and protector.

A present, loving God is the solution to what is most wrong with us. The saving God is one who *specializes* in delivering from self-dislike, self-delusion and self-centered self-sufficiency, if that's what's most wrong with us. A Redeemer not satisfied with simply attending to those symptoms which flow from such twisted tendencies of the inwardly twisted self. A Healer who sees the hurt underneath those destructive thoughts and deeds which skim across the surface of our minds and lives.

He was never supposed to leave. He was always supposed to be there for us. We were created to live in an ongoing state of God-consciousness; to move in that security which derives from being ever aware that the One who loves never betrays and always sustains. Jesus came with outstretched arms and said: "Come, be embraced by One who will not let go, for these human arms stand for (and contain) the arms of God."

The predominant human response to that, taken to its logical extreme, was to nail that embrace to a crossbar. The counter-response was, incredibly, a refusal of the refusal. God refused to accept that "no" as a final answer. Three days later a woman fell into those arms alive with new life. Three days later, those same hands broke a new loaf of bread and offered old friends Holy Communion. As Paul said: "For Jesus Christ, the Son of God... is not one who is 'Yes' and 'No'. On the contrary, he is God's 'Yes'; for it is he who is the 'Yes' to all of God's promises." (2 Cor. 1:19, 20, TEV). God refuses to take "No" for an answer.

To experience Salvation, we just say yes to the Yes. We must answer in the affirmative to the One who longs to affirm us. We will need to stop avoiding the truth that we were created to be leaners-in-love. To lean on the Lover as we lean on human lovers—but from a deeper part of ourselves and for a deeper reason.

To want to be saved is to want to keep on leaning on the Lover, for it is an ongoing process. What the Apostle said of a personal trial, we can say of the trial which our life has been, so bare of such love:

> "But this happened so that we might not rely on ourselves but on God, who raises from the dead. He has delivered us from such a deadly peril, and he will deliver us. On him we have set our hope that he will continue to deliver us." (2 Cor. 1:9-10, NIV)

The God who has, is, and will deliver or save us. Anything short of that is not enough. We don't need a "one shot" experience of Him. We need an ongoing experience. Faith is offered to us so that we can lay hold of precisely that.

Somehow we sense that habitual prayerfulness (or ongoing God-consciousness) is a gift. People who seem to find prayer their cup of tea; folks who crave and realize intimacy with God are "special"—specially gifted (in our general estimation), if we are able to accept that this really happens. And we are right. It *is* a gift and those who live this way *are* specially gifted.

What we most need is entry into Presence. The Presence which heals, delivers, saves, transforms. Prayer is the only way to the Presence. If Salvation is a gift which can only be appropriated through a prayer of the heart, then I need to be given both the prayer and the Presence, the access and the arrival. *Both* will need to be gifts.

Jesus taught the disciples how to pray, not primarily through a discourse on its essence, *but by giving them a prayer.* Not a formula-prayer, either. A flow of heart-sentiments addressed to One *they* could call Father (as He did), pleading first the priorities of the Kingdom, the urgencies of the Spirit — only to then focus upon the things *we* would call most important, the needs of the flesh, the insufficiencies of worldly existence. What God would call profound and what even we would consider trivial, the highest concerns of Heaven and the meanest matters of earth placed side by side, pointing to the day when Heaven and Earth will be One. A prayer-gift which will enable me to focus my heart on God, even as I focus my energies, now purified, upon the tasks before me in my present life is what I need and what I am offered.

What I need will not come through a prayer, it will come through prayer. It is not simply an absence capped by a reunion, but a wounded relationship restored to wholeness. Salvation is restored relationship. And the "cement" which keeps me in ongoing communion and communicativeness with the Beloved is prayer. Prayer, then, is not simply communication with Him or conversation: it is a love-dialogue of words and of no words as well, that wordlessness which only lovers know to be more illuminating and revelatory than the most eloquent of phrases.

We referred earlier to Old Testament prophecies describing the day when a new covenant would be given to replace the former. These prophecies, with amazing clarity, indicated the precise manner by which the new would surpass the old. Providentially, a great devotional writer of the last century, Andrew Murray, penned a magnificent little gem, *The Two Covenants*, elaborating this issue with great originality. It seems very appropriate, therefore, to include here a brief but eloquent excerpt:

The Old Covenant attains its object only as it brings men to a sense of their utter sinfulness and their hopeless impotence to deliver themselves. As long as they have not learnt this, no offer of the New Covenant life can lay hold of them...

Through the whole of the Old Covenant there was always one trouble: man's heart was not right with God. In the New Covenant the evil is to be remedied. It central promise is a heart delighting in God's law and capable of knowing and holding fellowship with Him . . .

"I will put my law in their inward parts, and write it in their hearts." When the Old Covenant with the law graven on stone had done its work in the discovering and condemning of SIN, the New Covenant would give in its stead the life of obedience and true holiness of heart. The whole of the Covenant blessing centers in this — the heart being put right and fitted to know God: "I will give them *a heart to know me*, that I am the Lord; and they shall be My people and I will be their God; for they shall return unto me *with their whole heart*"...

Individual personal fellowship with God, is to be the wonderful privilege of every member of the New Covenant people. Each one will know the Lord...

Instead of the vain attempt to work from without inward, the Spirit and the law are put into the inward parts, thence to work outward in life and walk."[1]

Salvation, despite what has been said about it by way of caricature, is not anything less than the freedom to have God as one's permanent friend. It is that friendship which supplies to us what is most missing in the inner us. That offer of a permanent love, relationship, however, is made to people who mistrust love instinctively; who are more comfortable with half-relationships than whole relationships; who are far more comfortable with controlling others than entrusting themselves into their care. Both the Garden, and what has happened since have conspired to make us that way.

Even if we'd become totally deaf to God or His revelation and paid no attention to either (with no possibility of being influenced by the Biblical interpretation of reality), we would surely still be forced to admit that the greatest human failure and the greatest human frustration lies in relationships which at best fall short of their promise; or at worst find themselves in a state of deterioration on the way to disintegration. Why should it be so hard to see, then, that this breaking-down of love-communication in human experience starts with our relationship to God?

People scarred by ailing relationships, frustrated by stalemated relationships, disappointed by failing relationships, frightened at the prospect of fresh relationships (or who are compensating for non-relationships by taking refuge in relationship with *things*) have spoken to so very many of us about God and how or why we need His Salvation.

No wonder, that we can be veterans of thousands of sermons (or even be impressively-degreed theologians) as we talk and reflect upon grace, law, Messiah, scripture, creed, church and even *love*; and it still comes across primarily as a matter of words and a priority of the head. No wonder that people barely in touch with their hearts, frightened of the risk of letting themselves go into *anybody's* arms and care have chosen to present faith to us primarily as a matter of asserting to doctrines, and clinging to the correct phrasing of revealed truth. No wonder that some of us are led to believe that the more theology, doctrine or even Bible you learn, the more you equivalently know God.

If I am living in the New Covenant (a covenant which means, if anything, the Holy Spirit now dwelling and speaking in my heart); if that New Covenant equally means my call to rest in that Presence and listen to what He says; if the call of that Spirit is to hear not just for me but for you; if this citizen of the Kingdom can hear Him say anything; if he can sense any special thrust to what He wants us to hear in this context, it is apparently this: so many words and so little wonder; so many prayers and so little prayer; so much talking at God and so little listening to Him; so much emphasis on sanctuaries of stone and so little focus on sanctuaries of hearts; so much emphasis on Church and so little emphasis on what Church is meant to lead us to *now*; so much needless over-complication of the message, so little burden to re-state it as simply as it was first stated; so much misrepresentation of God, so little repentance of it; so much respect for head knowledge, so little desire for heart knowledge; so much reverence for the Biblical past, so little expectancy of a Biblical present; so much attention to law, so little crying out for freedom from the law; so much self-preoccupation and Church-preoccupation, so little God-preoccupation or being burdened for others; so much talk about rebirth, so little evidence of it; so much protestation of belonging to the *New* Covenant, so much living in the spirit of the Old; so much manipulation via threat and fear into the Fold, so few fishers of men casting with "lures" of love; so many who are subjected to (and unimpressed by) a witness of words, so few who are drawn in by a witness of compassion; so much emphasis on Salvation as a precondition to the next life, so little proclamation of Salvation as healing for this life; so much attention to the externals of sin, so little attention what such misbehavior springs from; so much fuss about the need to be born again, so little call or inclination to *grow up* once you've been given that second chance; so much lip-service to how wonderful it will be to spend Heaven with God, so little talk about how important it is to spend *earth* with Him, too; so much talk about trusting God for this and that; so little testimony about entrusting *yourself* to *Him once and for all*...

Ever since Adam, people have been uncomfortable with the Presence. That's one big reason why prayer appears to us to be a drag, a chore, a distasteful necessity. It wasn't that the Couple couldn't communicate with their rejected Friend after the Fall, it was simply that what now transpired between them, was suddenly a strained, feeble caricature of what so recently had been. *Uneasiness in the Presence* is what has come down to us as part of that mysterious legacy, and unless we are healed of that, we are short-changing ourselves of what was won for us on the Cross.

We have been offered a "new heart and a new spirit" following upon the removal of a "heart of stone" which is to become a "heart of flesh" (Ez. 36:26). The promise of the new covenant is that God "...will give them a heart to know me, that I am the Lord; and they shall be my people and I will be their God, for they shall return to me with their whole heart." (Jer. 24:7, RSV). A wholehearted turning to God, a wholehearted entrusting of ourselves into His hands, a wholehearted seeking of His ongoing companionship, a wholehearted sensitivity to His will, a wholehearted will to do His will is *all contained* within the grace of Salvation. Anything less than wholeheartedness is somehow a denial of, or resistance to what is being offered to us.

We say affectionate things to (and do affectionate things for) one another constantly. And all that time, we are very often only half-listening, half-meaning what we say; half-meaning what our kisses and hugs say; half-promising what our promises promise. All the while we are easily convinced, of course, that the full thrust of our sincerity is backing all these things In other words, it isn't all that easy to always detect our less-than wholeheartedness, so practiced are we in wanting to always present the *image* of full sincerity of motive, full intensity of affection, etc.

When the profoundly gifted Rabbi Heschel writes of prayer, he frequently uses phrases like: "the soul gathered up into full focus" upon God. He is describing wholehearted attachment and attentiveness to God.[2] Anything less than "full focus" or the total gathering up of our heart's energies dishonors both what we want to say and the One to whom it is addresses. To be gifted with wholeheartedness, then, is to be gifted with the power to gather our spiritual longings into a focus that is fully sincere and truly vibrant.

This is what is coming down upon us all right now. Those of us who have never known a Salvation such as this, and those of us who already do. The grace to desire, receive and respond in wholeheartedness, not just once but again and again — always — to the One who loves us with all *His* heart and soul (cf. Jer.32:39-41) is what we are offered. Half-hearted prayerfulness is viewed by the prophet as dishonest prayerfulness: "...Judah did not return to me with her whole heart, but in pretense, says the LORD." (Jer. 3:10 RSV).

To enter any relationship guardedly is to enter that relationship with a basic mistrust or questioning, at least, of the character or good will of the one we approach. To enter with the thought of offering only a part of ourselves, while proposing to extend our whole person is, as we have noted, dishonest. Apart from being graced to do otherwise, we would probably fall into one or the other or both of the above tendencies.

"Father, having lived my life up to this time more in doubt of Your affection than faith; more in indifference to Your presence than sensitivity; more in reliance upon my own resources to save myself than in reliance upon Yours to protect and deliver me where I need it most; I now acknowledge my need to know You from the heart as One who craves my friendship. I am starting to see that not having You there, all the time to lean on, to be supported by, to be graced by, is to live a life that is less than life. Without your welcomed and acknowledged Presence in my inner heart, I have managed to devise all kinds of ways of hating myself and condemning myself. I have been forced to deny all sorts of hurts and inadequacies, summoning at times, a massive dishonesty, an enormous pretending-power in the service of making invisible that which can only be removed though self-honesty and Your Love. I have even convinced myself that all I really needed, deep down, was a better grip on myself, that I could be my own answer to myself, my own best security...

"If these are the things which constitute or point to what is most wrong with me, and the roots out of which have sprung all the failures in love of my life up to this moment, the sins which flow from the Sin, I want to be free of such things (or It), cause and effects, both.

"From the Cross in death's agony, Your Son prayed for me, that Your mercy would turn that moment's rejection of Him (and You) — which somehow contained and symbolized *my* not wanting You or Him, either — into a rejection of the rejection. Jesus pleaded that this, the greatest of all evils, You would turn to the greatest good: my full and free access to Your presence and His by the power of Your Spirit. And in raising Him from the dead, You said 'Yes.'

"I just don't need you now. I need you all the time. I need to know that I am loved by You, Father, Son and Spirit, in the deepest part of the inner me, with a love which never refuses and never fluctuates with caprice."

"I cannot live except out of dependence. If that dependence is not upon You, then it is on things outside of me which I 'pretend' are inside me: success, money, reputation, possessions, or power. Even people I have manipulated into substitutes for you. I want,then, to lean my whole inner weight on you so that I can re-relate myself to everyone and everything else in the right way for the first time. Your word to me is true about wanting to give me this.

"If I am to entrust myself, my whole self, into your hands with the intention of remaining entrusted, you will have to empower me to do that. If I am to let go into your arms, if I am to truly surrender myself to you, your love and your perfect plan for my life, you will have to grace me, with that letting go, pour into me that surrendering..."

If Salvation (as we have described it over the past four chapters) is the thing which we most need, then praying a prayer like the one suggested above will bring it to us; or open us up to receive it in the way were meant to receive it, with its full healing impact. We may need to repeat it again and again, as we are freed to pierce through a lifetime of layers of practiced insincerity. The early Methodists had a practice called "praying through," The Salvation prayer would be prayed over and over again until, as some of the writers of that day described, "...the Glory fell" and the one experiencing the call to grace "broke through" his or her micro-heartedness into that wholeheartedness wherein when God is finally able to answer such a prayer in the full power that He wishes to.

If, as many experts suggest, the roots of emotional suffering and psychological disorder lie in deep-seated feelings of inferiority or self-hate; stubbornly persistent and instinctively reflexive tendencies towards self-illusion; not to mention an unrecognized and shameless pride tainting and twisting so much of what is thought and said and done, then Salvation is something which has *everything* to do with relief from and the healing of those things, too. This book does not deny for one minute how much the piling-up of one negative influence upon another, particularly in the earliest years can inflict profound damage upon the psyche and has so very much to do with the formenting of personality disorders. We all have been wounded by

90

varying degrees of unlove which has left us inwardly impaired. The Scriptures simply seem to be saying that this deprivation of mine which is quite able to be passed on to you, if you are my spouse, child, or friend (insofar as my buried hurt or fear prevents me from giving and showing you the affection you need) can be traced right back to the Fall. The snowball which became an avalanche rolled off of a mountain called Eden.

Two extreme positions have so tended to dominate contemporary thinking about the relationship of spirituality and psychology, however, that it does not seem out of place here to underline such an assertion. One extreme is that Salvation is something which deals with the spirit alone and has little or nothing to do with the healing of so-called psychological difficulties. The other is that psychological woundedness ordinarily has little or nothing directly to do with sin, and therefore salvation or grace.

Contemporary psychology was born in a very non-religious environment because the Church at that time was frequently unable to find help to offer those suffering psychologically, with respect to the alleviation of their maladies. Now, tragically, much of the Church wants to play little more than ambulance driver to the doctors of the psyche. But doctors of the psyche cannot do anything to help people beyond pushing pills and getting folks to accept the fact of their unhealability unless they help them to see *that* and *how* they are unnecessarily hating themselves, deceiving themselves, or mistrusting all but themselves. In other words, help to bring them to a place where they *reject* what they've been doing as self-destructive and positively resolve to move into the opposite direction, even as they are accepted by the therapist with genuine concern, encouraged in a climate of persistent hope, and supported by a firm but gentle faith in their inner self-worth.

But that is repentance. It has to be the beginning of a turning from sin. Such is surely *more* than simply the adoption of a more positive mental outlook. It can only be a deliberate act of detaching oneself from selfishness, hate, dishonesty and pride. And that has to be a significant movement of the human spirit.

It would seem, today, that more psychologists are admitting that they are finding themselves crossing over the boundaries of the psyche into the territory of the spirit than clergymen are admitting that to want saving grace is to have to also want an end to that self-rejection, self-deception and self-inflation *without which neurosis and psychosis cannot exist.*

Prayer can be the very finest kind of therapy because it can lead us into a permanent relationship with the One, the only One, who can touch the profoundest hurt and deepest loneliness. No one suffers emotionally or languishes psychologically, or is out of balance mentally, unless they are simultaneously hung-up on themselves, overly, "into" themselves or needlessly imprisoned within the self. If the relationship which we need most of all is inoperative or barely operative, then the other relationships are necessarily affected in a negative way. That is why the call in the New Covenant to love our neighbor as ourselves follows immediately upon the summons to love God with all our heart, mind, soul and strength. To be suddenly and definitively freed from inner enchainment to self is to find that self both drawn and empowered to pour itself "upwards" towards God and "outwards" towards our neighbor: "The water that I shall give him (the believer) will become in him a spring of water welling up to eternal life." and ". . .he who believes in me as the scripture has said 'Out of his heart shall flow rivers of living water' " (Jn. 4:13; 7:37 RSV). The fountain upward, the river outward—our spirit now sourced in the Holy Spirit and channeled to flow *His* way.

Even if our fear of praying has been diminished because we have started to hand over our self-hate and are no longer as afraid of loving and being loved in the very place we felt most permanently blemished or nakedly ugly; even if our mistrust of living out of a whole new prayerfulness is moderated by the recognition that this new prayer-power will be the employment of a free gift rather than exercising the difficult and rarely-mastered skill we had estimated it to be, we still, most likely, are not home free, I'm sorry to report.

Our culture, the sum total of countless influences which have hammered away at us, formed and shaped us since birth, *directly opposes* such a way of being and living. Almost everything we have experienced at home, school and in the world of commerce and politics has conspired to impress upon us a message which comparatively few of us ever come to doubt: *you are only what you do or what you have; your value is measured by your achievement; doing is the only thing that matters; resting only makes sense insofar as it restores your energies, so that you can go back to doing———*

We were loved more when we did things which pleased our parents and less when we didn't. Then, we were more favored by teachers or coaches when we scored high marks or points and less when we didn't. And by that time, we are usually more than indoctrinated enough to be able to smoothly adjust to the "adult" world where recognition for achievement (which enables us to acquire more and more things) becomes all important. We don't even wince when the banker tells us that we're "worth" sixty thousand dollars or whatever, for most of us have fully adopted the attitudes which makes such sick vocabulary totally acceptable. We have come to believe that we are only worth as much as we have been able to do and what that doing has been able to bring us in terms of the possession of power — financial, social, political, etc. *It may even be the attitude which we operate out of most often, the conviction we cling to more tightly than any other.*

Occasionally, we look at this world of ours and remark that the pace is too unnaturally fast, the "healthy" competitiveness has become too infected by greed, or that the thrust to help bettering one's standard of living has gotten a bit too intense. Which means, of course, that we have basically accepted the promise of: "self-value is simply a matter of doing and having."

To be loved unconditionally is to be told that we are loved before we have *done* anything; that we are truly loveable, of such precious value to the one who extends this unmerited affection — not for what we have achieved, but for *who we are.*

God is only able to love us this way and if we are to "hear" what He says to us when he says, "I love you," then we have to somehow hear this, "I love you" in the way that is spoken, in the way that it is directed at the uniqueness of who we are, in our deepest self. Taking it in the spirit in which it is offered, is what is meant here. To do that, however, we

93

need to not only to be disabused of our suspicion of and resentment towards, other loves which once presented themselves to us as unconditional but weren't; but we also need to come to believe that it's *right* to accept a love which we haven't first "earned." Such inclinations towards mistrust are what we need to lift up to the One who loves this way, the only way which can truly save.

Paul Tournier describes our profoundest sickness as being caught in the apparently irresolvable tension between the two poles of thirsting so deeply for love and at the same time instinctively resisting it because of past disappointments in love and resentments about it.[3] Only Christ can fully resolve that conflict, if we allow Him to.

We need to be delivered from this false faith we have in the cultural lie and be graced to affirm to ourselves the opposite: "I *am* loveable for *who* I am and not what I am or what I've done or can do. I have every right just to be. *Who I am* goes deeper than any accomplishment I might achieve or possession I may acquire. I do not need to feel guilty, then, just for being. I can be, and rest, and not do, above and beyond simply energy-restoration intervals sandwiched in between slices of doing...."

To go into the Presence of the One who counsels me to be still and know that He is the Lord (Ps.46:9) is impossible unless I can allow myself to accept the fact that His acceptance of me (when I come) is because He *wants* to enjoy my being present with Him and wants me to do the same. While He does have things for me to do with Him and for Him, the affection He has for me is not based on that. *Let's just be with each other* is at the heart of my being invited to commune with Him.

If I should become seriously ill and bedridden for a long time or so seriously disabled as to be unemployed for an extended period, that experience might well show me how much I equate the value of who I am with what I can do. This counselor has seen men, for instance, ashamed to make love to their wives or accept the comfort of their affection, because not to be able to work is to be less than a man, in their own eyes. Their depression is far more than the frustration of not being able to work for a while or being confined to bed or home for a protracted interval. It is also the exhaustion resulting from inwardly berating oneself for no longer being a full person.

A person with a handicap in our society is called a "handicapped person." But to have a bum arm or a bad kidney is not to have your personhood handicapped (except in a world where doing is more important than being; where achieving is *why* you get loved), since love is the only thing that creates and keeps on creating real personhood.

We will never be happy just 'being' in the presence of the Beloved unless we are delivered not from the need to do but – to employ that necessary adjective again – the DESPERATE need to do, the frantic compulsion to produce in order to justify our existence and insure the flow our way of more love or love-substitutes. If there's a gift of prayer, then there's a gift of stillness, a gift of comfortableness with just being, a gift of knowing how right it is for us just to rest in the arms of the Beloved, to let go in His embrace.

Our focus at prayer's real beginning in our life will be undoubtedly pragmatic. The hurt, the heaviness, the guilt, the pain, and is He there to help (?). But, when we come to know that He is, and that He not only helps but *is the help*, the Helper, the Paraclete, we can then let Him free us more and more to just come to come. We will still need to talk about worries, threats, concerns and problems, from time to time; but we will know that we'd have come anyway into this special time and place of communing, even if those difficulties weren't burdening us. We will come into the Presence of the Father knowing that He knows what we need before we ask Him (Mt.6:8). In the spirit of the Lord's prayer: His name, His kingdom and His will, will assume increased priority over calls to be supplied with "our daily bread." We may start out seeking blessing for ourselves but He will give us the want and the prayer to be a blessing for others.

Martha's prayer to Jesus was: *Lord, help me – by helping my sister to see that she ought to be helping me clean house and fix supper.* His response was that she was attempting to enlist Divine Aid to support a frenzied lifestyle; and that unless she became more like Mary she's never pass beyond superficial acquaintanceship with Him into true intimacy: "Martha, Martha! You are worried and troubled over so many things, but just one is needed. Mary has chosen the right thing and it will not be taken away from her." (Lk.10:41-42, TEV)

Luke says of Mary that she had ". . . sat down at the feet of the Lord and listened to his teaching" (10:39, TEV). Jesus, of course, addresses not only Martha, but the "Martha" in you and me, as He says: *learn from the one who has learned from me — To just sit (still) and be there, lovingly, peacefully, in such loving attentiveness to who I am and what I might want to say.*

There is such a deliberate contrast between the "one" and the "many" here. Our natural impulse, apart from resting in and moving out of full heart-focus on the One who wills to love us and love through us (and have us always conscious of that in one degree or another) is to be distracted. Distracted from Him and from the "one thing" we are called to do, as well. We are so programmed to *do* instead of to *be* that we feel guilty even about doing, if the doing is "just one thing." If we can, our compulsion is to automatically attempt two things at once even while reaching out for a third, if at all possible.

It wasn't that Martha was to have no concern about supper, clean dishes, soiled clothing or dusty furniture. It wasn't that they'd all be fasting together that night while crusty pans languished in the sink and the trash bucket sat in the middle of the overflow of twice its capacity. It wasn't that the two sisters were to sit in some sort of mindless trance, oblivious to daily duties and worldly obligation, like hallucinating hippies, "freaked out" on beautiful colors temporarily blocking their view of the crash-pad's surrounding squalor.

The "one thing" (in this life) couldn't always be the luxury of silent, rapturous awe at the Presence, or exuberant, grateful praise for having been granted such a privilege, overflowing out of the heart onto the lips. The "one thing" would also have to include things like making supper and doing the dishes. From now on, however, they would be offered as an act of love, both for those who need supper and clean plates as well as the One who ever wants us to love more deeply and purely than we love at present, in the growing awareness of doing these things with Him and for Him.

We are called to do His will and His work in a noisy, busy world; but by bringing with us the peace and the freedom that comes from knowing that our value is independent of what we have done or can do. In the knowledge that in having Him, we have everything, we can return to a world nervously bent on acquiring or accomplishing as many things as it can, as quickly as it can, blessed with a radically different kind of need to have or do.

As Jewish writers would remind us, the Biblical notion of Sabbath was not that it was a day of rest primarily given for the purpose of recharging fading energies, so that one could return refreshed to the following week's work. It was supposed to be seen not as an interval between days of labor but as "the climax of living."[4] It was a call to rest in the Presence of God, who called us to be stewards of His creation, but never so busy that our relationship to the earth or those who live there would overshadow our awareness of Him, His goodness, His care, or His want to enjoy special moments of closeness with His children. The Sabbath, properly observed, would protect His sons and daughters from losing that crucial perspective on life, which, if it is not directed towards Him, ends of falling short of real living; just as humanity, when not directed at One above and beyond itself, finds itself bogged down in what is dehumanizing and so, a victim of its own inhumanity.

The message of the New Testament is that God of the Sabbath presence has chosen to make Himself even more present: that a God who only allowed intimate access to Himself once a year to one (the high priest), now offers an even more intimate access every day of the year to all.

We may feel like we're going through "the bends" or the "D.T's," for a while as we "withdraw" from addiction to this nervous need to do, this desperate desire to have. But we are simply adjusting to a whole new world, a whole new and living way. He will hold our hand and wipe our beaded brow, however, as He comforts us and somehow speeds the exit of these "toxins" out of the "blood" of the soul, drains these poisons out of the system of the spirit. It may take a little longer than we'd like, but it will surely happen so much more swiftly than we could ever have foreseen. And that will prove to us that it was His doing and that it's what He wanted us to have: "For thus said the Lord God, the Holy One of Israel, 'In returning and rest you shall be saved; in quietness and in trust shall be your strength . . .'" (Is. 30:15, RSV)

Martin Buber wisely points out in this regard that we are not surrendering here the "I" or the *real* self when we give ourselves up to God. We are giving up that self who would rather base itself on the security of things which can be held and controlled at will, so that we can be the self who will take the risk of relationship, with all the unpredictability and vulnerability which that exposes us to. We give up basing our lives on the having of things in order to be free to receive and keep on receiving a presence, "a presence as strength."[5]

To start with, we will have to set time aside everyday to be with Him. It is hard to see how anything less than twenty minutes a day will help us move into what Salvation is meant to bring us as a *way of life*. Some of that prayer will be pragmatic and related to external problems and circumstances of my life. Some of that prayer needs to be reflective of my allowing myself to be drawn beyond the practical or utilitarian. Just receiving the Love. Just receiving more of it. Letting Him love me. Letting that love flow into where I feel most hurt or upset or insecure or alone (even if I can't fully characterize what these stirrings of the inner person presently represent in my life). Allowing the Lover more intimate access to who I am deep down there. Then reacting with gratitude, awe, reverence, praise, joy — whatever seems most authentically "me," by way of response. In words, or without them.

Traditional spirituality has tended to view this more silent, more contemplative kind of praying as the privileged preserve of those more practiced in the life of prayer. The Holy Spirit seems to be saying, today, to many, that it's for everybody, right away — even if we can't immediately find ourselves comfortable with too much of it right off the bat.

(The *time*, by the way, should be the time when you find yourself most liable to be free of circumstantial distractions and physically not overtired. The position of the body should be one which strikes a balance between that which would make my body a distraction (through uncomfortableness) and that which would make my body so relaxed that I easily slip into the "twilight zone" between consciousness and being asleep.)

True prayer will bring real relaxation to the body as well as the spirit; but since, as we have already described, it is an energetic gathering up of our spirit's resources, a sensitive, expectant openness to receive and respond to what we have received. *It is not anything approaching semi-slumber.* This needs to be emphasized because many Christians, overjoyed with some of the beneficial side-effects of their new prayer-life (which will come to include a more relaxed nervous system) allow themselves to slide into a state where physical relaxation subtly but steadily overshadows what ought to be their dynamic response to the Presence, as the spiritual energy behind their receiving or responding to what they receive increasingly fades. If it is not dynamic, if it is not a moving in the direction of increased sensitivity to the spiritual; if it is not somehow heightening our consciousness of Who is there and how He is loving us, then we are not moving into prayer — but away from it.

Chapter 6

Healing Prayer (II)

Many people look to a spiritual thrill or state of inner excitement even accompanied, at times, by tingling emotions as "proof" that they have truly surrendered their lives to Christ. Once we have let go of enough self-rejection and self-condemnation or a sufficient "amount" of our need to be in control (even of relationships) and learn to receive, then we ought to be able to truly experience salvation as delight, joy, peace — different and deep "knowings" and our reactions to those "knowings" that we are loved. Never to have tasted the "first fruits" of Heaven; not to have received the "down payment" or "guarantee" of salvation, after having truly let go into His arms is still to be experiencing some kind of blockage problem. We are *all* meant to experience God here on earth, just as surely as we are all meant to experience love here on earth.

On the other hand, we need to be patient with ourselves and with Jesus, as He gently removes the inner hurt of many years and gradually replaces the "tissues" of our spirit (once dead or nearly so) with those which are able to pulsate with fresh and powerful sensitivity to the caresses of His Spirit. The real proof, however, that we have sincerely and wholeheartedly prayed "the" prayer and made "the" commitment is that we begin to experience ourselves as *new people*. (And, of course, that others find themselves impressed by and touched by this newness.)

The experience of new selfhood in Christ may not always be an immediately enjoyable feeling, however. It can be extremely unsettling, in fact. I have, after all, just stopped being a person whose whole weight was resting on herself and her self-appointed props and started being a person whose inner weight is securely anchored in God. I have ceased looking to myself for the ultimate answers and ultimate defenses and have begun to rely on Him for the most crucial guidances and protection. A whole lot of the deepest "me," has been suddenly and radically rearranged. Things that used to be there are just gone, or starting to go. Things that were never there or barely there are surprisingly and bewilderingly "settling in" to stay. I am a new person and surprised at how I feel. Responses not at all characteristic of the old me just seem to happen. I may feel positive about things I used to feel negative about. I may feel guarded about things I used to readily go along with. Attitudes I never had are just "there" and attitudes I always had just aren't.

I sense a certain uncomfortableness with formerly comfortable routines and an unfamiliar craving for the new and different. I no longer sense such a need to impress people with how good I am; the pressure of having to project someone I'm not, or qualities I don't have just isn't there the same way, anymore. Some of it is exciting. Some of it is scary—especially not being as much in control as I used to be. Whatever lightness I might feel at the release of so much piled-up guilt; however much joy I might experience in knowing that I have been unconditionally accepted; no matter how high my spirits are lifted up as a result of having been affirmed with such deep and inner resonance by the Lord Himself; that will not be enough to stop me from eventually experiencing a certain unsettledness and scariness of having to deal with a new "me."

I am not unlike the teenager who isn't sure whether he likes his now deep, now hoarse, now squeaking voice or not, tripping over feet disproportionately long, embarrassed about unaccustomed awkwardness half-wishing it had never happened, half-wishing it had finished happening. I am once again suffering from a crisis of identity.

To suffer that crisis is good. It means that *I meant* what I said when I said the prayer. It means that He meant what *He* said when He promised to answer the prayer. Identity crisis sounds a bit too technical, however. Let's just say that I'm hurting a little bit from growing pains. And *that's good*!

We don't go from the security of a sameness which turned out to be stagnancy—which turned out to be frustrating—which turned out to be insufferable, so that God can give us the security of a new sameness which won't lead to stagnancy, frustration and worse. God takes away our fenced-in little hothouse world so that He can give us a big new world—not a big new hothouse.

Fear leads to false securities. False securities are usually things or people treated like things. Real security only comes from love. His love and what His love does to our love by freeing it from dishonesty and possessiveness. His love, being perfect, casts out fear. Take in enough of it and it will cast out *all* fear. Then we won't need any false securities. Then we won't be slaves of time and place: locked into schedules, if not tortured by deadlines; imprisoned by properties, addicted to the acquisition of objects and equating all this with "peace of mind." It was a lack of love, after all, that frightened us into thinking that we could make up by doing and having for being so "shortchanged" on *being*—being loveable.

Sameness won't be so important, then, whether it's sameness of what we have, or sameness of who we are. *We aren't going to get freed from a "bad" sameness of who we are by receiving from God a "good" sameness of who we are.* We are going to get freed from a bad sameness of who we are by being freed to grow again. And not just again, but *better* than we ever did before, because our growing will be based squarely on *His* power and *His* wisdom and His love and not on our power or our wisdom or our love. We have been saved from non-growth (death) for growth (life).

Luke said of the adolescent Jesus that in addition to growing bigger and older he grew in wisdom and grace with God and man (2:52). The author of Hebrews adds that this wisdom and grace even increased through trials and setbacks, right up to the final trial and setback which His Father turned into triumph and victory (5:8; 2:7-9).

Even Jesus, then, was subject to the laws of spiritual and emotional growth: every day, more and more wisdom, more and more grace—Godwards and manwards. *Relationships:* intensifying and maturing day by day. What His Father laid out for him—our Father lays out for us—the freedom to grow, the freedom to never have to stop growing.

103

...Your Teacher will not hide himself any more, but your eyes shall see your Teacher. And Your ears shall hear a word behind you, saying, 'This is the way, walk in it...' (Is. 30:20-21, RSV)

I will put my law within them, and I will write it upon their hearts; and I will be their God, and they shall be my people. And no longer shall each man teach his neighbor... saying 'Know the Lord,' for they shall all know me, from the least of them to the greatest, says the Lord... (Jer. 31:33-34, RSV)

The New Testament speaks in different ways of the necessity of taking on a new attitude about ourselves, of accepting the fact that we really do have a new identity, once we have surrendered to the Savior's healing love. We have looked at ourselves for so long in one way, that unless we make a very conscious and deliberate effort to see ourselves as significantly different from what we were, the memory of the old self-identity will tend to overshadow, filter out our awareness of, and diminish increasingly the freeing influence of the new one.

One of the things we were most ashamed of, the profoundest nakedness, is now truly and wondrously covered by One who has no intention of refraining from embracing. In other words, the "dark veil of forgetfulness" covering that part of me has been pulled back, that barrier separating the conscious me from a part of me that I wanted not to be conscious of (out of fear and shame), is being taken away. Jesus is reconciling one "part" of me with another "part." I am starting to know now what He meant when He would ask: "Do you want to be made whole?" I can see that He's *already* asked *me* that. I may even sense that He's still asking me that, with no intimation being made that I hadn't taken all the healing I possibly could have at the first moment of saving acceptance.

Already, some of the fear of depth, the fear of going beneath the surface of me is gone, then. I am starting to realize that I don't have to be afraid of what used to be so effectively blocked-off from that "top" part of me which I wanted to believe was the *whole* of me. The deepest loneliness in me is being washed away. That's why I won't have to fear the "dark" anymore, the dark of being alone.

When I go apart to be with Him, I won't be alone at all. If I seek Him faithfully each day I'll discover that I really *was* more lonely for Him than for anything else and so, that strange apprehension about not having anyone with me to talk to, or that irrational need to be ever surrounded by some kind of noise will fade into memory. When it's time to go away by myself with Him, that "requirement" for constant social contact and the sounds of life will oblige me no longer with such absolute authority.

To meet that Lover deep within, then, brings not only the satisfaction of having known the thrill of such surprising affection, it also has meant healing for me. Suffering, which I had stoically accepted as an integral part of my personality is being permanently eradicated. To go to meet Him within, accordingly, is to go to experience the love that heals.

The hope I now experience is no longer simply attached to the prospect of external circumstances changing for the better. Now, my hope (which is somehow *His* at the same time) is instinctively focused upon the promise of *inner* circumstances yielding to ongoing improvement. I have already experienced significant inner change and there is no reason to doubt that this will not keep on happening. The burden of this change was on *Him*: the initiative for this transformation was His. And I sense that this is the way He wants to keep it. My burden was to accept what was offered and to cooperate by swimming with the flow of the healing and not against it. And it still is.

The Old Covenant experience of God at its purest and profoundest was always crying out for something more and something new. The Old Testament saint allowed himself to be taught by God that it was disloyalty to Him to remain content with any or all of His blessings, appropriated up to the present, as if that were *it*. Expectancy for *more*, even when one didn't know what that "more" was, made people like Mary, Elizabeth, Joseph, and John the Baptist "ready" for the events and revelations which would bewilderingly constitute the establishment of a covenant that would be "new" and "eternal."

The individual's being indwelt by the Spirit of God; his or her being able to know the will of the Indweller; an ability and an openness to understand what He was communicating —

a docility, a teachableness, *the gift of being a disciple,* a committed seeker after the wisdom of the Master, who would accept insights and learn truths directly from the lips of the Master — this is what was predicted and this is what has been given. We still need Spirit-gifted teachers; we still need the written word of God, but these are there to help us see more clearly and accept more readily that which is simultaneously being imparted to our hearts by Jesus through His Spirit.

When God offered King Solomon a "blank check" as it were, proposing to let him choose a gift of personal preference, the wise man prayed in response: "So give your servant a discerning heart..." (literally: a "hearing heart") (1 Kgs. 3:9, NIV). In a similar passage from the Book of Isaiah the prophet has the Suffering Servant describe himself in this way:

> The Lord God has given me the tongue of those who are taught that I may know how to sustain with a word him that is weary. Morning by morning he wakens, he wakens my ear to hear as those who are taught. The Lord God has opened my ear and I was not rebellious... (Is. 50:4-6, RSV)

The wisest man of the Old Covenant and the wisest of the New, both are people who have *the gift of hearing hearts* — individuals who know that when one goes to prayer, he must go as one who craves to be taught. Both had such a want to learn *for others;* but both knew also that somehow, what is offered to others must have first been tested within the laboratory of the self.

Self-wisdom, then, is one of the things we will expect to receive when we go to listen to the One who teaches within; and what we learn of ourselves and what we take to heart, healing-wise, as a result, is what we shall be equipped to take to others: the word to sustain the weary, the good news of what will make them free, even as we have been freed.

Nathaniel must have been a man who prayed this way, a man not only whose life but whose spirit as well spanned the two Testaments:

> When Jesus saw Nathanael coming to him, he said about him, 'Here is a real Israelite; There is nothing false in him!'

Nathanael asked him, 'How do you know me?' Jesus answered, 'I saw you under the fig tree before Philip called you. (Jn. 1:47-48, TEV)

It helps to know a little bit of geography and botany in order to find out what lies between the lines of this story for us: namely, that fig trees were very common, and still are, in Palestine. So, for Jesus to say, "I saw you under the fig tree" shouldn't have been the shocking or spiritually significant statement that it was to Nathaniel. Many times in his life he must have stood or sat under fig trees. We can safely presume, then, that within the very recent past, at a moment of crisis, Nathaniel had sought refuge from the hot Palestinian sun under a fig tree, even as he sought the face of God and answers from Israel's God as well. A prayer, somehow echoing the sentiments of what follows, must have issued forth from his heart:

"God! Why do I feel this way? Why do I feel as if something were missing? Why, in my attempts to observe the Torah and steep myself in our spiritual heritage, do I feel so frustrated? Why do I sense as much unfulfillment as I do blessing? Why won't You reveal Yourself and Your wisdom more clearly? ..."

So, when Jesus said to Nathaniel, "I saw you under the fig tree, He must have in some way been answering a prayer such as that: "My Father heard your prayer under the fig tree and is in the process of answering it. He knows your anguish and I am here on His behalf to set your heart at rest ..."

Nathaniel symbolizes Israel (the true Israelite) and Israel stands for the world in need of God. The fig tree of John's gospel of the New Creation is a sign of the fig tree of the original creation, the bush denuded of its foliage so that the Man and the Woman can hide themselves. The need for fig leaves, as we have already suggested, signifies an attempt to compensate for the lost love-covering of God's embrace. It likewise stood as a symbol of the new protective barriers they now felt they needed around them in order to be able to relate more securely to each other, now that they were inclined to mistrust and accuse one another.

Those fig leaves represented the Man's and the Woman's attempt to heal themselves of what happened to their relationship with their God, each other and themselves. A wall behind which each could hide from himself or herself, each other and Him. But only leaves from the *tree of life* were able to bring that kind of healing (cf. Rev. 22:2; Ez. 47:12) and they no longer had access to that tree. Only the Lamb would be able to restore that.

Nathaniel, in the discernment of Jesus, is a "man without guile," a man with "nothing false in him" because he has prayed for Salvation and it is *time* for Salvation and he has desired the heart of what Salvation is. This healing has already started in those who are ready and it is a healing of not only the Absence of God but of *guile*, of what is false, of what is instinctively crooked in humankind.

It is the Father in Jesus saying to the Adam in Nathaniel: "I saw you under the fig tree and I vowed then that I would not leave you in your shame, abandon you to your defenses woven in dishonesty; that I would restore your sonship to you and become Father to you once more..."

A favorite Old Testament conception of God is that He is a rock and a shield. The rock signifies, first of all, that He is the "ground of one's being" and experienced as such — the greatest possible source of security, because He stands under me in the "deepest within," so solidly and unshakeably. A shield is something held in front of me, over the precise part of me where I feel most vulnerable. God is my shield because He will assume the primary responsibility for standing in between me and what threatens to hurt me.

To experience the saving presence of the God who shields is to experience His assurance that we no longer have to resort to makeshift mechanisms of inner and outer self-defense. To move into the fullness of Salvation-prayer, accordingly, is to ask to be shown where pockets of dishonest self-protectiveness might still be operative in our lives without our fully realizing it. (It wouldn't hurt, at this point, to review what we've said earlier about defense mechanisms; and then to periodically pray, as the Spirit leads, for the personal wisdom we might need about how such things might still have a hold.)

Self-discernment of this nature, by the way, often comes not at the actual moment of concentrated prayer-seeking but later on, as we go through our daily life-routine: in the midst of social or business contacts, while we are engaged in casual or serious conversations with friends, acquaintances and especially people we find particularly difficult. Right then, or just afterwards, we are surprisingly (and often, annoyingly) shown how we dislike others (because they are too much like us); blame others for the very thing we have done; pretend emotions which are the exact opposite of the way we feel; do or say virtuous things to compensate for some inadequacy we don't care to face or deal with; try to block out immediately something we don't want to see or minimize as trivial that which we need to view as significant; blind ourselves to the weaknesses and flaws of those we love, even as we envision them possessing virtues and qualities they don't have, etc.

In an earlier chapter, we used the analogy of T.V. instant replay. Our well-practiced mechanisms are usually so well-oiled that a part from professional counsel ever so diplomatically applied, we might never be able to see them or admit their presence. But God's grace, gently but firmly, is able to perform the same service by showing us ourselves; by helping us "catch ourselves" at our game-playing, just as clearly and undeniably as the videotape's ability to bring back a moment otherwise gone forever, with all the crucial, though rapid movements almost miraculously slowed down for easy scrutiny.

Easy to see, but not easy to take. Unless I take all that He's giving me; the honesty to admit that *yes, I was doing or thinking that*; a hope that such dishonesty is well on the way out of my life; a courage to move out in the awareness that I am being graced with more than enough to handle this not-so-pleasant glimpse of self; a certain light-heartedness about what is still serious; a wry and gentle self-laughter; a God-given ability to laugh at myself for being so dumb, but somehow free of sardonic, self put-down.

Jesus picked up on the ancient scriptural imagery of the rock being a symbol for God as deepest security and gave it a new twist, as John Sanford points out.[1] Let's take a look at one of the key scriptures:

109

Every one then who hears these words of mine and does them will be like a wise man who built his house upon the rock; and the rain fell, and the floods came, and the winds blew and beat upon that house, but it did not fall, because it had been founded upon the rock... (Mt. 7:24-25, RSV)

In world literature the house has from the earliest times, been seen as a symbol of the personality. Jesus simply employs this traditional symbolism but stretches the rock symbolism from the security which comes from having God within into the security which comes from *hearing* the God within, being willing and able to listen to the Spirit who brings the love and wisdom of the Father and the Son, and what that prompts us to think and say and do.

Later on in the Gospel narrative, Jesus will call Peter a "rock" and promise to build His Church on that rock. But Peter has just been congratulated and commissioned because he acknowledged that the Master is the Messiah and God's son. And, as Jesus notes, he's learned this directly from the Father whom he'd obviously begun (at long last) to seek prayerfully, and whose voice he now was expecting to hear in response to that seeking.

We are only as strong as our want to hear; only as safe as our desire to listen to the One who communicates Himself and His ways: "See to it that you do not refuse him who speaks..." (Heb. 12:25, NIV); "My sheep listen to my voice; I know them, and they follow me..." (Jn. 10:27, NIV)

"Here I am! I stand at the door and knock. If anyone hears my voice and opens the door, I will come in and eat with him and he with me..." (Rev. 3:20,21, NIV)

While this passage has been admirably employed as a word of gentle invitation to those who have never really accepted that their Lord loves them (and is often used this way) it is important to see that these lines are specifically and immediately directed by Jesus at a church — which is a group of persons who have already accepted Salvation, an assembly of individuals who have come to know that their Father loves them. The imagery, then, would seem to indicate that Jesus is already in the house, namely that He has been allowed access to an inner person but that certain "rooms" are off limits to Him, bedrooms where hurts are hidden, closets concealing compromise, cellars and attics containing dusty or decaying souvenirs of a not altogether happy past.

"If anyone *hears my voice* and opens the door..." Wanting to hear the voice; ongoing openness to keep on listening at "door" after obscure "door" of the inner person for a gentle word that: "It's time to open *this* door today. Don't be afraid. We'll deal with this difficulty together..."—that is the way to progressive healing and on-going spiritual vitality. Wholeness comes *step by step*. The fullness of healing is appropriated, in God's wisdom, in stages which He wills to distribute with perfect, tailor-made suitability to the uniqueness of who we are and what we've been through.

When the door is opened, and Jesus is allowed entry, new victory automatically ensues and it's time to celebrate a wonderfully fresh intimacy with our Savior never before experienced at this depth: "I will sit down to supper with him and he with me...."

The rooms, I believe it is safe to say, could just as accurately be viewed as blind-spots, areas of self-blindness still to be uncovered and resurrendered. Put all the blind-spots together and you've got something like a shadow falling across the potential radiance of the inner self. When Jungian psychologists refer to "the shadow" or "shadow self," this is what the are talking about; and when they do, they are using symbolic terms or images much like the ones Jesus used when he referred to our struggles within as struggles between light and darkness.

> "Thy word is a lamp unto my feet and a light unto my path...The entrance of the words giveth light; it giveth understanding unto the simple..." (Ps. 119: 105,130,KJV)
>
> "Your eye is the lamp of your body, when your eye is sound, your whole body is full of light; but when it is not sound, your body is full of darkness. Therefore be careful lest the light in you be darkness. If then your whole body is full of light, having no part dark, it will be wholly bright, as when a lamp with its rays gives you light..." (Lk. 11:33-36, RSV)
>
> "...for once you were darkness, but now you are light in the Lord; walk as children of light ... Awake, O sleeper, and arise from the dead, and Christ will give you light..." (Eph. 5:8,14, RSV; see also Jn. 8:12; 1:9,11,14; 3:19-21; 12:35-36)

111

The Psalmist spoke of God's word being a lamp or a light which offered guidance to those traveling the pathways of life. That light, when allowed entry to the inner person, brought the gift of inspired understanding even to those not known for sharpness of intellect. The Evangelist saw more than that. The climactic "word" of God to man was a *person*. This word not only brought light, He was light. Light itself.

In our hurt and our fear we had inclined towards willful self-ignorance. That's what Jesus was talking about when He remarked: "If then the light in you is darkness, how great is the darkness!" (Mt. 6:22, RSV) The context is a comparison between the eye of the body and the eye of the spiritual "body" or inner person. If an individual is blind, then the "inside" of the body is in darkness. If an individual is spiritually blind, the "inside" of his spirit is in darkness. He has no inner light where he needs inner light, where he's hurting, hung-up or coming apart. His choosing not to see the inner difficulty (what Jung aptly calls somewhere, "malicious stupidity") not only amounts to a tragically needless sightlessness of the spirit, but actually leads to "double darkness."

It is "double" because it produces a blindness on the surface of things too. What we think, say, or do ends up being that which at the very least is tainted and at the worst controlled by those things we have chosen not to see. In a very legitimate way, as Sanford points out, we can be said to be "possessed" by those afflicted parts of the inner self that we have chosen not to be conscious of.[2] Any significant troubled "part" of the inner self we wilfully neglect and whose existence we deny becomes like an nearly autonomous rebel state which has seceded from the "country" of the soul and secretly plots to control the "federal government," namely the conscious ego.

The New Testament spoke of certain tormented individuals as being controlled or possessed by "unclean spirits." If, as the Scriptures suggest, Satan is allowed control over the inner personality it would seem that the reason for this is that we have decided that a cast-off part of our spirit should continue to remain unclean, in the dark, denied, and therefore unsurrendered to the light which heals. (Jesus, as Matthew records, stated

112

that the *unswept* house (spirit) was the habitation of demonic forces (12:43-45).

To the extent that some dimension of the outer person is controlled by a troubled and corresponding part of the inner which it cannot see, to that extent it can be said to be possessed. Paul Tournier, in one of his books, speaks of an Irishman whose solution to getting rid of his shadow was putting out the light. We all have done that. Jesus, however, has come to take away our need to ever again have to resort to such foolishness. To be afraid of *this* kind of darkness is hardly childish; to be afraid of this kind of light is downright stupid.

To go from a completely darkened room where we've been for a while into another, which is brightly illuminated, causes discomfort to the eyes and a squinting of the eyelids until our vision can adjust to the new environment of light. Jesus, who is the Light, once He is invited to dwell within, does not cause a corresponding degree of discomfort to the eyes of the spirit, however. His light is gentle, like a dimmer-switch which increases its brightness gradually and almost imperceptibly.

We saw earlier, the principle of "only one thing is necessary" when studying the encounter between Jesus, Martha and Mary. It especially holds true here. The Light is focusing itself upon one segment of my shadow self and I am being blessed with a certain piece of self-enlightment. When that realization about what's not right with me but which soon will be, as I accept in faith all that He's giving me healing-wise; and move out in that healing as He shows me, *then and only then*, will it be time for something else to be spotlighted. (If, when I pray or shortly thereafter), I find myself bombarded by all sorts of self-insights and summonses to break loose from old chains immediately if not sooner, then it is not the Light of Christ although a so-called *"angel of light"* (namely, the disreputable kind may have a lot to do with it.

"Jesus, I thought you said you loved me, just the way I am. How come you're apparently telling me now that I've got to change? What's the story here?", we may have already been inclined to ask in prayerful complaint.

He responds "Oh, I *do* love you just the way you are but I love you too much to *leave* you just the way you are," with a sly smile upon His lips and a gently teasing tone to his voice.

There are two laws of change which stand at the heart of the Gospel's call to humankind: from self-trust to trust in God's love (conversion); and from spiritual infancy to spiritual maturity, once we have allowed that rebirth to happen.

Our potential in Christ, a potential to grow and never stop growing is meant in a timing and according to a pattern which is *exactly right for us*. We should never allow the stagnancy of a standstill past and a "maturity" frozen into sameness by an attitude of "I've arrived" to taint our vision of who God is and what He is calling us to. It is we who give to *ourselves* that security which is attached to never having to grow. He gives us the security which is only needed by those who never intend to stop growing.

Someone whom I know well and whose good will I cannot doubt, shares with me a concern he has — about me. He sees me doing something which is counterproductive; but, because I am not seeing this, or seeing it as quickly as I need to, he feels that he has to mention it. Embarrassed and annoyed I immediately rebuff him (even though I sense that he's right) and later on that day, I recount "what happened" to another acquaintance to enlist his sympathy, completely distorting what my friend had said earlier.

This self-protective tendency (self-protectiveness, even against truth) we all have seen operative in our own lives at one time or another. It is often mingled with resentment or hostility towards the source of that truth (which has visited us without being invited) and can even operate in us when God is the source. A classic example of this is easily seen in the encounter between the Jesus of the Damascus highway vision and the recently raging, now cowering Saul: "Saul, Saul! Why are you persecuting me? You are hurting yourself by hitting back, like an ox kicking against its master's stick..." (Acts 26:12, TEV)

The above episode, for all its seriousness and all the confrontation it contains, is nonetheless softened and lightened by Heaven's humor. St. Paul-to-be is invited to grow in self-awareness by waking up to the fact that his present spiritual situation is very much akin to that of an irritated ox.

When we picture for ourselves what Saul must have pictured for himself, we see something like this: the huge lumbering beast is harnessed to a plow which is guided by the farmer who steers it from behind. When it's time to stop and turn, or start again after stopping, the farmer takes his goad or prodding-stick and pokes the ox on the rump or back legs. The ox neither wants to follow the farmer's direction nor does he feel that the goad has any right to inflict discomfort upon him. Refusing to move, he crankily decides to inflict revenge on the goad. Channeling all the moral outrage it can muster into one of his hind legs, the massive and clumsy creature lifts it, ballerina-like, and kicks it back into the goad. Foot and goad collide. "Don't let that happen again" that kick warns the "stricken" goad which must surely hurt a lot more than he does, even though the ox feels its smart, once again.

"Saul, can't you see that you are being just as preposterous as that dumb beast when you carry on this way? I am the farmer, the goad is the truth about you and about Me that I have been trying to show you. You are that ox wounding yourself on that truth, needlessly suffering because you chafe against the very thing which, if accepted, would heal you...."

Jesus is trying to help us to grow by helping us to let go of unneeded inner defenses sitting on top of hurts along with the fruitless, ultimately frustrating, outer compensations they spawn. He has to show us some things about ourselves which we're not going to be all that excited about owning up to. Saul's pain derived not so much from the truth but from all the fruitless energy and all the misspent rage he'd been venting trying to *avoid* that truth.

It is no different with us. If He is revealing to us uncomfortable truths about ourselves, He is gracing us, as we suggested earlier, with a simultaneous vision of the outrageous incongrousness between who we pretend to be and who we really are; a light and comic view of something serious, but about to be so no longer, if we'll let Him heal us.

He has given us all a sense of humor, one facet of which is to protect and promote spiritual (and, therefore, mental) health.

A balanced mind and a resilient spirit are impossible to maintain without it. If our temperament tends to be rather humorless, that only means that inner hurts have darkened our outlook on life and conspired to cheat us out of a God-given sensitivity to the ludicrous along with that spontaneous reaction to it, which we call laughter. The laughter which delivers, sets free, and therefore redeems. One of the ways that He saves us is by blessing us with a thicker skin, an ability to take a joke on ourselves that has no malicious intent, a sense, then, of our own periodic self-preposterousness.

Saul, as Luke informs us, was a consenting bystander, the day they stoned Stephen. The martyr's real holiness exposed the young Pharisee's homemade righteousness for what it was; and the fiery deacon's living faith in the living God threatened Saul's hitherto smug adherence to traditions enshrining the encounters of men now dead with a Lord now silent.

In order to deny this unwelcome realization, the studious young tentmaker became a fanatic persecutor of Christians. In this way he could keep his surface consciousness constantly engulfed in a pursuit designed to distract him thoroughly from something he couldn't deny in his inner heart: *Stephen is right and so is Jesus.* That's why he is confronted with nothing short of utter, naked truth on the road to Damascus: *Saul, why are you kidding yourself? — You're not trying to eliminate my followers, you're trying to eliminate Me.* ["Saul, Saul! Why are you persecuting me? (Acts 26:14, TEV), italics ours].

Saul hated God for being a living God; Jesus for being the unexpectedly-arrived Savior; and himself for not having the courage to face that. His striking out, then, was a symbolic striking out: not to adjust to the changing spiritual situation (a real, active and present God calling him to accept that the crucified Nazarene was the Messiah, through Stephen) suddenly left *Saul* exposed as the false believer. He projects his guilt about being a heretic onto the Christians and punishes *his* guilt in them. Beyond that, however, he is simultaneously attacking the available disciples because he is unable to get his hands on their Master, no longer present in the flesh.

Prayer can be therapeutic because Jesus counsels us from time to time when we pray, and good counseling is therapy.

Our Lord calls himself a Counselor, whose physical absence will be to no disadvantage to his counselees. He promised to send "another Counselor" to take his place after His death and resurrection, the Holy Spirit. That Spirit has come to dwell within our hearts and His role is to bring us everything that the Savior is, has and does. He "makes" Jesus present within us. A "second" counselor or paraclete brings us into immediate contact with the "first."

The New Testament Greek word is *parakletos*, a nearly untranslatable term, because it contains a spectrum of meanings, no one of which perfectly says it all. Counselor, Enabler, Encourager may well be the three best synonyms in this context. In short, it means one sent in to be of assistance where ordinary efforts fall short or prove inadequate; an expert or professional whose services can supplant or perfect the inexpert or amateurish attempts of one who cannot finish the job himself.

Because I cannot "put myself together" properly spiritually or emotionally; because I can't supply myself with all the wisdom I need to know and love myself the right way, and so be able to live in an ongoingly fulfilling way; because my self-counseling isn't good enough, I need a counselor who isn't me, *another* counselor. And that's where the Holy Spirit comes in. He is here to bring me the counsel of Jesus.

It may be in God's plan to bring me some of the personal counsel I need through a living human being who will be used as a channel for His wisdom for me. Much more than I realize, however, may be available to me directly in prayer and prayer's aftermath, if I will approach the Savior prayerfully with persistent openness to be counseled by Him through the agency of His Spirit.

One of the words used in the Pauline epistles for counsel is employed there in the sense of a "word of loving rebuke"; constructive criticism offered in the sensitivity of Christian charity. There is no growth, spiritual or psychological, without a matching willingness to be criticized constructively.

Few of us have any objections to the idea of constructive criticism, even as something that we might need from time to time. That doesn't always solve the problem, however. So many of us have been victims of *destructive* criticism in the

117

past; or recipients of criticism offered for "our own good" which was in reality little more than put-down masquerading as concern. Accordingly, we are instinctively resistant to the most gentle and obvious criticism of a truly constructive nature. A deep defensiveness which springs into play with incredible speed is firmly rooted in so many of us, empowering us to deny even Jesus His lovingly corrective word of healing discernment. We will need, quite a few of us, to ask the Deliverer to free us of this irrational fear of being cruelly criticized.

The Holy Spirit, as we said earlier, is the Encourager. Another New Testament word for ounsel has as its main thrust "that which brings encouragement." The root meaning of encouragement is to "breathe courage into." God's counsel breathes courage into us. The courage we need to face our faults and to change. The Counselor brings the words of Jesus to us, the right words for us: some of them right off the pages of the Bible; others spoken directly to our heart. In either case, He utterly personalizes them. He absolutely specifies them to the uniqueness of who we are—right now, at this precise moment in our lives.

That's why a passage like the one which enshrines that marvelous encounter between Jesus and the Samaritan woman at the well can be so pricelessly helpful.

He asked her for a drink of water as they stood by a well. Let's look for a moment at a few passages from the Scriptures which, I believe, throw significant light on the encounter:

> Keep your heart with all diligence, for from it flows the springs of life. (Prv. 4:23, RSV)
> All my springs are in you. (Ps. 87:7, RSV)
> . . . You shall be like a watered garden, like a spring of water, whose waters fail not. (Is. 58:11, RSV)
> Like a muddied spring or a polluted fountain is a righteous man who gives way before the wicked. (Prv. 23:26, RSV)
> The words of a man's mouth are deep waters; the fountain of wisdom is a gushing stream. (Prv. 18:4, RSV)

We have already made reference to the two times Jesus prophesies of his followers that they will be fountains of love surging majestically upwards to God, and rivers of compassion rushing powerfully outwards into the desert of their fellow man's despair (Jn. 4:14;7:37). These references joined with the ones above, at the very least, seem to say this: *If you would understand yourselves, look at the underground spring hidden beneath the earth, which, when allowed to properly channel itself out of what contains it, can become not only a well, but is able to express itself as a fountain or a river.* The well which avoids pollution by allowing itself to be drawn from; the well which can pour itself out as a river that brings life to everything it touches; the well which can even become a fountain spurting up to catch the light in its droplets, sometimes refracting it into rainbows, bestowing its bright and startling beauty upon anyone who sees it, even as it brings coolness and refreshment to those who stand near.

Personality, the Scriptures say out of this imagery, must flow both upwards and outwards, Godwards and manwards in love if it is ever to realize its true significance.

He asks her for a drink of water, but He is asking for more than that: I want to drink of *you. I want you to pour yourself out to me. I want the refreshment of your love . . .*

She is simply struck by the externals of it all and sees none of this, to start with, only that Jewish men do not address women in public and never ask Samaritans, men or women, for favors.

"If only you knew what God gives". . . Jesus remarks in reply to her superficial wonderment, shifting gears already from the trivial to the eternal. Somehow *He always says this* in one way or another when we come to Him with our complaints and shopping lists. It's not that these things are of no concern to Him; its just that our expectancy is so locked into the secondary, and so confined to the seeking of one or another of His blessings rather than thrown open to the Giver of all good gifts, Himself.

They have now arrived at the very heart of the matter, the very core of what the human personality can become when entrusted into the arms of the Savior — a feeble meandering trickle energized into a powerfully pulsating fountain, a fountain thrusting upwards into a higher kind of living and loving: *Drink of me and you will become that fountain.*

She is not seeing much of this, however. She is uncomfortable with symbolism, with hidden meanings and subtle suggestions, — precisely because her spirit has lain dormant all these years. She is like any of us. She wants it all spelled out, all nailed down — hard facts and quick answers. But she is being summoned (as we are) out of the attitude of "give me what I need to know, if I need to know things about God and my relationship with Him so that I can hurry back to the things that really matter, like work and paying the bills and getting a nicer house. . . ." She and we are being called into the "be still and know" kind of knowing, the knowledge of the heart, the poet's way of reflecting, the artist's way of seeing, and the clock cannot be allowed to ride roughshod over that. God has hidden things so that we would search; He has buried things so that we would dig; He's arranged that many things could be decipherable only in a climate of serene and silent seeking, sheltered from time's tyranny. He knows what we are made of and He's always known how hard it would be to extract us from the rat race which we see as life's normal pace.

She is not quite ready to see that He is her food and He is her drink, however.

"Go and call your husband . . . and come back" (Jn. 4:16, TEV), Jesus requests. She could have backed out then. She could have pretended that she had one, and left for home with no intention of returning. He gave her the perfect "out." He hinted at where she hurted the most and invited her to entrust that hurt to Him, by not denying it. It's the same Jesus who approaches us with the same gentleness. The gift of courage, the gift of honesty is given at moments like this!

She admits that she has been married five times. "You told me the truth *that time*" (Jn. 4:18, translation and italics ours) He teasingly responds, as He not only praises her truthfulness but simultaneously implies that she hasn't been as honest elsewhere. When someone suddenly remarks to us, with eyes rolled back or with extra volume and emphasis: "You can say *that* again," ordinarily they are challenging some understatement of ours, with gentle sarcasm. It's that kind of a wisecrack. *He's getting her to laugh at herself.*

120

She may have, but right about now she feels that it's time to change the subject. She asks Jesus about his position on a current controversy raging between Jews and Samaritans about which is the holiest mountain on earth. When Jesus gets too close for comfort; when He wants to heal something you're not "ready" to have healed; what better dodge than to drag out the Scriptural trivia or other irrelevancies: "Did you know that the word "grandmother" is only used *once* in the entire Bible?"; "What powerful foreign king in the Old Testament, had two z's in his name?"

Maybe we don't get *that* bad. We just read about the destruction of Sodom and Gomorrah, when the Holy Spirit is trying to draw us to reflect upon how First Corinthians Thirteen's call to love is so unanswered in our lives. When Jesus is trying to lay a few hints along the line of go-home-and-get-your-husband upon our hearts, we trot out the twenty-third psalm or some other inspirational tid-bit and recite it at Him or "praise Him to death" so that He can't get a word in edgewise. . .

But she doesn't get away with it. He untrivializes her trivia question and talks about the new worshipers who will soon be showing up not on the Samaritan mountain and not on the Jewish mountain but *everywhere*. People who'll be able and willing to pray everywhere and anywhere, at any time of the day or night. People comfortable with prayer because they're comfortable with God because they're comfortable with truth. The truth about Him and the truth about themselves.

We are being gifted to worship Him in Spirit and in truth, right now. To start for the first time or to keep on praying more Spiritually and more truthfully than ever before. He was so very gentle with her and yet so firm and so persistently determined to encourage her to not be afraid of the truth about herself, as He showed it to her. No put-down about her past; no looking cross-eyed at her present. Just a simple invitation to acknowledge the truth of past failure from One who obviously had so much faith in her ability to change and so much hope for her that she would. She'd felt so guilty, deep down. She'd had been so fearful of condemnation, both human and divine. He refused to appeal to either that guilt or that fear. He only wanted to take it away.

He was the not only the Constructive Criticizer and the Encourager but the Enabler too. He conveyed to her so clearly that He could do for her what she could never do for herself — make herself pure again, make herself strong for the very first time, make herself into a real lover.[3]

Richard Rohr has brilliantly corrected Transactional Analysis from the viewpoint of Biblical theology. Jesus' affirmation of us in our sinfulness isn't: "I'm O.K. You're O.K.," he asserts. What Jesus declares is: "You're not O.K. But that's O.K."

He accepts us in our "not-O.K.-ness," by loving us anyway. Once we come to believe that, we are then ready for a further word: "It's not O.K., however, to leave you that way. Allow me to love all the not-O.K.-ness out of you."[4]

Chapter 7

Healing of Memories

It was Eastertime and I wanted to somehow plug into the joy and the hope of Jesus' having risen from the dead. There was a problem, however. Ever since *last* Easter things had gone steadily downhill. One setback after another had come to haunt me. There was, on the other hand, reason to believe that things were getting better. But, somehow, the memory of so many sadnesses and disappointments crammed into such a comparatively brief period of my life was still there. Like a heavy weight hanging around my neck, inclining my head and therefore my face and gaze, downwards, even though the prospect of brighter days ahead was real and almost definitely in sight.

But to get excited *now* about Jesus' having come out of the tomb two thousand years ago, even if that did signify Heaven ahead for me, provided I remained faithful to my commitment to Him, somehow seemed contrived. If the Resurrection couldn't touch what was still burdening me so heavily at this precise moment in my life, its significance for the present was little more than a distraction whereby I could look back at something centuries removed from today, or look "ahead" to a future meeting with the Resurrected Christ in eternity and so not have to think, temporarily, about what had just happened.

I sensed that He wanted me free for what the *present* was calling for, cut loose from crippling connections to what no longer was. But *how* to link up with that remained unclear.

My favorite Gospel account of the Easter happenings was Luke's narrative describing the journey of the two disillusioned disciples retreating from Jerusalem, on that strange Sunday after so fateful a Friday which only Jesus' enemies would up to that moment be able to describe as being "good" (Chapter 24). After putting my Bible down at that crucial moment of unanswered questions, I closed my eyes and sat and prayed for the wisdom which had hitherto eluded me. It seemed right to picture the event in my imagination, as if I were watching a movie, or something along these lines. For once, it took no effort; it just seemed to unfold before my mind's eye. There was one startling difference, however, from the way in which the episode is described by the Evangelist. The two disciples and their mysterious companion (yet to be revealed as Jesus, raised from the dead) *all had Yiddish accents.*

The disciples were discussing with somber, yet almost feverish excitement, the events surrounding Jesus' arrest and execution. The Stranger is playing dumb, however. He pretends to know nothing of what has happened, as, with feigned curiosity, He questions them about it. Cleopas, just as in Luke, turns, and with tones of both gentle rebuke, and real amazement reacts with a counter-question: "Are you de only vun in all Jerushalem dat don't know vut happendt here in der last few days?"

And now comes the counter-counter-question that is delivered, in that strange inflection so commonly characteristic of Jewish people, where the tone of voice doesn't keep peaking upwards, as when we ordinarily ask a question in English, but prematurely shifts downwards and then maybe upwards again, but doesn't quite make it. With such crassly insensitive matter-of-factness; with such outrageously unapologetic ignorance, Jesus replies: "Sumpin happenedt over der veekend?"

It's such a put-on! He's stringing them along, and He's enjoying it too. It's like Peter Falk, doing his Columbo routine. I just can't help myself. I begin to chuckle. And then I start to see. *Jesus is making light of His own death.* He's playing dumb.

Betrayal, torture, mockery, abandonment beyond imagination — only three days ago and *its like nothing.* It's all behind him; it's totally turned around. He cannot be bothered about getting bothered about it. It's not just that what they did to His body has been undone; there are no ill-effects presently being suffered in his psyche or spirit either. There are no butterflies in His stomach when He thinks of it, no tightening of the neck muscles, no quivering of His nerves, no trembling of the hands, no shortening of breath, no lump in His throat. *This memory has no power over Him.*

The Jesus who was able to *make light* of what had happened to Him was present at that moment to help me to do the same thing—to make light of what had happened to me. The conclusion was inescapable. Even though I couldn't yet see *how*, it was enough for me to accept *that* it must be. That He willed it. That He willed that I will it. And as I did that, something knotted within began to come unraveled, something anxious started to relax, something very sad lost so much of its sadness. Just by giving Him permission to do what He wanted down there, and not knowing much more about the process or the object of the process, than that the inner pain connected with disappointments of my recent past needed to be healed, opened me up to healing which was both instantaneous and detectable.

Up to now, we have focused on Salvation as healing brought to bear on the Garden Wound. It is, after all, a healing of the deepest loneliness, the deepest fearfulness. More and more Christians today are seeing that what happens there in the depths of our hearts ought to be allowed to do all that it has the potential to do. If such Grace was never meant to heal buried or half-buried traumas which happened to me when I was three, seven or ten, all right. But if it is both able to touch and bring its healing powers to bear upon these things too, then we ought to let it.

One could certainly put together a persuasive argument promoting such a position out of an analysis of the healing and deliverance ministry of Jesus and the radical *personality* transformations which obviously resulted from it. The fact of the matter is, however, that people lately have just humbly and quietly prayed for the wisdom to avail themselves and others of whatever healing properties His saving grace might possess to rid us of the weight of a painful past. This writer is one of them.

Right now I am thinking particularly of Christians of both conservative and liberal backgrounds. Conservatives, so often "into" safer, time-worn expressions of the Gospel sometimes dislike the words "love" and "healing" having so much prominence when the issue of salvation is, after all, so undeniably linked to depravity, sinfulness, blood-atonement and getting to Heaven, etc. All this "inner healing talk" will just distract from all that. My answer is that the Good News is not just a matter of talk but of power (cf. 1 Cor. 4:20; 2 Tim. 3:5). People who have not only found Christ, but deep relief from life-long emotional pain will invariably turn out to be irrepressible witnesses to the *present power of God's love* and will carry that message to those characteristically least disposed to listen to it. Such individuals, by the way, aren't a bit surprised to learn that "salvation," the English word, is derived from *salus*, a Latin word meaning "health" or "wholeness."

As for you liberals, (some of you, anyway) I've just got this to say. Your call to the Gospel is so often seen as a summons to minister to society's ailments. Psychological suffering spawning only more psychological suffering in others is certainly one of the greatest blights tormenting contemporary society. If you're not taking all that the Gospel offers to people so widely and deeply afflicted, then your social concern may not be as Christian as you might think.

Inner healing is synonymous in many circles today with healing of memories. I believe that it is much more than that. That's why only one chapter of this book on the subject of inner healing will treat of healing of memories. On the other hand, pioneers in this area of Christian ministry like the late Ruth Stapleton and the Fathers Linn, S.J. have quite effectively used the submitting of memories of past hurt to Jesus as the starting point which can eventually lead to every aspect of the personality being brought under His healing influence.[1]

The memory which I referred to at the beginning of this chapter was really not a buried memory. It was an easily recalled remembrance of a series of unpleasant events which had only recently happened. When they had happened, however, not having a faith that was full enough, I could only react with a certain degree of negativity. At times, with resentment towards people who may have been trying to hurt me; even towards God, perhaps, for allowing such things to happen. At other times, with self-pity: I was just too nice a guy for this to happen to, and no one would ever fully appreciate the injustice of it all. . . .

If this misfortune had occurred, or something like it, when I was younger — being even less adequate at handling such threat or pain, the odds are fairly high that I would have tried to bury the memory of such unpleasant things. But if I had, I just wouldn't have buried the unpleasant memory, via a mind-game I played on myself along the lines of asserting or pretending to myself that it just hadn't happened. I also would have buried my reactions to those traumatic happenings. And that can be even more dangerous.

Precisely because my reactions to such things can be inadequate, less than balanced, needlessly negative, dangerously hostile — in other words, just plain wrong, they can end up being personally destructive. All the more so, should they be suddenly buried.

Buried resentment, buried fear, buried doubt, buried desire for revenge, buried bitterness, etc. are *just buried* — not dead, not truly disposed of, not really gone at all. Just out of sight, for a time. At the very least, they will occasionally surface; generally, in some disguised shape or form to temporarily plague (to my bafflement) how I feel or how I think in the present — coloring what ought to be a sunny-day disposition with cloudy negativity.

At the other end of the spectrum of damage, they may end up instigating what turns out to be a *life-long pattern* of instinctively reacting with hostility, suspicion, anxiety, manipulativeness, etc. in the face of a variety of circumstances *with no apparent connection* to something that happened and was "forgotten" years before.

I'll give you an example of what I mean. He had been, perhaps, my best friend in the fourth grade. And I hadn't seen him in almost thirty years. Now, I was quite unexpectedly looking at him again. A grown, tall, sturdy man — not a small and skinny playmate, anymore. He was unconscious, in the intensive care unit of a hospital, hundreds of miles away from the town where we'd gone to public elementary school together; and I was the priest they'd called to give him the Last Rites. I said the prescribed prayers and anointed him with the sacramental oil. Then I added my own prayers for his healing.

I left the hospital and returned to my car. I just couldn't bring myself to turn the ignition key. I sat back and point-blank questioned the Lord about what was going on here. Why this strange, frustrating reunion? What was Providence trying to bring about in the life of my childhood friend, which might be in its last hours or days?

For just a second, I could see it all again. Just the way it was that day when we were in the fourth grade. It was after school, in the basement of St. Mary's Church. A nun in the old-style starched wimple and black-robe-to-the-floor habit was conducting catechism class.

"Everyone who went to Mass last Sunday, put up your hand . . ." Every hand, but one, went up. "Peter — you *didn't* go to Mass, last Sunday?" He never got a chance to give her his excuse. In those days, there *weren't* any. He had missed Mass. He had committed Mortal Sin. If he had died before going to Confession, he'd have gone straight to Hell . . .

Once again, I could see him just the way he was that day. Tears of shame streaming down his face, scarlet-red with embarrassment. It didn't matter that his parents were farmers and lived five or six miles from Church. It didn't matter that they didn't go to church all that often and if they didn't take him, he had no way of getting there. He had committed just about the worst sin you could — the sin of missing Mass, the thing which probably angered God more than just about anything else.

Even if I had been shown *that* and nothing else, I'd have been so incredibly blessed. What I had forgotten and Peter had most likely forgotten, his Lord would never forget. How that little boy had been so needlessly and tragically hurt — all in the name of religion, all in the name of Christ.

Jesus, however, not only knew about what happened to scar Peter that day, but knew how that scar still continued to hurt him today. How it stood between the confused little boy still hidden underneath the self-assured, mature adult and the One who loved him more than anybody else. That scar had to be removed and some of the removing was somehow being accomplished while he lay unconscious and an old friend whispered prayers over his bed.

The next day I could actually see some of the healing happen. He had rebounded quickly. Twenty-four hours later he was awake and alert and pleasantly surprised to experience a reunion in that place with an old classmate from his youth. I was still his friend and he mine. We joked and reminisced. His friend, however, was also dressed in black, churchly garb. Now, he was likewise an official representative of the same Church. And where the nun had rejected, the priest accepted; where the former had seen fit to condemn, the latter was given the opportunity to affirm. I was somehow being used to make up for what she had done. Perhaps Peter would never need to recall what had happened on that painful day. With such delicacy and subtlety was the Healer at work. There's more than one way to heal a memory.

But Peter wasn't the only one getting healed. So was I. I had never experienced directly anything quite as negative as he had, that day; but I'd grown up in the same Church. So much of what wasn't healthy in Catholicism at that time had, I began to see more clearly than ever, had done a scarring work inside of me. The harshness, the inflexibility, sometimes even the self-righteousness of many priests and nuns (I also had been blessed to have known gentle and warmly human ones, too) had left me apprehensive, at the very deepest levels of who I was, about who God was. A God who would send you to Hell for missing one Mass was someone to be terrified of. You don't have to suffer a "massive" trauma like Peter to become equally wounded. A lot of "mini-traumas" can add up, and so end up, being the equivalent of a big one.

Even after I had seriously started to accept by way of personal experience that God really *was* Love, pockets of buried fear of His alleged cruelty, submerged anxiety about His supposed judgmentalism still remained and were not immediately or readily let go of upon conversion. So very many of us need deep healings of wounds deriving from a clearly unnecessary harshness in our religious upbringing.

An Episcopal nun, Mother Elise, in her doctoral thesis at Columbia offers some amazing documentation, along this line. In investigating the possible negative influence of authority figures on children's images of God, she discovered an unhappy common denominator. If God is like my parents, pastors or teachers then He is probably the *unfair goal-setter* and the *capricious punisher*.[2]

Whenever old doubts return, which in effect suggest that God is cold and condemnatory, I often just think of the Jesus of Peter's bedside. The Jesus who had grieved for a little boy's hurt and would not be comforted until that wrong had been righted.

I had mentioned this episode by way of example. An example of how past, buried hurt could affect present behavior without our even realizing it. There are a lot of Peters walking around, saying to themselves "I'm just not comfortable with Church or even the idea of God or prayer. I can see how it's O.K. for some folks but I'm just not disposed that way . . ."

What they may not realize is that they might well have buried a nasty memory, or two, of being turned off by a minister, teacher or parent, etc. who told them about a God they couldn't possibly trust, let alone love. A *pattern* of distrusting God or of automatically and unconsciously associating distastefulness with the very thought of Him may have been initiated in episodes as apparently simple and as brief as the one recounted above.

Years later we may find little difficulty in coming up with a lot of apparently reasonable, mature or sophisticated reasons as to why we can't be believers or committed believers, and all the while it's probably rooted in a little boy or girl's confusion or hurt.

Before we go any further, perhaps we need to talk briefly about whether this healing of memories business is really in our best interests. Is this discussion setting us up to go probing around in our past and priming us to start digging up unwanted remembrances?

In a way, you could say that the most self-aware people in the world are psychotics. They are so focused on their (supposed) inner selves that they are no longer in meaningful contact with the world around them.

Pronounced neurotics come in second. These folks are forever thinking about themselves, their problems and their hurts. They generally manage to fulfill what they perceive to be their primary responsibilities in the world. Even these things, however, in some way or another they view as distractions — necessary evils to be endured only until they are free to return to life's only significant function — thinking about themselves.

Selfishness, then, a jealously guarded "right" to be constantly thinking about *me* is at the heart of emotional disorder. I will, therefore, never be healed inwardly *by getting help* from God (or anyone else for that matter) for the purpose of enabling me to think about myself even *more* than I used to. *Healing will come through a lessening of self-preoccupation and not the opposite.*

So, before we talk about the possibility that Jesus might want to heal a traumatic memory of ours; or how He needs to show us a destructive pattern of response in our lives flowing out of that, let us say, right off the bat, something which might seem to contradict such a suggestion, but in reality only sets it in true perspective: *God is not really anxious to get us rummaging about in our past.*

Jesus came to teach us how to live in the *now*, to live with God in the now, to do with God in the now. He was well aware that the two greatest enemies of living in the now are preoccupation with the past or anxiety about the future. We do no violence to the Gospel, I believe, by paraphrasing it this way. Jesus *forbids* us to go into our past or to try to project ourselves into the future. If He wants to give us a vision of what He would like us to be or do by way of a free choice to cooperate with His grace — *fine.* Otherwise, no crystal-ball speculation about "fate" or "destiny" denying the significance of freedom and choice. If He wants to show us something about our past, as it presently relates to the way we are today because past hurt is intimately connected to today's hang-up, all well and good. We have commended our past and our future into His hands. Only He, then, should be able to grant permission to us to look back to what was, or ahead to what isn't yet, but can be (by His favor and our cooperativeness).

"I will not go into my past, Jesus, unless You call me there . . ." is a prayer which those embarking upon a path of inner healing might well need to pray. That way, as we petition for insights and wisdom about how He wants to heal us, or even where He wants to heal us, (if He should choose to bring our past to mind). He will bless us with a peace signaling that *He* was the one who drew our attention to this difficult moment from our earlier days. He will also flood us with a hope that healing will soon be the gentle outcome of such prayerful reflection. If, on the other hand, we experience a marked absence of this peace and/or hope at such a moment, that seems to be reason enough to terminate our considerations upon the matter, as probably not prompted by God.

We spoke just above about the frightened, "guilty" little boy hidden "within" Peter, now a grown man. A small boy or little girl is hidden within so many of us, tragically and needlessly imprisoned by the shackles of a certain immaturity but ready to reveal himself or herself in the twinkling of an eye, at the dropping of a hat. If this is not always to our own embarrassment, then it is much to the embarrassment of those who are not only forced to be victims of the muted or boisterous poutings, etc. of a wounded child dressed up as in an adult's body.

Just about everyone is familiar with Jesus' parable of the Good Samaritan. Its immediate, obvious meaning applies to our "neighbor" in need who, as the Teacher surprisingly demonstrates, may even be a stranger, whose distasteful-appearing wounds may initially stir uncomfortableness within us and whose urgent needs may assault our convenience, or force us to open our purse. We are informed that he is our responsibility — we, who like Cain are often inclined to question the propriety of even having to be our (blood) brother's keeper.

John Sanford suggests that the parable may also apply with unique pointedness to our inner lives as well. The man who has been beaten and robbed by thieves and left dying by the roadside can also be seen as a symbol of the wounded inner person. A part of me concealed from immediate view (lying in a roadside ditch) has been robbed of what is rightly mine (health and strength). The Pharisee and Levite, (the part of me "into" appearances and respectability) refuse to acknowledge the destitute and "bloodied" side of me, a "stranger."

A Samaritan comes by, however, (Samaritans were half-breed "heretics" despised by most full-blooded and "right-believing" Jews of Jesus time). He is the only one who will help. He is repelled by neither the torn, bloodstained clothing nor the death-like pallor of the victim. He is the disguised, despised Christ who is not afraid to associate himself with the woundedness and destitution of the inner me.

He is "disguised" because it is nearly unthinkable that the Resurrected, Victorious Savior-King would ever want to reveal Himself as one who stoops with such incredible concern over that which is ugly and hidden and deathlike: *That can't be Christ.*

He is "despised" because He associates Himself most immediately and determinedly with that part of me I despise the most, what I want to "leave for dead," hidden from sight what isn't worth bothering about. The "Priest-Levite" or "Pharisee" part of me is inclined, then, not only to despise that dimension of me, but anyone who would draw attention to it, even out of love. It is possible, accordingly, not only not to recognize the one who concerns himself about my inner woundedness but also to be bothered by the One who chooses so to care; to resent this intrusion; even to despise *Him* even as we despise ourselves for being so impaired as to have attracted His attention. And so, we are tempted to protest. *That can't be Jesus.*[3]

We said earlier that the call to prayerfully examine a troubled moment from our past should not be listened to unless we sense ourselves graced with the requisite peace and hope. That is not to say, however, that such blessed assurance cannot exist side-by-side with a certain degree of discomfort. The discomfort of the wound itself; the discomfort of having something so long hidden brought to the light of day; the discomfort deriving from the knowledge that Jesus is the One who is insisting upon this "surgery" that we'd up to this moment declared unnecessary. The exciting prospect of the new freedom and health soon to be ours (hope), as well as the assurance that the surgeon is gentle, skillful and brilliantly successful (peace, born of trust), will undoubtedly more than sustain us.

On the day the doctor tells us about a hidden tumor and suggests an immediate operation, we might not be inclined to like either the news or *him* very much. Some will reject such a suggestion (not to mention the surgeon) with anger and contempt. But we know how foolish that is. We dare not dismiss the recommendations of the Divine Physician.

We also can't afford to assure ourselves by the way, that *we* love Jesus *too much* to ever give Him the brush-off like that. It's possible we never have. Perhaps we never will. But, if so, it will be because of His incredible sensitivity to our thin skins and unbelievable patience with our self-stupidity, as He maneuvers His way around all our resistances, forced to draw upon nearly all the infinite Wisdom at His disposal. And *not* because we were so devoted to Him, so desirous of being healed, so expert at recognizing His presence and will at first glance.

As Matthew and Dennis Linn so simply summarize, when we get in touch with what we most need to hear, we are hearing Christ.[4] The more we love a person, the more we will trust what they say and conversely the less we shield ourselves from their gaze. This is what needs to keep on happening with Jesus. The closer we come to Him, the more enlightened as to our own hurts we shall surely find ourselves. With such a gentleness will He speak of them, in such simplicity, with such firm conviction that now is the time for their painful power over us to be ended.

If there's one thing true about human personality, it is that it scars and it scars badly. We know that about recallable bad memories. Which of us, for instance, doesn't have the conviction that there were certain unpleasant things that we've been through that will never be able to shake? That we will have to carry the sad weight of these things to the grave? We also need to see that unremembered past and wounding experiences are able to exercise a similar scarring impact on the way we look at how we must travel through life.

Even so, what's the problem? Why can't we just say to God: "All right, I understand now that you want to heal my memory. So here it is. Cleanse it. Change it. Transform it. Remove from my buried memory of the past anything which presently cripples, inhibits, wounds, or troubles me still — *right now*."

Some of the difficulty has to do with the phenomenon of our *wanting* to hold onto scars. What a strange thing. What a curious suggestion, that we should want to be scarred, that we might have no intention of ever wanting to let go of scars or wounds from the past.

One day, as I was counseling with someone, it became increasingly obvious to me that he really didn't want to let go of the disfigurement of past hurts. As I silently prayed for wisdom, for some way that I might demonstrate to him both the fact and the foolishness of such a pose being presently struck in his life, the following parable came to me:

A man had been in the military service. While serving in the heat of battle, he became badly wounded. After a long recuperative period in the hospital, his doctor approaches his bed with the news: "Well, you're physically recovered now. You may be released today, if you wish. There is, as you know, some bad scarring all over the chest area. Newly-developed techniques of plastic surgery will be able to remove most if not all, of this unsightly tissue. Since the army will foot the entire bill for this procedure, we suggest that you soon arrange for this plastic surgery and the removal of the scars."

But the soldier responds: "Oh, no! Thanks anyway, doc. I want to get out today, and that's it. Just as soon as I can, I'm going to go to the beach and stroll up and down. I want people to see these scars. I want them to see what I've suffered for my country!"

Many of us are like that soldier. We've seen some rough action; we've come through some scary battles; and for precisely that reason, we feel we have the *right* to wear scars. We want people to know what we've been through. We want folks to realize that we've been really kicked around in some of life's nastier conflicts.

We said of Jesus' Resurrection-healing that He was able to handle a discussion about His arrest and execution, *as if it had never happened to Him.* Now, *that's* healing. To be able to recall a past painful event and not to presently suffer any ill-effects spiritually, psychologically or physically. That's a memory with no harmful power over us. No reason, then, to want or need anybody's sympathy for what we've suffered. No reason to cling to the identity of someone who needs to go through life obviously scarred. It can be hard, nonetheless, for some of us to be brought to the full want for "No more sympathy! No more scars!"

By now, some may be mistakenly thinking that healing of memories is some sort of meditative self-analysis. Certain methods of therapy involve extensive emphasis upon intricately examining negative influences from one's past and relating them to the attitudes and behavior of the present. The memory healing we speak of here, however, is ordinarily a much briefer and simpler process. *The One who loves me can be trusted to lead me to any significant past inner hurt I need to see.* As we saw earlier, an essential guiding principle is still "only one thing necessary." I will only be shown one area of past hurt at a time. "At a time" means a *comfortable* period. Comfortable, tailor-made, perfectly suited to who I am and what I am able to handle.

We tend to see ourselves as a leaf-bare tree, from the top down. Hundreds and hundreds of branch ends giving the appearance of the tree's complexity. All kinds of tangled and twisted sub-sub-branches, coming off of sub-branches, coming off of branches coming off the trunk. It's awfully hard to see the trunk from that perspective or the simplicity underlying all that apparent complicatedness. God sees us as if we were the same tree; but as a person who is standing underneath, looking upwards, would. He can see the trunk (Original Sin) and then four or five main branches (the key hurts of our life), finally, all the sub and sub-sub branches coming off of these, (the current maze of confusion, anxiety, anger, dishonesty, guilt, fear, self-pity, resentment, or cynicism etc. currently paining us and mystifying us in whole or in part, as to their cause). If He can get us to allow Him to deal with the trunk and main branches, the sub-branches and sub-sub branches will practically take care of themselves, so rooted in and fed by the trunk and branches, they happen to be.

Original Sin and usually three or four key satellite hurts (in this counselor's experience) — sometimes more, sometimes less — are all that are basically needed to be submitted prayerfully, patiently, and persistently to the Healer for the radical and permanent personality change He wants to bless us with to happen in our lives. If we will let Him give us the cake, the frosting will also be there in time, too.

It's so important that we don't allow ourselves to be intimidated by our own apparent self-complicatedness or the complicatedness of our present personal problems. He knows how to look at the "tree" the *right* way. He knows how to deal with it with a remarkable simplicity, and with unexpected swiftness. A branch, or even a tree that took years to grow, can be felled in a matter of minutes. A problem that has been around for so long a time that it appears to be permanent can be significantly reduced, on the way to being even completely removed, in a relatively short time when the Divine Physician is given a free hand to "do His thing."

We will now touch on a few of those "branches." We will suggest very briefly some common areas of hurt which can often be targeted by the Healer of Hearts for healing by way of prayerfully drawing our attention to a past hurt; giving us wisdom about how our present is still somehow negatively connected to and influenced by that past hurt; and finally by severing, with our permission, that destructive connecting link, once and for all.

Something bad happened to us. Generally, we were small and therefore relatively ignorant about the full significance of what was happening or of the best way to defend ourselves. The hurt landed. And then we reacted.

It's the combination of the hurt and *our reaction to the hurt* which comprise the power of the negative memory. If someone walks up to me today and says to me: "You are a worthless idiot." I won't like it and I'll regret that such an unfortunate episode had to occur. But hopefully, I will not do certain things by way of further reaction:

1. I will not choose to believe the accusation — I am not worthless; and while I will have to admit to you that I have done an idiotic thing or two in my past life, that still doesn't make me an idiot.

2. I will choose not to resent that mistaken individual or wish him future evil. I may flush instinctively with a bit of anger and get a little red in the face, but I'll give the anger to Jesus and I'll ask Him for His patience and forgiveness; and

137

He'll give them to me. I will not bury that anger, then, and let it secretly smolder within (resentment).

3. I will not opt to feel sorry for myself for having been subjected to such an indignity.

4. Finally, I will not deny to myself that somebody actually would ever even consider that I was an idiot, let alone openly accuse me of it.

But were I four years old when that episode had happened, I might have done the following:

1. Wondered whether he might be right; and even come to the point of believing the "truth" of a point made with such forcefulness and authority.

2. Fall into the full flow of resentment directed at the accuser and/or *myself* for being someone in the position of being susceptible to such criticism.

3. Feel very sorry for myself for having been subjected to such a terrible predicament.

4. Decide that I can't handle all the pain which this embarrassment, resentment, self-doubt, etc. causes me and block the whole episode out of my conscious awareness. Tell myself it never happened. Pretend to myself that no such thing ever was said. Deny, repress — with amazing speed and apparent effectiveness, the whole business.

So, then, one problem has now become multi-faceted. The suspicion that I just may be an idiot. The hatred I have for the one who "noticed" it. The hatred I have for myself for not being able to hide it. And finally the *covering* under which all that unresolved, negative emotion lies, the artificial forgetfulness separating all that unpleasantness from my surface awareness of myself and life as it now is.

Picture a saddled horse standing in front of you. Everything looks as if he's ready to go, prepared to receive and even cooperate with the soon-to-be added burden of the rider's weight. But there's a burr underneath the saddle; and when the rider mounts, the pressure of his presence from above added to the hidden presence of the burr will create pain and ensuing problems for both horse and rider.

The "rider" is the ordinary burden I ought to be able to handle without any difficulty. (I am the horse, in this case.)

The saddle (my conscious awareness) is not only rightly being used to help me relate to the burden at hand; its "underside" is wrongly being used to conceal something which shouldn't be there, the "burr" of unpleasant memory.

That's why we sometimes *over*-react and can't understand why. Why ordinary pressures and challenges mysteriously present themselves as an extraordinary burden, occasionally. The evident pressure from without is merging with a hidden pressure from within. That's why, too, a prayerful seeking of God for wisdom about *why we over-react today* or why we keep over-reacting in similar situations may include as part of its answer, a sudden recollection of childhood moment, when we found ourselves unjustly hurt and frighteningly helpless.

A dimension of the tragedy of little folks being forced to deal with unpleasant, untruths (masquerading as truths) by denying their reality, pretending that they are not there, is that they grow up to be big folks who do exactly the same thing, when faced with unpleasant *realities*. Any reality perceived to be in the least bit unsettling is immediately excluded from consciousness: "It just wasn't there; it just wasn't said," etc.

If we are ever to be fully healed of buried past hurts, we will have to come to see that at the heart of our problem wasn't that we were wrong to choose to forget bad things, it was that *we forgot them the wrong way*. Ironically, we were right when we instinctively recognized that to keep something so negative constantly before our minds' eye would only needlessly prolong a bad moment. We were right to see *forgetting* as part of the solution. We were wrong however, to do our forgetting via mind-manipulation: using that instrument created to tell us what *is* for the exact opposite of what it was intended, — to "disclose" to us that what is really there really isn't. We didn't know any better then. We ought to know better by now.

We may need to be shown that we are still people very much afraid to be in touch with our true feelings, who instinctively cut ourselves off from what our insides are trying to tell us. If so, it will be in a gentleness, if we allow Him, and with such encouragement that we do not need to walk that way ever again. To be healed of bad memories, is to be healed of the "lid" on top of them as well, the spirit of pretending to ourselves the opposite of what stands before us threateningly.

A major healing of memory many of us need is in the area of guilt. We talked earlier about how some adults never get to trade-in the small-fry's super-ego for an adult conscience. We also discussed some of the reasons for such a phenomenon occurring, especially, the situation of being exposed to parental correction given in an unhealthy way. (cf. Chapter 3).

We needed to be corrected. Many times we couldn't tell the safe thing from the dangerous one; the right way to do things from the wrong way; etc. Parents, teachers, and others were there to show us and show us the difference. Especially when we understood what they told us and chose to ignore their counsel, did we need to be set straight. And sometimes, it came not only with firmness but unnecessary severity. With an unneeded violence which could be verbal as well as physical.

While it's indeed quite possible that some of us may be ongoing victims of child abuse, physically or sexually, because we carry around with us a buried memory or memories of something that terrible, many more of us tend to be victims of verbal child abuse. We were corrected with *something unnecessarily violent* in the choice of words, or tone of voice. It could have been something which happened only once or twice. Most likely it happened a number of times. The anger in their voice might have literally terrified us. The tone of condemnation might have made us feel that we were dirty, perverse or morally worthless. The mocking adjectives might have led us to believe that only someone witless, crazy or idiotic would ever have done such a stupid thing. We ended up feeling unbelievably guilty. Finally, the chances are that we then repressed the whole thing and artificially "forgot" the whole episode.

A young woman I know had an abortion a few years ago. At that moment she decided that she wasn't going to feel guilty about it. She refused to look at the implications of such an act, either with reference to its general rightness or wrongness or her own deepest convictions about the practice. It was simply the most convenient and practical thing for her right then. Two years late she started to feel terribly guilty about "nothings," awfully anxious over trivial problems. As we counseled, it became increasingly clear to her that she was really experiencing guilt over the abortion. She needed to ask for God's forgiveness. She had to ask His help to forgive herself. Then the real *guilt* finally left her.

But there is another kind of guilt. False guilt. Believing in the lie which says that you're responsible for something that you're not at all responsible for; or that you bear major responsibility for something that you only had minor involvement in. If, in childhood, we were made to feel guilty about something we never did, or very guilty about something minor, it may be that Jesus will want to grant us some self-insight to that effect; a brief recollection of a characteristic episode, now able to be seen from the so much more balanced perspective of the adult. His grace will enable us to realize how distorted the accusation was and how unnecessary it was for us to have responded with such feelings of guilt. In other words, He will stand in between us and the lie which harmed us, reassuring us of its falsity. He also will contradict the secondary lies which parasitically connected themselves to the first, lies like "You're an idiot!" "You're no damned good!" "You will have to keep on punishing yourself for something this terrible." "You'll never be able to do a first-rate job, no matter what you try." "You'll probably be punished terribly, maybe eternally, someday, for such behavior," etc.

If we are quickly made to feel guilty, that is, if we discover that we tend to be easy targets for manipulators who can get us to do just about anything they want, or leave us feeling terrible for having refused them; then, chances are we need a memory healing in this area. If, on the other hand, we feel a constant need to correct people, reform other people's behavior, or constantly find ourselves setting friends or family "straight" we also may need the same basic memory healing. Rather than suffer this "over-reaction guilt" ourselves, we could be projecting it onto others and punishing it in them. Either extreme could well be victims of this kind of childhood guilt-trip and its scarred aftermath.

Perhaps the greatest source of unresolved guilt is hatred of parents. Sometimes built-up resentment of parents comes out of conflicts based in the correction of real or imagined childhood misbehavior, sometimes out of other situations. Either, way it's something very hard to handle. I can still remember the day in catechism class nearly forty years ago, when I was a first or second grader, as sister explained the fourth commandment to us. She described the hateful, unspeakably obscene boy or girl who not only refused to honor their father or mother and constantly rebelled against their authority, but even hated them. No sin could be more terrible. We shuddered and sweated as we listened. None of us would ever do *that* — not that we ever had . . .

We somehow instinctively know that we were created to love them. We somehow sense that their guidance ought to be correct and their care for us, consistent. And when it isn't, we can't handle it. It throws us into confusion. We somehow realize that our identity ought to be that of a reasonable grateful, dutiful, loving offspring. The last thing we want to be is the opposite of that. And then, one day, something happens to make us feel the opposite. We find ourselves resenting them; what they say, or don't say to us; what they do or don't do to or for us. We all, I suppose, have not only disliked them when they corrected us in some way justly and for our own good, but even borne a grudge or two over it.

But what about mistreatment or neglect? How then could we have avoided entering into a habit of resenting them? Not hating them "across the board," but resenting them for this or that repeated, unfair provocation; for this or that sin of commission or omission? And if so, how could we have avoided hating ourselves for hating them, resenting and condemning ourselves for having become a parent-hating monster? And how could we have accordingly avoided "burying" this so unwanted a piece of "data"?

We can love and hate the same person at the same time. That's a fact of life. I can really care for you generally and resent you specifically. But so often, we kid ourselves with spurious logic such as this: "I can't possibly hate him. After all, I love him, don't I?" It's the same logic some of us used as we repressed from awareness, both our resentment of our parents and our accompanying self-condemnation for the same;

and we may still be employing it to keep the "lid" on. As we suggested earlier, adult "over-devotion" to parents is often a cover up for repressed, childhood hate. A lot of us need to have our memories healed in precisely this area. We need to be open to have the Lord lead us back to a point or situation where we started to resent him, her or them, etc.

If so, we will find ourselves graced to "understand" them better. To identify with their "taking out" of their inner hurts on us because we, as adults, have done similarly irrational things, when *we* punished some innocent scapegoat. We will be enabled to hurt with Jesus for them and whatever caused them to be thusly scarred. We will also see how He grieved over our being scarred as well. We will see that He understood why we resented, and why we then denied. We will see that it is the time to let His forgiveness flow to them in the light of these fresh realizations, whether they are alive or dead; for, even if they have passed on He assures us that they are alive to Him and that His forgiveness passing through our hearts will still be able to reach them.

Perhaps the worst thing we see ourselves as having done in our past life is having hated a parent. Perhaps it is something else. Whatever it was, God loved us before, during and after that misdeed. We may need to be brought briefly back to such a "worst moment." If only to see that He didn't condemn us, but was standing there, ready to forgive and encourage. That, in fact, He's never left. That He is still at our side ready to help us resolve that needlessly negative impulse, ready to give us the forgiveness we need for others as well ourselves — right now.

A young woman who belongs to our prayer community shared this with me the other day and now I share it with you. She was praying about her praying: Why, when I pray for legitimate needs to be fulfilled do I feel so defeated and frustrated, so often? The problem (like the one described just above) is related to the silence and the waiting. God's apparent silence in the face of our urgent requests. The waiting we sometimes have to do before even the hint of an answer reveals itself.

Surprisingly, she could see herself as a little girl again. Her mother and father were arguing, as usual. She needed something. Her presence was briefly but barely acknowledged, and some sort of promise was made about taking care of her need. Then, the argument resumed. She was soon forgotten and so was her request. They never got around to fulfilling it.

You think I'm that way with you when prayer comes hard, or the answer comes slowly was the insight she believed Jesus had given her. An inner bitterness about promises from people who *say* they love you was still inhibiting her ability to trust present promises. Promises of affection. Whether they came from man or even God. After a while, the little girl had surrounded her inner self with defenses. Defenses against further disappointment, further broken promises, further love-betrayal.

About a year ago, a woman sat glued to her chair after the prayer meeting ended and just about everyone else was engaged in casual chatter over soda and cookies. After most of the people had left, I noticed that she was still sitting there. I sat down next to her and noticed that her hands were trembling. After quite a bit of struggle she finally blurted out what was going on: "Tonight while I was praying, a very unpleasant memory came to me and it wouldn't go away. I kept asking Jesus to remove it and He wouldn't. I don't know what's going on . . ."

She could only have been nine or ten years old at the time. Alone in a room with her uncle. He approached and embraced her gently. But then something seemed wrong. He began to stroke her private parts. She felt both bad and yet good at the same time. There was something so pleasurable and new about it. But his manner was strange and he warned her sternly not to tell anyone about it. It would be *their* secret.

Now it was time to break the power of that secret. It was Jesus who had led her to share it with me. We talked about forgiving that man and forgiving herself. About letting go of not only unresolved guilt about the episode, but also a buried attitude as well. An attitude that sexual activity, for a woman, is, somehow always connected with being taken advantage of. An attitude that the privacy presently connected with it (in her mind) still had to do with covering up what wasn't good or honest. In time, this woman came to experience a whole new freedom in her relationship with her husband; a whole new ease in giving and receiving marital love in intimacy.

A similar breakthrough occurring in a marital relationship came out of a different sort of memory healing. A friend of mine felt frustration over the fact that her relationship with her husband didn't seem to be deepening. The stagnancy that she felt there was brought to prayer. In time, the answer to her prayerfully persistent waiting was a clear recollection of a long-forgotten childhood disappointment.

She saw herself recoil in shock, as she overheard one of her closest friends criticize her, cruelly and unfairly, to a third little friend of theirs. Because of the pain of this breaking of faith, she witnessed herself resolving, *as a five or six year old*, never to allow anyone to ever come as close to her again as she had once allowed that playmate who'd just betrayed their friendship. Only when she surrendered that wall, erected in childhood against overly-close relationships, would the distance separating her from her husband begin to diminish.

All three episodes, just mentioned, while externally quite different, had this common denominator. They all resulted in the raising up of barriers, the establishment of defenses. Each of these women, as a result of these negative circumstances, felt the need to close themselves off in significant ways from the reception of another's love. Each harbored for different reasons, a secret bitterness against love. To believe, however, that love rips you off, even while it does bring some apparently beneficial and transitory side-effects is to simultaneously believe that life rips you off. A bitterness against life is the inevitable by-product of a bitterness against love.

You know the saying, 'A little bit of yeast makes the whole batch of dough rise.' You must remove the old yeast of sin so you will be entirely pure. Then you will be like a new batch of dough without any yeast, as indeed you actually are. For our Passover Festival is ready, now that Christ, our Passover lamb has been sacrificed. Let us celebrate our passover, then, not with bread having the old yeast of sin and wickedness, but with the bread of purity and truth. (1 Cor. 5:6-8, TEV).

Leaven is a sour or corrupting piece of dough used to ferment a new piece of dough. It is something old hidden in the midst of something otherwise new. Paul tried to show the Corinthian Christians that they could secretly hang on to some "piece" of the old to the detriment of the new. He attempted to demonstrate to them (and us) the possibility of the health of the new life in Grace being infected, and therefore weakened by, the presence of a decaying remnant of the past. That would certainly include sour memories and a bitterness towards love and life which they promote.

Which of us feels free from bitterness, a sour taste still in our mouths even though the wounding, disappointing experience of love or life happened years ago? Only the person who has seen fit to truly surrender these memories into the Savior's cleansing care. Otherwise, there is work still to be done.

It may have been the death of a parent when we were so young and it may have seemed to us that he or she freely chose to leave and abandon us. It may have been a sarcastic comment about a wrong answer from a teacher when we were in the second grade. It may have been seductively dishonest promise of love on an early date, where only our body was wanted for a "one night stand." It may have been unremitting pressure to achieve and succeed from over-ambitious parents who needed us to succeed academically or athletically to compensate for their real or imagined childhood deprivations. It may have been a mother or father who loved but just couldn't touch or embrace-or ever allow their true feelings to surface. It may have been a string of attempts to succeed or achieve recognition on our part which met with repeated failure and led us to feel that we must therefore be a failure. It may have been fear at the sight of a drunk and angry father or anger at a silent, retreating mother who never fought back. It may have been learning that you were born outside of wedlock and therefore coming to believe that you didn't have the same right to be on this planet as those born "legitimately" have.

Or so many other things. Things, after which we could no longer look at life the same way anymore. Things which gave us new eyeglasses through which we would thereafter view the world. Lenses which would forever darken the way life looked. Lenses which would ever distort the way life looked. Life. Love. Situations. Relationships. The Present. The Future. Everything from that moment on somehow tinged with and twisted by the negative.

"But if you harbor bitter envy and selfish ambition in your hearts, do not boast about it or deny the truth. Such 'wisdom' does not come down from heaven but is earthly, unspiritual, of the devil. For where you have envy and selfish ambition, there you find disorder and every evil practice." (Jas. 3:14-16, NIV). James focused in on jealousy and ambition here, as he talked about one aspect of wisdom we all know too well. The "wisdom" of those who feel that they've been short-changed or ripped-off by life and have no intention of letting it ever happen to them again. The "wisdom" of walls. The "wisdom" of embittered suspicion. The "wisdom of never again allowing oneself to be vulnerable. The "wisdom" of a heart self-deadened to further love-hurt and therefore further love. The "wisdom" of "knowing" in advance that people are "always" self-seeking, dishonest and out to take you for a ride, even before they get a chance to open their mouths or shake our hands, by way of introduction. The "wisdom" of never trusting anyone again. The "wisdom" of never again allowing ourselves the luxury of childlike openness and expectancy.

So inclined we are to want to have our cake an eat it too! Thus, even if we become Christians, that doesn't mean that we instantly want to let go of our walls, our defenses, our "wisdom." Even if we want to be "born again," that doesn't at all necessarily or automatically mean that we are really asking Jesus to make us like a child again. Many of us want *both*, a fresh start spiritually, free of guilt of past moral failure but by no means disarmed of our demonic wisdom, our "knowing" cynicism about the other person's dishonesty or lack of integrity. We could, after all, easily find ourselves in the position of wanting to love Jesus and even wanting to have His love for others, "even if they are never to be trusted"!

Who needs healing of memories? Who *doesn't* need healing of memories? Those who have read other accounts of healing

147

of memories may have noticed that up to this point no recommendation has been made along the lines of trying to prayerfully picture the moment of key hurt even as we envision Jesus standing beside us at that moment, shielding us from the "blow," counseling us to forgive the one who was determined to hurt us. What is sometimes called healing by means of the "creative imagination."

At certain times and with certain personalities this writer has found such an approach appropriate and extremely helpful. Faith, as the author of Hebrews instructs us, is the "evidence of things unseen." By faith we are empowered to see with the "eyes" of the heart. We are enabled, in this instance, to see what actually was *once the case*, even though at the time we weren't aware of it.

At the moment I was wounded in childhood, for instance, Jesus *was* there "right beside me" loving me, longing to protect me with the armor of trust in His love and the power He gives us to forgive. I just couldn't "see" it then. So, when I pray for a healing of a painful memory via the "technique" of creative imagination, I am simply allowing myself to "see" *now* what was in fact truly operative *then*. My protector and Healer present and ready to do His "thing."

In prayer, then, I am thereby equipped to presently take advantage of what, through lack of faith, I was unable to take advantage of previously: His protection, wisdom, forgiveness-power. I accept His counsel. I allow Him to reassure me that even this threatening and negative happening He is able to be worked to good (Rom. 8:28). I allow the Lord who can see the tragic inner hurts in the hearts of those who intend to hurt me to give me His compassion for them in their woundedness; even as He gives me not only His own prayer from the cross, but the unconditional forgiveness which inspired and empowered it: "Father, forgive them, they don't know what they are doing."

We do not "psyche" ourselves up, then, when we pray this way. We don't play a mind-game on ourselves as we pretend to ourselves a nice thing that never really was. His way of seeking healing is not a form of spiritual "make believe." It's belief for real. It's practical faith. It's employing the imagination to facilitate what we can know, even without employing the imagination's power to picture things: God's love and the power of that love to heal.

Chapter 8

Healing of Identity (I)

We live in a society which itself is suffering the bewilderment of a massive identity crisis. That makes the embarking upon finding out who and what one is or ought to be, today, is especially painful. So few have the "luxury" of something culturally or even spiritually solid against which to measure or brace themselves, let alone to catapult themselves off of.

In addition, there is a striking parallel between two poles of contemporary Christian theology and contemporary secular psychology. Both theologians and psychologists end up saying that uniqueness and enduring selfsameness are ultimately important and enriching, even as some of their counterparts attempt to sell you on the alleged selfishness and stupidity of anyone's wanting to hold onto a firm sense of being special and unrepeatable.

Then, we Christians have always maintained that to acknowledge one's need of a relationship with God as one's Father and Jesus as one's Savior is to become a new person. We live, however, in an era of proliferating cults whose adherents give evidence of massive personality transformation. What, if anything, differentiates the enthusiastic "reborn" believer from the grinning cult "clone"? Here are just a few of the key issues swirling about the problem of finding out who you are in relationship to the world around you, and even God.

Identity, today, in both popular parlance and professional lingo, is used as a synonym for, more than anything else, *role*. What you make of yourself by way of professional, social, or financial achievement is seen to be your identity. Only to the extent that one is successful in one's chosen vocation is a person seen to have achieved identity. I *am* "someone" because I am a recognized success in the business world, for example. In this view, the "who" and the "what" of a person are nearly, if not totally, identical. The "what you are," i.e. the status achieved in society, is asserted to be the equivalent of "who you are."

We are, of course, meant by our Creator to feel the thrill of accomplishment, the fulfillment derived from *doing*, even as we tackle the tasks life confronts us with, if we, and those we are responsible for, are to be fed and sheltered, etc. Yet, it is also clear (from a careful overview of the way He confronts men and women both as groups and as individuals, from the beginning of the Bible to the end) that the God who reveals Himself there is far more interested in first affirming people for *who* they are than in praising them for what they've accomplished. It's not that He isn't ready to acknowledge diligent and obedient service to Himself or His people. It's simply that He wants it made abundantly clear that He values people with an infinite valuing—just for who they are; that He loves individuals with limitless love—just for being John or Mary, even before John decides to accept the call of an Apostle, say, or Mary the mission to mother His Son.

In fact, the more closely we look at the "Johns" and "Marys" of the Sacred Scriptures, the more we recognize that it is precisely because they *know* they are "beloved" and are so delighted to be beloved (and thus, happy to be who they already are) that they succeed so eminently at their appointed tasks. They may well end up accomplishing phenomenal things; but, unlike today's everpresent workaholic, they aren't "into" accomplishing in order to assure themselves that they are worthwhile. Rather, it is precisely because they *know* they are worthwhile, above all, in the eyes of their Divine Lover (and, so, in their own) that they are able to give themselves to their work in a way that is so obviously free of that compulsion to "prove."

He was first known about town as "the carpenter's son." Later, He referred to himself as God's son. Yes, the boy would surely have answered to the name of Jesus, and so would the man. Jesus was both son of earth and son of Heaven, child of Mary and child of the Eternal Father. He never lost sight of either His earthly or His heavenly roots. They were both forever a part of Him—what came to Him from the Virgin and His foster father, the carpenter, His land and His people, as well as what came to Him out of His going apart to be alone with that God who taught and encouraged His child to call Him *Abba*, papa, daddy.

There were moments when being both carpenter's son and Yahweh's son at one and the same time was no easy task. Jesus must have felt more than once that He was close to being torn in two, pulled in clearly conflicting directions. *Abba*, for instance, once said to the 12-year-old, "Stay in the Temple and speak My wisdom to the rabbis," while Joseph said, "It's time to get back to Nazareth and the carpenter's shop." The choices that came out of these crises were choices surely made in pain, choices ultimately made out of obedience to God rather than to man; choices made in fear and trembling, even as they were born out of the prayer of faith (cf. Heb. 2:17-18; 5:7-9).

Jesus is the unique Son of the eternal Father. But you can become a unique son or daughter of His, too, the Scriptures suggest. If you don't examine these texts in the framework of their immediate contexts, as well as against the entire unfolding of God's marvelous plan, however, you could end up thinking that the end-product of becoming a believer is to lose your own individual identity; that you're called to get swallowed up in *His*, never to regain personal self-awareness again. Such an understanding, however, has to be what some individuals have chosen to read *into* the Bible, rather than what they got out of it, this writer maintains.

"If you don't know that you are God's child, then you've only come up with *half* your identity thus far," Divine Revelation surely asserts. But a lot of folks don't even know whether they are their *own* parents' child. That amounts to having even less than half an identity, we would not hesitate to add.

Let's look at the second assertion first. Some of us, of course, don't even know who our real parents are. Some of us were orphaned or given over for adoption before we were able to get to know them. If you fall into this category, you may well have a special identity hang-up, based in wondering whether you have a full "right" to be here on this planet.

You are not "an accident," even though you might be inclined to think so. God intended that all children come to birth out of a man's and a woman's commitment to faithfully and exclusively love each other and have children who would be the embodiment of that love. But He foresaw that some parents would fall short of this intention. He decided to made good on their inadequacies, nonetheless.

Only when we take questions about our own personal birthright into His presence, with a *listening* heart, will we be able to hear Him say to us, "You are no accident. You are part of my eternal plan. Know that I want you to *be*. Know that I want you to see yourself as placed here by My will. I am glad that you *are*. I want *you* to be glad that you are. I want you to know that you are My child, so special to Me . . ."

But even if we don't have to deal with that specific difficulty of being an orphan, we will still have to deal with being somebody's son or daughter. Somebody *imperfect's* son or daughter. Somebody-not-so-easy-to-get-along-with's son or daughter. Somebody-who-was-too-preoccupied-with-their-own-hurts-to-fully-attend-to-their-child's-hurt's son or daughter. Somebody-who-may-have-been-inclined-to-be-possessive-or-overprotective's son or daughter, and on and on we could go . . .

We had problems with them and probably still do, years after our 18th or 21st birthday. We were in a position to know their faults, best of all. Thus, we were often quickest to condemn those flaws. We soon discovered, however, that we didn't just bear a "family resemblance" to Ma or Pa, but that we now carried, if not those same defects, ones just as glaring and just as apparently unshakable. And so, we tended to move beyond just wanting to be independent of them in order to be our own person. We may well have even experienced the temptation to deny our connections with them, or at least any connection between the way we are and the way they are or were.

As long as we foster walls and barriers between ourselves and them, however, we simultaneously cut ourselves off from who we really are. We are defrauding ourselves of part of our rightful inheritance, something essential to our true identity.

By the time we are able to be parents ourselves, we have begun to experience how impeded *we* are by inner hurts. It is then that we can finally admit to ourselves how we are prone to taking out our frustrations on those close to us, and we are finally prepared (as much as we'll ever be) to understand them, and so to forgive them. In that forgiveness and reconciliation, we are finally reconciled with *ourselves*.

They are properly part of us, because they have been forgiven and, accordingly, taken into our hearts in love. Or, they are part of us because they are denied, deep beneath the surface of our consciousness where our unforgiveness for them fuels that compulsiveness, cruelty, stupidity, selfishness, or countless other ugly traits which force us to resemble them — the way they were when they were at their worst.

The choice is now up to us. He who loved them despite their woundedness, despite their unloveableness, will enable us to do the same. And, as we do, we will be pouring love upon those hurts in them, even as that love simultaneously pulls our own splintered spirits into wholeness. Even if they have passed into eternity, Grace still mysteriously seems to be calling us to be reconciled anyway, somehow assuring us that it is not too late, even though we are unable to grasp why.

To some extent, being less than perfect, they failed to affirm us or affirm us as much as we needed to be affirmed. "Affirm" is such a good word. Literally, it means "to make someone strong." It refers to that act whereby we find value in another and then express to that other that we see their value and are glad about it.

As Thomas Kane beautifully expresses it, affirming happens when someone reflects my goodness back to me.[1] It is *truth*, therefore. This provides the experience, to borrow Bernard Bush's imagery, of seeing ourselves and so knowing ourselves *truly* because we "see" our image reflected in the eyes of someone who loves us.[2] More than anything else, this is what enables any of us to experience himself or herself as being special and to know from within that it is good and right that I am me and I am here.

Affirmation is the gift of myself to myself *from another*, we could say. When I go apart and try to tell myself that I am good and wonderful without having first been given that compliment from another, the words inevitably sound hollow and unconvincing. Strictly speaking, we cannot affirm ourselves, as we said earlier. We cannot give ourselves to ourselves, even though many will try. There is an old rabbinical saying, appreciative of this position: "Within each of us there is a candle waiting to be lit; but no one can light his own candle."

Affirmation, even though it comes from someone who cares about us and someone who wants in some way to be in relationship with us, as John Powell points out, always upholds the other as *other*.[3] If it says, "I want you to be mine," it does so only after first having clearly respected the other as being his or her own person, and so, not anybody's possession. Or, as Dr. Conrad Baars has wryly suggested, we "forgive" the other for being different from us.[4]

We said above that affirmation is making someone strong and an act of finding value in that person. Yet such a definition can be somewhat misleading, for affirmation proceeds far more from a state of *being* than doing. It is, first of all, the phenomenon of simply allowing ourselves to be truly and fully present to another with all that we are and have. Our being-lovingly-and-attentively-present to the other says to that other that she is worth the "effort" we are "making" to be fully there for her. This is precisely what brings strength to the other and stirs her to do the same in response.

When anyone reveals oneself as being both present and present as a lover, the one so graced with such presence and love is ultimately encouraged to respond in precisely the same way. (All the pages of Divine Revelation are there, by the way, to persuade us that He is there, fully and lovingly present to us. If we will open ourselves to *believe* that, then we can turn and make ourselves lovingly present to *Him* in a mutual act of self-revelation. [cf. 1 Jn. 12; 2 Jn. 13])

Richard Rohr, in one of his many fine taped Bible teachings, speaks of a young woman who had thanked him for always "believing the best" of her. That love which affirms, despite its powerful focus on the present, also looks forward in faith to the future. It believes the best of the ones we love. It somehow sees them "already" matured, "already" freed of hang-ups, "already" whole. It liberates the other to likewise believe the best about themselves; to look to how they can and will someday be, rather than remain forever focused upon, and so forever linked, to today's insecurities. Affirming always contains this dimension of believing the best of the one affirmed.

This brings us back to identity, our parents, and God. Earlier, we suggested that our parents failed us. To the extent that they didn't clearly or consistently get that message across to me about how loveable they found me or how special I was in their sight, I was to that extent *left unaffirmed.* I was left with doubts about my loveableness and specialness. Doubts that may still be there buried deep within me, camouflage by my denial of their existence, perhaps, but still there, silently gnawing away at my "innards" like termites chewing on the support beams of an unfortunately infested house.

Parents, of course, don't fail to affirm because they can't see our loveableness. They generally fail to affirm because of their own inner and outer hang-ups, which occupy their attention and so weaken their ability to fully focus their love upon us. "You are my beloved son or daughter," they wanted to say, but it came out weakly at times, or they were going to say it and/or *show* it, but got distracted. Something like that.

Even when Jesus was a grown man, the Scriptures record, He heard his Father in heaven affirm him as a "beloved son in whom He was well pleased." He must have often gone to prayer with ears wide open to hear it, again and again. Surely, He never tired of "hearing" those words, of being caressed by that sentiment.

Coming out of this recurring experience, He could then teach: "He's *your* Father, too. When *you* pray, you may now call him 'Father,' as well." This carried the implication that we were able to become sons and daughters, somehow as He was, because of and out of His unique Sonship, and the Redemption He won for us.

"Let my Father call you 'My son,' 'My daughter,' just as He does with me" — this is the clear import of His teaching. This happens above all in prayer. Prayer that is *dialogue* prayer. Prayer that gives the One we address time and space to *talk back* to us. Prayer that leaves a heart open to hear in its own way.

The heart can "hear" peace. The heart can accurately and unmanipulatingly translate wordless, inflooding assurance into the vernacular of "my son" or "my daughter." The heart can know the hug of invisible "arms" that embrace eternally (cf. Deut. 33:27). The heart can recognize the Lord of the beaming countenance; the face that flashes recognition, welcome, acceptance. . . (cf. Deut.6:24).

Such is able to make up for what our parents couldn't give us. It can wash away decades worth of encrusted fear of unloveableness and blast away wall after wall of false feelings of unworthiness, if we would only reach out and keep reaching out embrace-wise, in the expectancy of faith.

And yet, it isn't just there to make up for defects in human love. It is there in its own right. For there is a part of our heart that was created for Him and Him alone. He may have come to us in and through the love of others and will continue to do so, but we desperately need the experience of being apart with Him, too, so that He can speak to us the special name (Rev. 2:17) that only He knows, that is given to no one else.

Jesus never wanted anyone to think of himself or herself as simply a part of the whole, or as a face in the crowd, even when that whole or crowd happened to bear the august title of "People of God," royal and holy. Part of our identity is surely meant to be derived from seeing ourselves as brothers and sisters in Christ, going "home" together. But just as a Father gazing at his assembled family sees not just "the kids," but Peter and James and Judy and Mary, so we are likewise seen and known, individually: "I know mine and mine know me. . . I call each by name." (Jn. 10:14,3).

When Jesus said to grown men and women that they had to become as little children again, surely part of what He meant was that we never outgrow the need to be affirmed by another, that we never stop needing to hear from another (whether that other is God or man) that we are known, that we are loved, that we are special.

Anyone who has, in his prayer life especially, "matured" beyond this need for being affirmed *has matured into a false maturity.* This need can never be outgrown. Certain well-known contemporary spiritual writers speak of "transcending the I-Thou," of leaving behind the need for mutual affirmation, as one simultaneously lays aside one's "selfish" identity, or surrenders it to a God who has all this time been waiting for us to "repent" of it. In good faith, no doubt, they have managed to misread the Scriptures. *The point of God's self-revelation is Person-to-person.* Then, it's person-to-person in a new way because of the dynamic presence of that Person drawing all people together. Which means that the whole amazing, divinely unleashed process is supposed to get more and more personal, not surprisingly; and never supposed to stop becoming more personal.

We have quarreled earlier with that concept of identity which focuses so exclusively on a person's "whatness" as to downgrade or ignore the importance of one's "whoness." We must now quarrel with another extremely popular notion of identity, one which encourages people to see themselves, more than anything else, as an ever-changing bundle of reactions and sensations; or, as an ever-flowing stream of consciousness.

This point of view would generally quarrel with the notion that there is something solid about oneself that always remains. That there is something fixed and permanent about us which always stays with us, despite the many physical, mental, and emotional changes which everyone experiences as she passes through life, is misguidedly erroneous and even detrimental, its proponents would insist.

Psychologist James Kilpatrick has written an exceptionally engaging and illuminating book, *Identity and Intimacy*, unfolding this very problem and conflict.

He is quite straightforward about his own problems with contemporary Christianity and his inability to find it providing, or articulating relevant answers to the "gut" problems of contemporary man and today's society.[5] Nonetheless, his position on the meaning of human identity is, ironically, as about as close as one could come to what the Bible elucidates, about who and what a person must become if he is to enter into what the God revealed there wants him to enjoy.

The points which Kilpatrick makes in criticism of what he sees as the Human Potential psychologists' erroneous understanding of human nature, cannot be far removed, if removed at all, from the arguments which Jesus must offer, as He makes the ancient pages of the Hebrew and Christian Testaments a living and freshly applicable word of His. How does one adjust to the bewildering change or society-wide instability of the 1980's?

By always changing, yourself, the Human Potentialist answers. Not just in the sense of always adjusting to new circumstances; but in the sense of finally coming around to seeing yourself not so much as a self, but as a succession of new selves replacing discarded former selves (who no longer have any importance). Or, to put it a little differently, you accept yourself as a "self in process," as a self automatically and "naturally" unfolding from within. You spontaneously "go," therefore, with what you're most inclined to think and especially feel most strongly at the present moment, even when this is in high contradiction to what you formerly may have thought or felt, even yesterday. Identity is fluidity. Today's self may not and need not hear any resemblance to yesterday's self. Surely, this is the kind of person best equipped to adapt to the ever-changing, rarely predictable climate of today's world.

Before we go any further, it needs to be said that it is not simply two radically-opposed theoretical models of personal identity that we are discussing here. The theoreticians are, after all, simply describing where people "are at."

Identity is, to a significant degree, a matter of choice; and many, carried along like a piece of spinning driftwood in a current always rushing along past changing riverbanks, decide that the only stable element in their makeup is its ever-changingness. They choose to see themselves primarily as some sort of embodied response, ever engaged in spontaneous, nearly automatic reaction to the most attractive or powerful stimulus at hand.

But how is anyone able to honestly and authentically say to another, "You can count on me" or "Trust me," asks Kilpatrick. How can a man and a woman say to each other, "I am yours forever. I will be faithful and true to you as long as I live."?

Only if the person making so bold or courageous a statement is endowed with a well-founded confidence in himself or herself that he or she has something durable or permanent about himself or herself. My *self* is the guarantee I give you that such a commitment is to be kept. I believe about myself, (a belief partially based upon past performance, evident both to me and to you) that there is a primary or central "me," that *lasts* despite physical changes, and even psychological ones, (the periodic self-adjustments and "redefinitions" of who or what I am).[6]

I am not simply Jim and Paula's child, now grown up. They kept saying to me, not just, "I still recognize you as being my boy, Jack." They kept saying, "I still recognize you as my boy, Jack, whom I repeatedly find loveable." Beyond that fundamental affirmation, they also affirmed me *out of faith*, "seeing" fully developed qualities in me that they were sure I'd be able to make my own, before they were actually there. By constantly encouraging me to be honest, forgiving, or courageous, for example, they helped me to believe that I could be this way and so helped me to *decide* that I *would* be this way. Because they kept believing this of me, I eventually was able to believe this of myself.

Thus, the "something permanent" about me, the selfsameness of me would not simply be the fact that, genetically, I forever carried "part" of both of them with me through life. I also carry with me the fruits of their affirmation of me. Not only the deep conviction that I am loveable, and capable of returning love; but that I am also able, as well, of being consistently faithful in my love-commitments; that I possess as a permanent part of me the qualities mentioned above, or others like them.

For the sake of brevity, we have omitted the parallel affirming influence of siblings, playmates, other relatives, teachers, etc. We also have not spoken here of how this "ideal" is never realized, or only partially so. Finally, while we have noted elsewhere the "un-affirming" that can also happen to children and even predominate in childhood, we shouldn't fail to mention that telling a child continually that she is "no good," always dishonest, or that she'll "never amount to anything" can have disastrous results, often pushing the child towards an adulthood in which she will find it savagely difficult to break free of such false prophecy still ringing in her "inner ears," prophecy that she feels so driven to fulfill.

Erik Erikson, the renowned psychiatrist who devoted much of his professional life to studying the meaning of identity, sees its authentic unfolding as something which occurs only to the extent that one successfully passes through a series of eight stages or crises.

In the first, for example, the child so internalizes parental love as to begin to believe himself loveable and even trustworthy or conversely, he fails to and begins to nourish a basic mistrust of itself, of others and so, eventually, even of life itself.

In his teens, he reaches the fifth stage, wherein out of a "look back" upon the outstanding identifications of his previous life, i.e. key people, attractive situations, compelling circumstances, admirable values, etc. which he's identified with (some of which may be contradictory); and out of a searching look forward towards marriage and career possibilities, he finds himself faced with the need to discover a realistic common denominator between who he has been and who he'd like to be. If he successfully weathers that agonizing period, and does not attempt to indefinitely postpone the key life decisions which necessarily must bring it to its conclusion, he thus overcomes the prevalent temptations to lose his shaky sense of self, usually by merging with the crowd and parroting its identity. But not to lose one's identity in the crowd is not necessarily to escape the trap of losing one's identity by grafting it on to that of another.

Thus, the next crisis generally attaches itself to romance, and to whether one looks to one's possible mate as a person who will fulfill one's already somewhat secure sense of self or as one who will *substitute for one's unsteady sense of self.*

The succeeding crisis can be stated this way: will one allow an interest in nurturing and guiding the next generation to emerge or will it be repressed in favor of indulging yourself as if, as Erikson says, you were your own "one and only child"?

Erikson does not assert that the struggles of one stage are definitively over at a certain age, never to be repeated at a deeper level of one's growth. *Trust vs. Mistrust* is not just the baby's struggle, for instance. It's the young man's, and the elderly woman's as well.

What is particularly relevant in his thinking to our considerations thus far is that he designates these stages as "crises." Crisis means more than "time of particular stress or upheaval." Its root-meaning is *decision*. A crisis is "rough" time because we're called to come up with a "rough" decision. Out of each of Erikson's eight crises comes a choice ultimately positive or negative, progressive or regressive. These choices are not momentary ones, either. They will affect the way we are for the rest of our lives.[7]

As Kilpatrick similarly argues, an individual *becomes* a self *out of her choices*.[8] She "creates" herself out of her choices; or, as we Christians would say, God continues to create or call her into her unique personhood, by guiding her into making the right life-decisions. This means that our identity, while it is to some degree the product of outside influences, is far more than that. It is based in our healthy or unhealthy, honest or dishonest, hopeful or despairing, loving or unloving *responses* to those influences. Not *automatic* responses or reactions, but free-choice responses, formed out of often painful struggles, made after sometimes painful deliberation. Decisions that *I intend* to be a consistently honest or caring person, for example, or decisions *not to now retreat* from one's earlier commitment to honesty or sensitivity to the needs of others, despite the pressures of the moment to do so.

Identity, in its original sense, is thought to derive from two Latin words: *Idem*, meaning "same" and, perhaps, *similitas*, meaning "likeness." Likeness to oneself, a certain ongoing sameness with oneself is at the core of its meaning. Erikson and Kilpatrick, as well as the Scriptures long before them, insist that one's selfsameness must go far beyond not failing to own up to one's parental, racial, ethnic, or national roots; that we are given a freedom to decide who we are to be and that it is crucial that we exercise that freedom properly.

Rollo May, in much the same vein, argues that freedom and consciousness of self need to go hand in hand if a person is ever to be able to authentically contribute to her own development. In other words, only by choosing to be conscious of how we acted in the past while remaining open to reflect on the appropriateness or inappropriateness of these actions, will we be able to grow in the ability to modify, if necessary, how we will act in the present. This is precisely what provides humanity with the power to stay free of "the rigid chain of stimulus and response." The less self-aware we are, the more we will be controlled by forgotten conditionings, drives, inhibitions or instinctive reactions from our past, he argues.[9]

In the book of Deuteronomy, Moses is shown summarizing for his people the meaning of the Ten Commandments and their call to live in Covenant with the Lord:

> I call heaven and earth to witness against you this day, that I have set before you life and death, blessing and curse; therefore, choose life that you and your descendants may live, loving the Lord your God, obeying his voice and cleaving to Him, for that means life to you and length of days. (30:19, 20, RSV)

Kilpatrick comes closest to restating the eternal Biblical message, when he insists that this strand of continuity connecting who we have been, who we are, and who we must continue to be, cannot be separated from what we have come to believe about what is ultimately right and ultimately wrong.[10] For the believer, of course, this is more than simply the fruit of one's sincere reflections on what is moral or ethical versus their opposites. The Christian has come to realize that his own lights are insufficient even as his own (unaided) will power is not simply enough to insure his persistent adherence to right actions arising out of right intentions. He knows that he needs the enlightenment of God's written word which is made living by the Holy Spirit who ever accompanies its being read, when the reading is done in faith, and out of an honest seeking or real truth concerning the situation at hand, i.e., out of a sincere crying out for the most loving response possible. (This will go beyond, by the way, doing something simply because the Bible says so, or avoiding it because the Scriptures or Christian tradition forbids it. The mature disciple of Jesus is someone who has so searched out the truth of the matter as to have come to the realization *personally* of something's inner rightness or wrongness.) He also knows that only by relying on God dwelling within him will he be fully free to choose and do the right thing.

Morality and identity become inseparably intertwined. Our convictions of rightness and wrongness become an essential dimension of the inner fabric of who we are. Almost every one of us, of course, even the most devout believer among us, has revised her stand on this or that aspect of what is right. If we are to grow in His love and wisdom, as He calls us to, we will be repeatedly struck by new perspectives and find ourselves grounded in deeper sensitivities which don't really contradict our previous understandings of God's revealed truth (unless they were mistaken) but certainly lead us to modify our previous view of how that truth was to be best appreciated, as well as applied. But this is not the same as constantly changing one's ethical position.

To constantly "redraw the moral line" at which an individual will make his or her stand, says Kilpatrick, is to run the risk of erasing one's sense of continuity with one's past; of not only blotting out the connection between who we are now and who we used to be but even of eradicating so many of these moral lines that we start to feel that underneath the contradictory roles we play, that there is nothing left of us, that in fact we are nothing.[11]

Kilpatrick quotes a section from Bolt's magnificent play, *A Man for All Seasons*: The central figure of that work is Thomas More, a spiritual man of the highest principles, as well as a skilled lawyer, who is repeatedly able to so turn a phrase or redefine his position, as to escape major conflicts with those who are radically opposed to him. In other words, he knows how to make certain adjustments or strike certain compromises without compromising his basic position. But the day comes when he has used up all the tricks in his bag, or as Bolt puts it, the demands of his opponents call him to withdraw from "that final area where he located his self." To betray his principles there was to *betray his very self*. He saw that he had no choice but to draw a line and stand fast. Beyond that mysterious line, adds Kilpatrick, lies ". . . Something indispensable . . . the essence of what we mean by identity or the self."[12]

Never having studied Shakespeare's *Hamlet*, in which is proposed the counsel, "to thine own self be true," I was initially deprived of the opportunity of having a teacher or classmate explain its meaning to me. When I first started to wonder about the significance of that oft-quoted expression, I suspected that it might mean nothing more than narcissists' contemporary proverb: "You've got to look out for *old number one.*"

What it *does* mean, of course, is that we have a true self, not so much an ideal self, as a self imbued with ideals — and that if we are not loyal to those ideals we will have ended up being disloyal to whom we really are or whom we ought to be striving to become. Obviously, the Bard knew a lot about identity.

The word which both Kilpatrick and Erikson use most frequently to describe the quality which insures that we will have something solid and ongoing about our identity, and therefore something permanent and consistent residing in our relationships with others is *fidelity.* It means precisely, being true to ourselves and so to others, loyal to ourselves and so to others, faithful to ourselves and others. The word used most frequently in the majority of Bible translations to describe this quality is *faithfulness.* It will be helpful here to sample some representative quotes from both the Old and New Testaments using (or implying) this word as it applies first to God (including the God-man, Jesus), and then to men and women, as their Creator and Savior calls them forth into mirroring that divine quality.

With reference to God:
And the LORD passed before him [Moses] and proclaimed, the LORD, the LORD, a God merciful and gracious, slow to anger, and abounding in steadfast love and faithfulness, keeping steadfast love for thousands . . . (Ex. 34:6-7, RSV)

Know therefore that the LORD your God is God who keeps covenant and steadfast love with those who love him and keep his commandments, to a thousand generations. (Deut. 7:9, RSV)

If we are faithless, he [Jesus] remains faithful for he cannot deny himself. (2 Tim. 2:12, RSV)

With reference to humankind:
Let not lovingkindness and faithfulness leave you; bind them about your neck, write them on the tablet of your heart . . . (Prv. 3:3, RSV)

Let a man so account of us, as of the ministers of Christ and stewards of the mysteries of God. Moreover it is required in stewards, that a man be found faithful. (1 Cor. 4:1-2, KJV; see also 1 Sam. 2:35; 22:14; Neh. 9:7-8; Ps. 31:23; 101:6; Prv. 3:3; 1 Cor. 4:19)

Out of their many experiences with the Lord, two qualities of His repeatedly stood out to the Jews, as the distilled essence of who He was: His lovingkindness or compassion, and His faithfulness or loyalty. Not only did He tell them that He was that way, as we just saw above; He also proved to them again and again from how He dealt with them and what He did for them that they could count on His being that way. Thus, a person after God's own heart, a person truly in His image, was the faithful person.

First, they came to believe in Him, believe that His words were true or that He was true to His promises. Because He could be relied upon, they could entrust themselves into His hands, confidently hand themselves over into His care. Out of that experience of being constantly cared for, faithfully loved, they came to see that they were able to not only be people of faith, but *faithful people*; not only people who trusted, but *people who could be trusted*; not only people who relied upon God but who could be relied upon, themselves, as His people. To be a man of faith then, was to be a *faithful* man; to be a woman of trust was to be a trustworthy woman. Thus, when the Jewish elders translated the Hebrew Old Testament into Greek, the word of the prophet "The just man will live by faith" (Hab. 2:4) was rendered "the just man will live by faithfulness."

But the just man also falls seven times a day, their wise men reminded the Jews (Prv. 24:16); that is, he sometimes falls into unfaithfulness. And the prophet reminded them that even the most righteous man wore soiled garments (Is. 64:6).

Faithfulness was not only a rarity; even the rare faithful person could never claim perfect faithfulness. The New Testament therefore called for a new *mistrust* in a person's ability to enter into flawless virtue. Only then could he be gifted or graced with a new trust in God's ability to make him what he could never make himself: holy as His heavenly Father was holy; compassionate as His heavenly Father was compassionate; even perfect as His heavenly Father was perfect, on account of Jesus' dying and rising for all.

"I give my judgement, as one that hath obtained mercy of the Lord to be faithful," Paul said (1 Cor. 7:25, KJV). He "boasted" that he was genuinely faithful both to God and man, knowing that his faithfulness was a *gift* that he'd receive from Jesus, a gift that he'd accepted out of faith in what his Christ had done for him on the Cross. This new faith in the new thing that God had accomplished in and through Jesus was aimed at *producing a new faithfulness* in His servant, the Apostle insisted.

What the New Testament would proclaim bluntly and uncompromisingly, the Hebrew Testament at its prophetic climax was already strongly hinting at: that we would need God's special intervention in order that we might be made to realize our own lack of faithfulness, and in this knowledge come to be healed of it.

> . . . The LORD has a controversy with the inhabitants of the land. There is no faithfulness or kindness, and no knowledge of God in the land . . . [so I, the LORD must intervene and] . . . betroth you to me forever; I will betroth you to me in righteousness and justice, in steadfast love and in mercy. I will betroth you to me in faithfulness and you shall know the LORD. (Hos. 4:1, 2:19, RSV)

Jesus loved to quote Hosea as a prophet who caught most succinctly and proclaimed most pointedly the Old Testament climax — revelation of a God who loved unconditionally and so invited love's response. He likewise focused in His own teachings upon the paramount importance of faithfulness. In Matthew's gospel, He is shown painting in parable the picture of the good and faithful servant, suggesting that those two adjectives would comprise the heart of the Savior's verdict upon, and the Father's welcome to the loyal disciple on the last day (Mt. 25:14-30). In Luke's gospel, however, He is shown teaching much the same thing in a different context: "He who is faithful in a very little is faithful in very much; and he who is dishonest in a very little is dishonest also in much . . ." (Lk. 16:10, RSV).

The key to growing in faithfulness lies in humbly attending in wholeheartedness to the tiniest of tasks; in never looking upon minor responsibilities as beneath one's dignity.

Here he contrasts quite surprisingly, yet most perceptively, faithfulness and dishonesty, arraying them as if they were opposites. And so they are, in the sense that only when we are true to our true selves (the person we know we are called to be) are we really faithful. When we deny our true selves, we in effect tell ourselves that *we never were* that person, or never really wanted to be that kind of person. Or, we tell ourselves that we didn't just now violate our ideals, when we most certainly have done precisely that.

The author of Hebrews (as Luke does) sees Jesus as someone who must grow up into the fullness of the beautiful qualities which adorned His personality. Even faithfulness came to Him out of His grapplings with opposition, misunderstanding and other trials; and so, these traits will appear with increasing evidence in the words and deeds of His followers in precisely the same way:

> Now Moses was faithful in all God's house as a servant to testify to the things that were spoken later, but Christ was faithful over God's house as a Son. And we are His house if we hold fast our confidence and pride in our hope (i.e. Jesus) . . . He had to be made like His brethren in every respect, so that He might become a merciful and faithful high priest in the service of God, to make expiation for the sins of the people. For because He Himself has suffered and been tempted, He is able to help those who are tempted . . . Let us hold fast the confession of our hope without wavering, for He who promised is faithful . . . (Heb. 3:5-6, 2:17-18, 10:23, RSV)

He tackled the challenges that life threw at Him and "[Jesus] . . . became . . . faithful . . ." He grew into fidelity by trusting in His Father's love and support; and so, He is the faithful one who loves and comforts His followers at all times. Keep looking to Him, the New Testament writers counsel, to put faithfulness in you as you confess your inability to make yourself faithful; and keep on looking to Him in the midst of struggle and the experience of your apparent powerlessness, so that He who is faithful and true may make you even more faithful to God and more true to yourself. "He who calls you is faithful and He will do it," Paul insists. Do what? Why, keep you faithful, of course. "His blessing is there to keep each of us sanctified wholly, to keep us sound in spirit, mind and body and "blameless" right up to the coming of our Lord Jesus Christ." (cf. 1 Thess. 5:23-24)

Chapter 9

Healing of Identity (II)

We have already spoken of the possibility of laying aside negative qualities of personality which we once had considered to be a permanent part of us. And, we have also encouraged the reader to believe that positive qualities of personality hitherto absent from our make-up, could nonetheless be "grafted in" later and truly become an essential dimension of who we are. We have therefore, argued, in effect, that personality change is often necessary and desirable. Even radical personality change. That, however, is one scary proposal. To suggest such a thing to people who live in an era of ever-present and newly-spawning cults is surely to invite instant anxiety and automatic suspicion. The cultists not only promise, but *produce* example after example of pronounced personality change, with a stunning degree of success. So much as to leave, perhaps, even the majority of us standing at full-alert guardedness for ourselves and our loved ones, not simply against cultism, but even in opposition to any kind of personality change: "Better to avoid all of it than get caught up in the wrong kind, even if there is a *right* kind. The risks of mistaking the counterfeit for the real are just too great."

But there is no real Christianity without conversion; and conversion means a one hundred and eighty degree turn-around in at least some major "segments" or dimensions of who we are. The Bible is from beginning to end a book filled with stories of men and women who experienced radical transformations of character, as a result of having encountered the living God. And the believer's task is not simply to accept these stories as true and therefore see them as somehow part of her spiritual heritage. It is to face up to the fact that she is called to enter into the very same kind of encounter and likewise emerge from such a meeting, a new and different person.

Our challenge, then, is to discern the true from the false; to search out whether and how we might be able to distinguish the authentic from the forgery. First, we shall need to examine the common denominator which, I believe, can be found to be underlying all cult personality change. Then, hopefully, we will contrast it with "graced" personality change and demonstrate how essentially different they are, despite certain surface similarities.

When our American missionaries and businessmen first emerged from Chinese prisons, soon to be followed by our P.O.W.'s, likewise liberated from their Chinese or North Korean captors, in the late forties and early fifties, the Western world gasped in amazement. Severe mental and emotional changes were so shockingly apparent in the personalities of not a few of these former captives. Lifelong capitalists now declared themselves to be dedicated Communists; career military men now bitterly questioned the rightness of America's attempts to block the spread of totalitarianism; dedicated priests and ministers now looked upon years of hardship they'd endured for the sake of spreading the gospel in a foreign land as a wasted effort, primarily motivated by economic exploitativeness, whose chief effect was to inflict further poverty and misery upon a people already poor and miserable. They had been "brainwashed," we were soon told, as a new word found its way unsettlingly into our vocabularies.[1]

After a while, the word generally seemed to fall into disuse, until nearly a quarter-century later when it suddenly re-emerged to once again haunt nervous conversations. Neighbors, sons, daughters, brothers, sisters or cousins, bright young Americans all, apparently normal males and females in their late teens and early twenties, mostly, had in large numbers gone off to the gurus or joined the cults. They soon would smilingly and exultantly describe themselves as "different people." Their families and former friends unsmilingly and despairingly found themselves forced to agree: "They're so different . . . they must have been brainwashed!"

In popular parlance, "brainwashing" is suspected as the real reason for the personality changes evidenced in both the former prisoners of oriental communists and the temporary cult

172

convert. In other words, the man on the street is saying that he doesn't believe that an authentic, spontaneous or healthy personality change has happened in either case. This writer believes that the man on the street is right. We *are* dealing with a form of brainwashing or ingeniously deceitful personality manipulation, in both cases.

In many cases, the Communist brainwashing victim was subjected to physical torture, but this was always secondary to the application of psychological torture. Physical abuse was often applied to speed up the process by weakening the victim's resistance, but there is enough documentation of effective brainwashing in which no physical torture was applied, to demonstrate that it does not constitute an element essential to the process.

The psychological torture, generally worked this way. For long periods of time as he stood before his captors, the victim was forced to listen to a constant harangue leveled against himself and his way of life, prior to arrest. When finally allowed to return to his cell, the victim would not thereby be brought to a place of relative rest or comfort after such an exhausting experience. His fellow prisoners would invariably turn out to be brainwashing "graduates" who were "atoning" for past "crimes" by attempting to assist their captors in their attempt to rehabilitate this presently "unrepentant" cellmate.

Eventually, the constant physical and emotional assaults (or just the emotional assaults alone) bring the victim to the breaking point. He is now ready to make a confession. Usually, a wildly self-accusing, self-condemning outburst wherein he admits to just about anything and everything. At this juncture, his captors change. The tone of their voices softens. Welcoming and approving smiles and expressions replace the anger-and-condemnation masks they'd hitherto worn. Chains are removed from their captives' legs and wrists, if previously applied. In time, they will "kindly" assist the "repentant" victim to re-write his confession. The nearly delirious guilt ravings (which generally bear little or no resemblance to the truth) are replaced by a carefully re-assembled collection of events from the prisoner's past life, which either really happened or "almost" happened that way.

173

These events or "almost-events" are, of course, seen in an entirely new light — the "light" of official Communist doctrine. A doctrine which almost always views any non-communist's motives as consistently exploitative of the people, or subversive of their welfare. A new and highly negative interpretation is now given to key events in one's past life. An interpretation which the victim comes to increasingly believe in, as being true.

Our "penitent" often experiences a tremendous catharsis at this point in time. Signing the confession allows him to slough off his formerly "corrupt" way of life. He has "died" and is now ready to be "reborn." This rebirth will come through "re-education," as his captors (almost "brothers" now) warmly and enthusiastically initiate him into the Communist way of life, as they gently assist him to re-interpret the whole of reality through the lenses of Marxist doctrine. When he comes to understand and accept the entire package of that doctrine as right for him (and so, right for everybody) he will have experienced the "fullness" of rebirth. He will see himself, and others will see him, as a *new person*.

We have examined briefly the "what" of brainwashing. It now remains for us to examine its "how" or "why." Its power, I believe, is the power of guilt. Guilt about what? *Guilt about who we are.*

But why? Especially, if we are honest, productive and law-abiding citizens of the State; or even the Church, as well. Why should we carry guilt around with us, which focuses itself upon who we are? *Because we are who we are only in relationship to others, the significant others who have influenced our lives.* Because we are who we are in relationship to institutions and values which have also influenced our lives as well.

Almost none of these, however, have been perfect expressions of personhood, institution or value. Our parents, for example, have not been perfect and so we automatically tend to harbor at least some negative feelings about our relationship with them or who we are in relationship to them. Our church, if we belong to one, has not been perfect and so we probably have negative feelings about it, and, therefore, who we are in relationship to it. Again, most likely, guilt is predominant among those feelings. In like manner, I may not be one hundred percent positive in my feelings about being a resident of a particular state or a citizen of a particular country.

In each relationship to a significant person or thing, I've had to weigh the positive against the negative and say to myself that "there's a lot more positive there than negative here, so this relationship has basically been a good one for me; it's helped me discover who I am, what I want and where I want to go in life." Much of what comprises our identity has been formed out of such identifications, *positive* identifications, that is.

But what have we done with the negative aspects of those relationships we have generally deemed to be positive and so productively influential in our lives? Maybe faced up to them and so, resolved our negative feelings over those negative aspects in a positive way.

Most of us are unlikely to have done much of that, however. The overwhelming evidence seems to be that by far the majority of us prefer to bury such uncomfortable realizations rather than confront them; to minimize their significance, if not to deny their reality altogether.

Dad and Mom get a 98 if not 100 in my book. My country right or wrong—or better, my country's right even when it is wrong. My church taught me about God and His goodness—after all, and that must mean that its leadership could not possibly have done or be doing anything in direct contradiction to the meaning of such a beautiful Gospel.

Deep down, then, it's impossible to be one hundred percent comfortable that I'm not-all-that-perfect Mr. and Mrs. so-and-so's son or daughter; or a member of a not-so-holy church; or a citizen of a not-nearly-as-just-as-it-ought-to-be state, etc.

Buried doubts about how right my church is, how good my country is. Buried fears that my parents may not have been all that honest with me about their love for me, or that they may not have been as ethically and civilly law-abiding as they appeared to be. Buried hatred of myself for hating my parents on a day or at a time when I felt they'd let me down. Buried insecurity even about how good God could possibly be, buried, perhaps, on that day when I was first confronted with the horror of some evil that He allowed to happen, and allowed with apparent indifference. Buried guilt over the fact that I may have significantly betrayed ideals or compromised standards I told myself I just had to stand by, in order to maintain my resolve to remain a good Christian or loyal American, etc.

All kinds of doubts like that down there, merging into one big nameless Doubt. All kinds of insecurities like that down there merging into one big, homogenized Insecurity. All kinds of self-hatreds, self-condemnations or guilts down there merging into hidden, floating but massive, "blob" of self-hate, self-condemnation or guilt. And it's never been really taken care of. It's never been honestly faced up to, so that it could be properly removed, *and the brainwasher is banking on that.*

The brainwasher has forced his victim to admit that despite surface securities and the facade of having things pretty much together he or she is inwardly loaded with much of the opposite. When such victims are brought to the point of no longer being able to bury or deny all that camouflaged hurt, when they are in the throes of suffering it, the mind-manipulator moves in to provide an outlet for all that unbearable pressure and release from all that terrible pain.

At such an extreme moment of vulnerability most people are only too willing to accept *any explanation* as to why they feel this way, so long as in the accepting of such explanation they are thereby able to feel free of such terrible tension. The confession of past sins (as the brainwasher defines sin) and the embracing of the new doctrine leading to a new lifestyle, provide just that outlet.

For a while, it doesn't seem to matter that you've repented of the wrong things and grabbed hold of a system laced with inconsistencies. The feeling of release make it seem as if it had to have been the right repentant step to have taken and the right world-view to have embraced.

But what has the victim done? He has been persuaded to *reject his former self.* Already significantly infected by an inner self-hate arising out of his un-faced-up-to doubts, fears and insecurities, he now enters into a new and *conscious* act of self-rejection. He now does, in an across-the-board way, on the surface what he had been doing all along in a fragmented way, and underneath the surface of his personality. Despite immediate and momentary feelings of elation, in the long run, this can only leave him more in bondage to hatred of the self than ever before. Hatred is surely no cure for hatred.

The "clean slate" upon which the story of this "new" person's life is now to be written is, like slate, black and hard, effectively blocking out from the conscious mind the person one used to be. How easy to believe with such an effective cover interposed between the present you and former you, that the old you is dead and gone forever!

This new self is now based squarely upon an outpouring of hatred not only upon one's former self alone but upon one's former self — in relationship to the significant persons, institutions and values once dear to the person he used to be. The victim has been taught how to translate secondary or incomplete contempt, attached to key elements in his past, into full-blown resentment of what once constituted the core of his former life.

Another crucial change however has also happened, that is just as devastating; *he has ceased to be an individual.*

Experiences like looking up at the sky on a clear and starry night sometimes fill us with emotions quite different than the awe and wonder we often feel at such moments. At such moments, when we are unmistakably confronted with the vastness of material creation, we are frequently forced to acknowledge that each of us constitutes a part of that immense expanse; a very, very tiny part in comparison to the whole.

Such acknowledgment is more than simply a mental note that you or I constitute a quite infinitesimal fraction of the entirety of what is. A sickening feeling at the pit of our stomachs, a tightening of the nerves and muscles, accompanying such a realization may also mean that we simultaneously have begun to wonder whether we are nothing more than a grain of sand on the shores of outer space, a mere microscopic molecule, in a close to infinite cosmos. Or we may have just suffered fear, the fear of personal insignificance, the fear of personal powerlessness, as we briefly viewed ourselves against such an immense and powerful backdrop.

Some would say that it is our greatest fear. It certainly is in the running for the top two or three spot in the hit parade of human insecurities. What one does with this fear of insignificance or the sense of powerlessness it spawns is clearly one of the key challenges of life. Most of us do not care to tangle with such a behemoth-sized fear, and so we don't. The question it raises: "Does my personal existence really count for anything? is just too scary; and so, it rarely gets asked.

Many of us are compulsive do-ers, desperately and endlessly running about trying to do one "significant" thing after another in order to prove to ourselves or others that we really *are* significant. That's how we try to answer the question. That's how we *prove* that we've never properly answered it or even asked it.

Which brings us back to the brainwashing victim. He gets a real answer to the question, a solid solution to the problem. Or, rather, it gets handed to him: *There's no such thing as individual significance, personal importance.* The individual by himself is without significance. The person by himself is without power. The individual is crying out for significance, but he will get it only by merging himself with a significant whole, by joining up with a movement or organization whose purposes are genuinely significant. The person is tormented by his feelings of powerlessness but he will only be able to lose them by fusing with the organization or movement which unquestionably possesses power.

Domination now becomes salvation. Becoming a part of an allegedly significant whole, he can bask in the pleasure of being a "significant" part. He has finally accepted himself as being an atom; but he no longer has to be threatened by that, because he is a *significant* atom rather than a lone atom floating, unconnected and therefore useless and powerless. To be dominated by what is so obviously good could never be bad. The new self is a *self under domination.* It feels good to be that way because the nagging, eternal question which refuses to go away has been so "positively" and definitively answered; the threatening powerlessness swallowed up in a surge of power.

As Eric Fromm points out, such a person is "saved" from ever having to make painful life-decisions ever again.[2] He is "saved" from having to be responsible for his life's meaning, as well as having to deal with doubts about life's meaning itself. He is "saved" from any further wrestling with who he is or who he ought to become. Now, one of the many, he has been delivered form the torture of having to be compared with others and so the fear of being exposed as inferior.[3] As Eric Hoffer has pointed out, to the extent that we are dissatisfied with being ourselves, to that extent are we gripped by the compulsion to be like others.[4]

After a period of facing unwavering and never-to-be daunted all-knowingness on the part of the ones who are calling for his conversion, he cannot but eventually help feeling jealous of them: "If only I could be *that* secure. If only I could be *that* serene. If only I could be blessed by having a world-view that stills all doubts, answers all questions, banishes all insecurities . . ."

He becomes envious of what he *thinks* is their faith. A faith which leaves no room for doubt. A faith which never has to wrestle with apparent contradictions to the official doctrine or inconsistencies in the lives of the movement's leaders. A faith which bestows not just assurance, but *absolute* assurance. It is not faith, then, as the Bible defines faith. It is "faith," rather, as the psychologists define *reaction formation*.

We saw earlier that reaction formation is one of hurting humanity's instructive ways of trying to fend off further hurt. That it is a defense mechanism. Like the other mechanisms, by the way, it usually operates more unconsciously than consciously. When it is operative, a person pretends on the surface of her personality the exact opposite of what she is feeling beneath the surface of that personality, at the core of who she is.

The more, for instance, that others appear to believe that you are happy when you're really unhappy or that you're secure when you're really insecure, the more *you* tend to believe what they believe: that you really *are* happy; you really *are* secure. You manipulate your mind and emotions so effectively that your original experience of unhappiness or insecurity is temporarily stilled, and you are left believing, for a time, that happiness or security is what you are authentically experiencing. Reaction formation is a variety of self-illusion.

The brainwash victim (or the cult candidate) is made to feel jealous, then, of the apparent personality strength of the committed "believers" surrounding him. In reality, however, he is being made to be envious of a super-human strength or certitude. A strength or certitude which humanity is never able to authentically experience in this vale of tears and threats. He will come to share this "faith," if he wishes—but only after he has learned to grab onto the official doctrine, as if it were the last available life jacket after a plane crash; only after he has been filled with such fear and suspicion of differing points of view so as to allow them not a second's consideration; only after he has been convinced that the teachings of the movement and its leaders must be ever interposed between himself and everything he experiences—only, that is, after he's promised to view reality exclusively through the "official" lenses, through what Hoffer calls, "the fact-proof screen";[5] only after he learns not to face doubts or fears about the movement or its worldview, but to banish them from consciousness with split-second timing; only after he's learned, then, to *repress* all over again (now, with authoritative permission) all his doubts and fears, even as he ruthlessly summons all the necessary energy (from wherever it is within him) so as to be able to bravely parade the opposite; only after he has become expert in seeking and finding the powerful refuge of reaction-formation. Then and only then, will he become "one in faith" with the "supermen" he so tragically admires.

From time to time throughout its history, Christianity has sometimes allowed itself to become side-tracked because of its misreading of the Scripture; or in its overemphasis of one aspect of God's intent, while underemphasizing another. The result, as we shall see, has led devout Catholic mystics and Protestant reformers, for instance, to inadvertently misrepresent key elements in the dynamics of conversion. In other words, now and again, both have ended up, in effect, introducing to their readers or followers one or another of the *brainwash-conversion elements*, rather than the biblical steps of surrender (which they in some way caricature). We will need, therefore, to attach some examples of this past and (to some degree) present tendency to our recounting of the comparatively simple Scriptural viewpoint.

[*One further note.*] It will be obvious to many by now that the heart of the brainwashing process is very close to what even the non-expert knows to be common practice among many of the well-known cults. The Cultist is very often: 1) someone who has been poisoned against his past, and is accordingly

180

persuaded of the "need" to now exist in alienation (and isolation) from parents, family, and former friends; 2) someone who, therefore, has rejected with vehemence the sheer "ignorance," "crassness," or "selfishness" of *not just parts* of his former life but of *its overall fabric*; 3) someone who embraces the cult's doctrine not so much as a key to being able to now "see" spiritual realities (hitherto unseen) but as a screen used to filter out any reality which would contradict the cult's official way of looking at life; 4) someone who has gladly traded in his ("useless" and "spurious") individuality for the *great feeling* of being a part of a "glorious" movement, or the extension of a "powerful" personality.

I. *Brainwashing aims at leading one to a definitive, across-the-board rejection of one's past.*

By severing past connections with family, country, church, etc., the brainwash victim simultaneously severs connection with most, if not all, of his former identity. What kind of attitude about one's past, in contrast, is demanded of the Christian convert?

"God shows his love for us in that while we were yet sinners Christ died for us" (Rom. 5:8, RSV). "But God, who is rich in mercy, out of the great love with which he loved us, even when we were dead through our trespasses . . ." (Eph. 2:4-5, RSV). "He (the Father) is kind (even) to the ungrateful and selfish" (Luke 6:36, RSV).

These scriptures clearly show that God loves the unconverted before they are converted, the unbelievers even before they come to believe. In other words, as anguished as He is over their indifference to or ignorance of Him, that anguish does not prevent Him from loving them. He sees what is bad within them but He also sees the good, which the bad increasingly threatens to overcome — if not squeeze out altogether. Their unloveableness does not over-shadow or entirely cover over their loveableness to Him, even though it may to everybody else. He is able to find some good within them, for He (like we) is only able to love what is good.

No one, for instance, was more aware of his sinfulness than Zachaeus, the tax collector, and undoubtedly his simply being in the presence of Jesus made that self-awareness more acute. But he was made even more aware of how much Jesus loved him; he was even more touched by the fact that Jesus called him by name. Jesus found some good in him *that Zachaeus didn't even know was there.* Jesus discerned a lovableness within a man for whom just about everyone else could only find contempt, including that man himself. The shady little man melted into repentance in the face of such love and acceptance, along the lines of the following: "If Jesus already finds me good and lovable despite the evil and unlovableness he has to see, I will let him remove my evil and unlovableness and trust him to make me wholly good and wholly lovable."

Zachaeus then proceeded to recall his past: ". . . If I have defrauded anyone of anything, I restore it to him fourfold" (Lk. 19:8, RSV). With God's help, he will make right what was wrong in his past life. The Father will help him to be reconciled with his past — not help him to obliterate it. Well, . . . not exactly. Part of his past *will* be obliterated — his sinfulness: "Though your sins are like scarlet, they shall be white as snow . . ."(Is. 1:18, RSV).

In the chapter on healing of memories, as well as earlier in this chapter, we have spoken about how the Gospel clearly summons us to forgive from the heart all those who have in any way hurt us; and so enlists us, at least from our side, to reach out in reconciliation. Jesus warned his prospective disciples that their families' might turn on them, should they decide to follow him, but never counseled arbitrarily cutting oneself off from them. He warned against parental love's periodic possessiveness and manipulativeness, but never against parental love, that Man, who taught us that we should look upon God as a father. Some Pharisees he encountered were in the habit of giving money to the church which they should have provided in support of their elderly parents. Jesus, in response, could only cry out against such "religion," made to be falsely competitive with devotion owed to one's father and mother.

There are times, of course, when love is not true to itself unless it expresses itself through anger. Only then will it have a chance of bursting through barriers, of dissolving inner self-illusions, so that it might do its cleansing, healing work. Jesus, for instance, didn't speak very softly that day He spoke to those Pharisees about their neglect of their parents. But that doesn't mean that when He started speaking to them, appealing to them, at the beginning of his public ministry, that He didn't speak softly and gently. The sharp rebuke toned with impatience and warning-of-the-time-running-out came at the climax of a careful process of reaching out again and again, as diplomatically as the situation allowed. The day simply came when diplomacy had to be junked, because only a shout still offered Him the possibility of His being heard.

So, sometimes God has to shout. Sometimes, His prophets, in times of particularly widespread deliberate deafness to his call, sound as if they are ravingly obsessed with man's irreligion. Sometimes when folks have just about decided that sin ought to be totally abolished, not only in fact, but in name, God's messengers must scream out to us that our righteousness is "as filthy rags" and that our hearts are "desperately wicked."

If we look just to those times and the Scriptures which record these events, then we may well tend to think that God sees no good in us; that He finds us utterly repulsive; and so, will accept us only if we are prepared to totally reject our totally evil past, and therefore, our totally evil past identity. Such passages need to be seen, of course, in their proper context and contrasted with the many other passages of a different tone (represented by the ones we quoted at the opening of this particular section).

If the prospective Christian convert gets the Gospel explained to her in accordance with the way it was written, she will be enabled to understand that: a) some of her past self was lovable and therefore good; God's saving, healing work will therefore be directed at elevating, magnifying and intensifying that lovableness and goodness; b) some of her past self was connected to people and things through relationships, partially good and partially bad; these relationships will have to be significantly purified and modified; c) some of her past self was connected to things essentially destructive and poisonous; such connections will have to be radically severed.

Job's well-meaning, but deceived friend, Bildad the Shuhite, was anxious to persuade him to repent of sins he'd never committed in order to regain God's favor. He suggests to Job that man is a "maggot" and a "worm" before God. Great servants of God, particularly as I have suggested, Catholic mystics (past and present) as well as Protestant reformers of the past and some of their evangelist "descendants" of the present have allowed *Bildad's* view of how God sees us to replace Jesus's view of how God sees us. If Bildad is right, God reacts to us in our sinfulness, in much the same way that you and I react when we look down at a maggot: "Ugh! How disgusting!!!"

This likewise means that many holy and well-meaning men and women have counseled (and still counsel) prospective Christians to reject not just their former sins but their former "sinful" selves. Not merely in part, but their entire former selves. They are unwittingly calling forth, like the cultists and communists, a new self-hate which is supposed to sweep away the old self-hate and so make the heart receptive to the saving influence of God's love.

But the handiwork of love was never meant to be founded upon the handiwork of hate. Instead of counseling: "let God's attitude towards you with its love and acceptance of you, despite your sinfulness, be your own attitude towards yourself"; they are saying: "see yourself as the maggot that God sees you to be and so let yourself be as repulsed as He is!". They leave the baby Christian forever viewing his past life and self through the dark lenses of rejection. Even though God has somehow redeemed the individual, there is absolutely nothing redeeming about who he was prior to his conversion. He is led to believe he has not only repented of his sinfulness, he has repented of being himself. *That's a lot more than God ever asked for.*

Much literature, modern and medieval, penned by mystical writers of the Christian tradition see fit to contrast the *true self* and the *false self*. While, at times, the meaning of these two terms varies, generally what these authors signify by the true self refers to that "part" of the human spirit (or inner person) touched by God's saving grace. The false self (or outer person) refers to the remainder of human personality — all sense of self based in family background, nationality, love-attachments to people and things, personal accomplishments, etc. In order to mature in Christ, many of the mystics assure us, we must accept *only* the inner person as being the true self. All sense of self derived from contacts other than with God can only be hopelessly contaminated with sin. Therefore, it must be thoroughly cast off before the individual can be allowed to become fully at one with God.

Before fully rejecting such a position, it is right, I believe, to look at the grain of truth it contains — a very important truth, at that. Before coming to know the God whom Jesus called Father, almost of necessity, the unconverted person adopts the self-image of one *who has put himself together.* Namely, the image of someone who is able to carry himself through life, without the necessity of having to draw constantly upon God's love, and without the need of having to ask for His forgiveness. Sin, as Thomas Merton eloquently demonstrates, before it is a malicious thought or destructive deed, is a *false identity.* And we are not fully delivered of that sin or its power, until that identity has "died."[6]

"Truly, truly, I say to you, unless a grain of wheat falls into the earth and dies, it remains alone, but if it dies, it bears much fruit." (Jn. 12: 24, RSV). Surely, Jesus was talking about the death of the egotistically self-assertive identity when He spoke of the death of that seed. While one must beware of pushing such analogies farther than they ought to be pushed, it seems safe to say that the following is implied by it: the seed doesn't really "die"; only the outer kernel decays and dies, while the core of the seed survives. It not only survives, once the husk gives way to the warmth, moisture and chemicals of the soil, but surges upward and outwards to display its potential in the color and visibility of a new plant.

When we give up our shell (the exterior, false self-identity) and allow our core to be touched by the surrounding environment (God's love), a new outer expression of the inner self starts to reveal itself. Yes, the seed's core does send its roots downward or inward (i.e., grounds itself in the reality of God's sustaining affection), but it simultaneously gives a true expression to itself on the surface of life, offering its beauty or nourishment to the world around it. The outer self, then, is not simply discarded in favor of the inner, *period.* It is discarded in favor of the inner so that it can thereupon attain to a freshly transformed outer self.

Let's try to focus in on this process in terms a bit more concrete, briefly surveying the formation of normal human identity and investigating what, out of this identity, needs to "die" in order for the individual to experience the fullness of what it means to be "born again."

Sara Smith hadn't been raised as anything. Her parents had been respectful of the religious beliefs of others, but felt no need of organized religion: "For some people, that can be good. Your mother and father don't feel that they need it. You'll have to make up your own mind about it . . ." Upon reaching adulthood, she She surrenders her life to Christ.

The question presently at hand is: what part of Sara has to go? What is the false identity that she needs to surrender if she is to make an honest commitment and grow to maturity in this new life? If the inner self of Sara is now to come alive and blossom, what part of the old outer self is presently being called to die?

Jesus is now her Savior and brother, More of a brother than Paul Smith. Jesus' Father is now her Father, too. A heavenly Father that even grownups need to lean on, listen to, cry in front of. When she prays now, she begins to sense this in different ways. In some ways, in time, she also starts to sense herself being involved in another relationship — that of a bride. Somehow God is her passionate lover and she responds by submitting to his advances and embrace . . .

She has entered into a whole new series of relationships. These relationships do not supplant the previous ones. They supplement them. She does not have to stop being Joe and Sally Smith's daughter in order to be the Father's child. Nor does she have to disown her brother or sister in order to have Jesus as her Brother. Finally, she will not have to divorce her husband in order to experience that romance which is initiated by the Holy Spirit. The new identity builds on and completes the good things that were at the heart of her old identity, formed when she was ignorant of God, just as Abraham's new name given him by God allowed him to keep part of his old name, Abram.

There were things, however, attached to that "first" identity which were illusory and egocentric. The Smith's were white and Anglo-Saxon and Sara one day detected within herself, while praying, a deep self-declaration which said that she was a better person than people who didn't have the bloodline and social status which she enjoyed with and derived from her parents. She also discovered an attitude, that because she was prettier and more successful, worldly-wise, than Sheila had been, that this meant that she was a *better person* than her sister. In time, she came to see as well that she had believed, on the deepest level, that it was all right to love her husband and child possessively and manipulatively, especially when she felt threatened, even if their well-being or freedom were infringed upon at such moments.

Finally, in addition to these and many similar self-revelations, she also found out, (even though she had meant what she said when she promised to live her life in loving dependence upon the God who sustains) that there were many practical areas of her life where she not only gave no thought to her Lord but felt no need to seek His strength, love, or immediate will. Pockets of self-sufficiency. Places in her life where, it would seem, she had no need of God's support, let alone the need to be aware of His presence.

Sara's instinct for egoism and illusion may not have been as practiced or developed as that of others not so blessed by a relatively "storm-free" childhood, and so her need to discard, with Divine aid, the false self, might not appear to be as pressing or as extensive as theirs might be.

But we all have the same need. Some of us are further along than others in this area, sometimes allowing the false self to all but eclipse what remains of what the love of father and mother, sister and brothers, etc. have created in us — not only the potential for good but the potential for God. Those who believe in love will always have an easier time in coming to believe in the God who is Love than those who aren't sure whether or not love really exists.

A God-given identity comes in the same way that a parent-given identity does, except in a deeper part of us. It is not

187

meant to replace that first sense of one's unique value, but rather to heighten it.

Accordingly, it may be strongly argued that any approach, which, in effect, counsels the rejection of every vestige of one's earthly identity, even as it promotes the taking up, in one's inmost center, of a mysterious identity given us by God, *in place of the other*, is a reckless disparagement of what God intended to remain as a permanent dimension of who we are. A profounder integrating of all that makes us human; a full reconciliation of flesh and spirit, our inner person and our outer, is surely what is envisioned by the writers of the New Testament.

2. *The brainwashers or cult mind-manipulators offer their convert (who has just rejected as basically evil not only the "sins" of his past life [as officially defined by one's captors or the cult leadership] but, in effect, his former identity) a new way of looking at life, as he experiences release from guilt and the burden of who he used to be.*

We said above that the convert is given both the equivalent of a new bible and a new faith. The "bible" or official doctrine which reinterprets "reality" for the new believer (usually from every conceivable aspect) is made "one's own" by exercising a new "faith." This "faith" is expressed by dismissing immediately from one's consciousness any doubt or fear arising from facts which apparently contradict the authorized doctrinal viewpoint or party lines, now embraced as infallible truth.

How does this differ from the Christians' acceptance of the Bible as God's inspired word; and how does faith for the Christian differ from reaction formation?

This Bible, or Book of Divine Revelation, is *not primarily* a book of revealed truths. It is rather a book which attempts to open one up to the fact that God is somehow a Person (or three persons-in-one, as the New Testament teaches) and that He is intent on revealing Himself to persons. He is, of course, communicating *truths* about Himself through *words* and *ideas* spoken to and written down by, his appointed messengers. Those words and ideas are communicated, however, to assist each human person to accept the unimaginable reality of a Divine Person wishing to enter into a truly personal relationship with him or her. All knowledge, facts, words, and ideas deriving from God's revelation, even though some of these may be partially or temporarily aimed at your "head" or mind, are ultimately given so that each of our hearts would fully open up to the reality, power and experience of heart-knowledge, the knowing that only lovers are able to have one another.

In order that this love-relationship might be established and this mutual heart-knowledge begin to be enjoyed, an act of faith must occur and keep on occurring. This act of faith ordinarily builds upon, and operates, according to the same pattern as the act of faith which the child comes to make regarding, for example, the essential goodness, tenderness or faithful love of his mother. She has shown him that she is good, tender and loving, again and again. Because of this, even though he has no absolute or infallible proof that she won't turn out to be evil, cruel or unloving in the future, he decides to *trust* that she will continue to be caring. In addition, because he trusts her, when he is able to understand her words, he will accept *them* as being true also.

The believer has given God a chance to demonstrate His love, by opening up to His acceptance of her as she is and His free forgiveness of past misdeeds. She has no absolute proof that God won't capriciously turn on her and reject her unexpectedly, somewhere on down the road. This new love, however, brings a mysterious assurance along with it, a deep inner knowing that God's embrace will never refuse to relax, an assurance which matches the promises made to that effect, written down in the Scriptures. Because she trusts in this loving God, she will trust whatever God has said or says about who she is, who she is to become, etc.

"To have faith is to be sure of the things we hope for, to be certain of the things we cannot see . . . " (Heb. ll:l, TEV) Faith, according to the Bible itself, brings *certainty*, provides a sense of being sure about things we otherwise couldn't know about. Ironically, however, this verse from Hebrews which partially unfolds the meaning of faith to the believer, introduces a chapter of Scripture which simultaneously prepares that same believer to get ready to live a life by no means free of uncertainty. Each one of these examples of men and women who lived and walked by faith place before us someone who had to give up the security of the known for the unknown, the security of what they were sure of for something they weren't sure of. "(Abraham) . . . left his own country, without knowing where he was going." (Heb 11:8, TEV)

This involved not only giving up material securities such as home, family, cultural ties, etc., but even spiritual securities: for these people of faith constantly also had to accept the new and surprising ways in which God would deal with them, directly or indirectly. They couldn't just fall back on former experiences of God (their own or anybody else's). If they were to adequately face up to the situation at hand, they invariably discovered that His presence had to be constantly sought afresh. These heroes of faith enjoyed the security of knowing that God was good; that God was with them; the assurance that, despite the adversities of the present, God would surely intervene and deliver them. That didn't mean, however, that they were exempted from having to wrestle with doubts, tremble with fear, or that they didn't feel strongly tempted to fall back purely upon their own devices as they patiently, and sometimes nervously waited for His intervention. Gripped with terror at the prospect of the Cross, Jesus, Himself, sweat blood even as He chose to trust anew that His Father would not fail to vindicate Him. On the other hand, these living examples of faith did give witness again and again to unexplainable hope, in their darkest moments; an amazing serenity in the midst of incredible vexation; a persistent confidence that God wouldn't let them down even when the odds seemed overwhelming that He already had.

We are often troubled but not crushed; sometimes in doubt but never in despair . . ." (2 Cor. 4:5, TEV) Paul said, perhaps best summarizing the apparent contradiction of living and walking by faith in God's faithfulness and kindness, and yet still having to live and walk through a world which provides each of us with more than enough apparent reason to write off such faithfulness and kindness as inconsistent with what we personally have experienced by way of evil.

They didn't block out, then, any awareness they had of the apparent contradiction between God's care for them and their present dire straits. They didn't beat down beneath their consciousness any doubts of His loving kindness or bury anxieties about His evident inaction on their behalf, by self-hypnotically focusing on inspirational Bible verses (and so, thereby, manipulating Scripture to help them deny reality). Instead, they objectively faced the realness of what opposed their well-being and then opened their spiritual eyes to focus in faith upon another Reality, a God somehow still there beyond and above the doubts and anxieties, a God who could never cease to be faithful, never stop being a Savior, a God unable to forget that He is Love: "From such terrible dangers of death he saved us, and will save us; and we have placed our hope in him that he will save us again . . ." (2 Cor. 1:9-11, TEV). Their faith had nothing to do, therefore, with what Rollo May calls that "compulsive escape from uncertainties." Rather, it had everything to do with taking courage in the face of them.

Each stage of identity growth that Erikson lists involves a moving from the known to the unknown, from the safe to possibly unsafe, from what we're sure of to what we're not sure of. But Erikson has only attempted to isolate and describe the major stages of growth that God has built into the dynamics of the human personality. Why should we be surprised, then, by a paralleling of these crises-of-moving-out-into-the-unfamiliar if we are ever to mature out of our rebirth-in-the-Spirit? And why also should we prove to be any more willing to move out bravely into the unknown, free of uncertainty in the spiritual side of life than we are in the so-called natural side? A crisis is still a crisis and they're always a bit unnerving.

Either we end up becoming more and more flesh-and-blood individuals, because we have taken the risk of taking new steps into the previously uncharted realms of the spirit, or we end up just clinging desperately to our Scriptural certitudes and going nowhere. We either live by the kind of assurance that God gave to Abraham or Paul, and move out in faith as they did; or we memorize their biographies and simply spout the words they spoke or wrote, and try to make ourselves secure in a *world of words* about *other* people.

Biblical heroes were people who refused to use God, other saints of His, or even the Bible itself as an excuse for not living their own lives and making their own unique contribution. Any part of the Bible they knew, or were privileged to hear, they could only view as a launching pad catapulting them into real life, life with God and life with people. They didn't need to clutch grimly onto God's words in order to prove themselves right. They loved God so much in fact, that they were even willing to *risk being wrong* as they searched out fresh ways of speaking of His saving love, ways that perhaps no one had used before. That's why Hosea isn't a carbon copy of Jeremiah or John a Xerox facsimile of Paul, etc.

The inspired word of God, as we mentioned earlier, can be wielded in the same fashion as the cultists' fact-proof, anti-reality screen. If so, it is being employed for the exact opposite purpose of what it was given us for. We can, sadly, so limit our focus upon God's promises and then mentally fix that focus so intensely as to thereby use His truth as a shield against reality.

3. *The brainwasher brings his convert to an inner act of submission, wherein, he psychologically ceases to be an individual and so now finds his significance in being a special part of a "glorious" whole.*

The question we must answer here is, does Biblical Christianity, when it calls for new personhood in Christ through conversion to Him, also counsel "part-of-the-whole-ism, as it enlists its converts to enter into a crusade against ignorance of God and the evils which result from this? People like Eric Hoffer have insisted that it has. We will now attempt to demonstrate the opposite.

Eric Fromm, in his classic work, *Escape from Freedom*, argues persuasively that personal identity, whereby the individual first sees himself as an individual, and only secondarily as a member of the society to which he most immediately belongs, does not emerge as a widespread phenomenon in Western Civilization until the time of the Reformation-Renaissance. I am sure, nonetheless, that Fromm would agree that persons like Socrates and Jesus possessed a truly personal identity, many centuries prior to this breakthrough from cultural identity to uniqueness of individuality. Socrates never ceased to be a Greek or a representative of Greek culture, just as Jesus never ceased to be a Jew or a representative of Jewish culture; but both men found themselves forced to stand against many of the prevailing attitudes and values of their day. Only if they were able to see themselves as more than just a part of the whole, however, could they have done this. Only if they'd come to see themselves as unique individuals who had to hold to certain standards, even if the whole world differed with them, or otherwise *lose who they were*, were they able to take such stands.

Jesus, before He was suspected of perhaps being the Messiah, was first believed by many to be a prophet (Lk. 7:16). Among other things, it was surely His individualism which gained Jesus this title. When a Jew demonstrated such a quality, he almost couldn't help but be compared with the great prophetic leaders of Jewish tradition. They were always individualists. But in what sense?

First of all, they were individualists in the sense mentioned above; in the sense of having the guts to stand publicly and firmly against aspects of public opinion or popular mores. But they were understood to be individualists in another sense, also. They were seen as persons who were able to go before Yahweh alone; as individuals who had enjoyed uniquely personal intercourse with the Holy One of Israel. There is no doubt that the Old Testament Jew saw himself primarily as a part of the whole, in relationship not only to society but even when he sought the face of God. As H. Wheeler Robinson points out, the overall situation in this period of Jewish history is not characterized by the fact that there was little or no individual self-consciousness.[7] It simply was distinguished by the fact that individuals were *more conscious* of being a member of a group. Each person had his own distinctive name, but when he went to prayer, he went as Israel, or as one of the children of Israel. God was seen to be uniquely individual, a Person; but a Person who had entered into covenant with a nation, with a people as a whole, and not with individuals.

Within that context, however, powerful elements moving towards a greater sense of the individual's importance were at work. As he sought God's help, the king or priest would lay aside the "we" and pray at times, in the first person singular, although he would be still praying in the name of the whole group. The prophets prayed this way, too. But, as Robinson reminds us, these prophets were not only the mouthpiece of the people towards God, they were also the mouthpiece of God towards His people (Is. 29:10; Jer. 15:19). Because the prophet was allowed to go before God as an individual, praying alone, apart from the group; because God not only answered him with a response for the nation, but with personal direction and words of encouragement meant directly for him, the beginnings of a realization that individuals could relate to Him, person-to-Person, as well as nation-to-Person began to dawn. Out of each encounter with the Lord, furthermore, the prophet would return to the world of ordinary experience not with a sense that he had merged with the Divine, not with the conviction that he had lost his selfhood, but rather with a heightened awareness of *how very different* from God he was.[8]

Jesus, as we have noted, if He were anything, was a unique individual and saw Himself as such. But everyone He encountered, He seems to have viewed in the same way. All of the gospels picture for us not just a Jesus who ministers to crowds but to crowds of individuals and often to individuals, apart from the crowds. We spoke earlier of Zachaeus, and how he found himself singled out, called by name and called into a new sense of identity. An even more powerful example of how Jesus refused to simply see people as a part of the whole is touchingly concretized in the story of the woman who suffered with the twelve year hemorrhage. (Lk. 8:42-47) It just is not enough of a miracle that God would see fit to heal an incurable through the ministry of His Son. She will not simply come to know God as a Healing Force. She must see the acceptance of the Eternal Father beaming at her through the facial expressions and welcoming words of Jesus. She must know that the Healer has healed her because He knew about her long trial; somehow suffered along with her; and now, out of love, releases her from this burden, this dear child, whom He knows and loves personally.

No one saw this more clearly than John and no one felt a greater burden for the infant Christian Church that this incredibly wonderful new light of God's Self-revelation not be overlooked or understated. He left that church (as well as today's) a Gospel of intimate encounters, a Gospel of one loving dialogue after another occurring between Jesus and a chosen individual. Sometimes that individual was wealthy or powerful like Nicodemus or Pilate, but the majority of them exemplified precisely the opposite. They were otherwise the poorest of the poor and the weakest of the weak. The folks most inclined to view themselves as people who didn't matter — as almost nameless, almost faceless specks out the teeming multitudes. And He left them feeling that they were so precious and special to His Father, as well as to Himself, so foreknown and fore-loved; left them in amazement that they were deemed this *important* to the Lord and His Messiah. He left them, as Fosdick says, awakened with a "transforming respect" for the significance of their own individual lives.[9]

Archaeologists have recently unearthed adjoining tomb markers in Bethany, Israel, judged to be about two thousand years old, bearing the names of Martha, Mary and Lazarus. Perhaps, the very man Jesus had raised from the dead, as well as his two sisters. So, maybe posterity would still have known a little about Lazarus, after all, even without that mention of him in John's Gospel. But we needed to know about his brief reprieve from death. We needed to know that Jesus didn't just call back a body to life, but *the whole person*. That body, catching just part of the uniqueness characterizing the warm heart of a once-and-for-all personality called Lazarus. Different from all other men; different also, of course, from every other Lazarus. "This friendship must not and will not die," Jesus effectually proclaimed in the act of bringing him back, " . . .this uniqueness is far too precious to me and my Father."

And so, the resurrection of Lazarus, anticipates slightly the resurrection of Jesus; the Jesus who promised a like resurrection to all who would believe, and keep on believing in the Love. Nothing ordinarily symbolizes our being different from everybody else than how different our appearance is from everybody else's. The body must be restored, among other things, so that we would be enabled to believe the unbelievable, that who we are matters, matters to God for all time; that He who asserted that, "I know mine and mine know me . . . I call each by name," eternally values our never-to-be-repeatedness (Jn.

10:14, 3, RSV). He will see to it that this uniqueness is preserved, just as He will see to it that the body which expresses that uniqueness will surely be raised and glorified.

"Now you are the body of Christ *and individually members of it . . .*" Paul remarked to the Corinthians. (1 Cor. 12:27, RSV, italics ours) See yourselves as forming a glorious whole together, he says, but don't lose sight of the fact that each of you has his or her unique importance.

". . . God shows his love for us in that while we were still sinners, Christ died for us." (Rom. 5:8, RSV) ". . . the life I now live in the flesh, I live by faith in the Son of God who loved me and gave himself for me." (Gal. 2:20, RSV) Died for us. Loved me and gave himself for me: I'm a part of the human race and He died for all of us. I'm Paul from Tarsus and He did it out of love for me, personally. Once again, we see the same balance between the group and individual.

In an earlier chapter, we noted that the image apparently used more than any other in both the Hebrew and Christian Testaments to help us understand what and who we are is that of the fountain or well-spring. Personhood happens when one pours oneself upwards towards God and outwards towards one's fellow man. We become more and more the self we were intended to be as we reach out to lean-in-love upon God, and offer ourselves as a presence that welcomes His wanting to commune with us. Likewise, we become more and more the self we were intended to be, as we reach out to lean-in-love upon those available to us as friends, even as we offer ourselves to them that they might receive the same from us.

The Biblical self, then, is always a self-in-relationship: "Remain united to me, and I will remain united to you. A branch cannot bear fruit of itself. It can do so only if it remains in the vine. In the same way you cannot bear fruit unless you remain in me." ". . . you will (come to) know that I am in my Father, just as I am in you . . ." (Jn. 15:4, 14:20, TEV)

A self isn't a true self until the self is a lover. A lover who always somehow carries her beloved within her as the heart of her heart, even as the beloved does the same thing in response — no matter what physical distance might separate them.

196

There are individuals who attempt to build themselves up in selfish independence; individuals who attempt to affirm themselves in isolation through an egoistic using of people and things: namely the self-made, "pulling-your-own-strings" representative's of today's "me generation." Such persons, in Jesus's view, are building for themselves an anti-personality and constructing a hollow selfhood. They are straining towards that ultimate isolation and extremity of self-preoccupation which is Hell: "He who finds his life will lose it, and he who loses his life for my sake will find it." (Mt. 10:39, RSV)

The supreme paradox of the personality growth called for by Jesus occurs when a person takes the risk of pouring himself out again and again Godwards and manwards, with everything that he has. It would seem that this extravagant pouring out of self would leave you with no self left for yourself, however.

"That's not how it works," Jesus would surely counter: what you end up with is *more* you, not less; a more defined you than ever, not a blurred you; a more heightened you, rather than just a shadow of the person you used to be, His teachings clearly imply.

Christian history, as we've suggested earlier, has very often been the sad story of how the Church failed to remain in touch with it's Biblical birthright. While it is dangerous to attempt to summarize many centuries in just a few lines (which cannot contain genuine exceptions to the general rule), it is, nonetheless, not inaccurate to suggest the following.

Catholicism, (which developed directly out of the root of Church really experienced as family, as Christian community) ended up retaining the "body" of a close-knit external unity and loyal obedience to leadership. On the other hand it gradually lost much of the "soul" of that original community's warmly mutual love, caring closeness and experienced equality. In effect, the Catholic tradition ended up effectively, even if unofficially, reinstating the Old Testament believer's view of self in relation to God: You dare go to Him only as part of the whole; only the kings, priests or prophets may directly commune with Him (popes, bishops, and priests). The ordinary believer found herself miles away, then, from intimate fellowship not only with God, but also miles away from ever being able to see herself in a very real way as an equal to, or worthy to be an intimate of that Church's leaders. Only the hierarchy were viewed as being "special" to God; and they, like He, might only be approached with awe's lowered eyes, or bended knee.

The Protestant Reformation rediscovered the importance of the individual and re-encouraged the ordinary believer to see herself as having just as much right as anybody else to enjoy full access to God's presence. In doing so, it was reacting strongly against the cold impersonalness of Catholic worship and the sad anonymity plaguing not only the Catholic believer's relationship with God, but her relationship with her fellow believers, as well.

Yet, while the Reformers restored to the individual believer, the awareness of her personal importance to God, as in the early church, it frequently failed to reemphasize equally the parallel need of relating to one another familiarly in a community of love, where each and every one personally knew the Spirit's anointing for ministry. As a result, much of the current non-religious and selfish individualism, along with it's exaggerated need for independence, so characteristic of Western society today, can be eventually traced back to the former spiritually-based and unselfish striving of the first Protestants.

Our heritage in Christ is not simply being a part of a glorious whole (Catholicism), or being able to approach the Divine Presence singly (Protestantism). It is the freedom to find ourselves becoming ever more unique selves. This will happen, however, only to the extent that we reach outwards in love towards our fellow human beings in search of authentic relationship with them, even as we simultaneously look upwards in affection to our Heavenly Father through His Son.

True Christianity may genuinely be looked upon as a glorious cause, the cause of Love. But genuine love always respects the uniqueness of each person as created in God's image. When Christians are encouraged to either lose themselves in God or in the extending of His Kingdom, as they often have been, significant dimensions of God's identity, the Church's identity and the individual's identity (against Heaven's stated will) end up being tragically and needlessly eclipsed. Whenever the true interests of personhood are diminished, especially as they touch

198

upon our uniqueness (actually or potentially), the true interests of God are simultaneously and equally diminished, His word never tires of telling us.

Chapter 10

Healing of Identity (III)

"This is all that I have learned; God made us plain and simple, but we have made ourselves very complicated." (Eccl. 7:29, TEV).

In the final analysis, it would seem that we choose to develop into one of two types of persons, exemplified in the image that follows. One person looks into a mirror and sees himself reflected back. Another person looks into a mirror which has been somehow shattered and whose pieces hang at different angles. He accordingly sees his image reflected back, say, a hundred different times. A hundred little "Jims" staring back at him. The first man symbolizes the person who wants to be one, integrated, truly together. The second symbolizes the individual who's fascinated by his fragmentedness, proud of his complicatedness. So many of us would appear to fall into this last category. We'd rather be many persons than one.

The persistent refrain of the Old and New Testaments, climaxed especially in the clear insistences of Jesus, is that God wants us to be one; that His heart grieves over our double-mindedness and double-heartedness; that He is offended by our pretentious, self-induced complexities; that His healing grace is, accordingly, aimed at restoring to us a simplicity which was originally ours, but was lost through a foolish fascination with the Serpent's cunning. (cf. 2 Cor. 11:3)

Jesus was well aware that people were not one with themselves. That's why He did not fall into the trap of encouraging people to strive after an at-oneness with God or their neighbor, without insisting that they needed to be drawn into an inner wholeness, transparency to self, or unity with self, at the same time. He not only encouraged us to aspire after an at-oneness with ourselves; but even more importantly, He made it clear that His Father's love was poised to fulfill that very wish for us and in us.

We know, of course, about severe splits of personality, like schizophrenia with it's unhealthy divorce of the emotional side of an individual from the intellectual. We've all likewise heard of multiple personality from books and films like *Three Faces of Eve* or *Sybil*, wherein an individual (because of severe damage inflicted in childhood) unconsciously and compulsively assumes another personality and name temporarily, as if the conscious, day-to-day identity didn't exist.

Most of us are not schizophrenics, but few of us enjoy consistent balance of our emotional and intellectual sides. All too frequently, our thinking and our feeling do not dwell alongside one another in a "marriage" all that happy. How often do we go from being the coldly detached analyzer of the world around us to the hot-headed, overly emotional reactor to certain things on that same world that we do not like?

Most of us are not Sybils or Eves, either. But countless numbers of us are far more a collection of multiple selves than a balanced unity of many qualities blending together into, and expressing the uniqueness of who we are. Like the nice guy at the bowling alley; the Sir Walter Raleigh holding the door for the pretty girl; the uncomplaining servant of the boss's wishes, who at home, who, on that same day, shows himself to be constantly negative and short-tempered, generally and unromantically indifferent to his wife, an absolute dictator, as he barks order after order at his cowering children. Not exactly Jekyll and Hyde, but not all that far from the proverbial street angel and house devil. So very many of us are like that — a bundle of contradictory qualities, traits and ideals. As Fosdick so wryly comments in this regard, we'd know ourselves a lot better if there weren't so many of us![1]

The word "personality" comes from the Latin root *persona*. *Persona* first meant *a face mask* worn by an actor; and so, *the character* played by actor; then finally, *person* as it does most commonly today. *Persona* is a composite of two smaller Latin words, *per*, "through," and *sonare*, "to make a sound." In Greek and Roman plays, actors wore masks representing the major traits of the character portrayed. These masks contained a mini-megaphone through which the player could project his voice to the audience.

The actor or actress, of course, wore the mask because he or she did not want to be recognized as somebody's next door neighbor, but as, say, Jocasta the Queen of Thebes or Teresias, the famous seer. The face-covering helped them to become somebody else, temporarily. How ironic that the word "personality" is derived from the situation wherein, and the device whereby, somebody pretends to be somebody else!

And yet, this is precisely one of the deepest splits tearing at the human identity. There isn't a person alive who hasn't felt it. There isn't one of us that can't remember being compelled, apparently by the circumstances at hand, to project to those about us a personality other than the one we felt ourselves most rootedly to be.

There are those, even representing schools of psychological thought, who proclaim in one way or another, that the mask is the person and that if all masks are thrown away, you have no one left. There are others, also represented by professional personality theorists, who see the person as having two distinct parts to her make-up, her external, social mask and her true self behind the mask. These latter, to some degree at least, mirror the position clearly exposed in various ways and places by the Scriptures. The New Testament speaks, for example, of "the inner person" (implying thereby the *outer*).

Paul Tournier has written at length about this two-fold tension underlying the personality's make-up, adding wise observations and reflections derived from his own personal experience to the pertinent insights of men like Jung and Adler.[2] He insists that, while every personality has these two dimensions — the external social self, (which he calls *the personage*) and the mysterious inner core-self (*the person*) — they can never be completely separated. Ultimately, either an interior self (which we have increasingly got in touch with) is accurately expressed by and through the external image we project; or an exterior self (in bondage to social conformity and artificial posings) so sits on the inner person as to leave it blind to so much of its unrecognized potential.

Rollo May tells us of a client of his who described himself as a cluster of mirrors, with each one reflecting another aspect of what other people expected him to be.[3] The expectations of parents, teachers, bosses and other authority figures had become at some point, or at many points along the way, excessively overbearing and artificially arbitrary. He became so frightened that he dared not veer away from, or question the appropriateness of these expectations. He *became* his outer person. He *became* his masks.

I had first met the young man I was now counseling five years before when I'd known him as a scrappy teenager, always ready to take on all comers, driven to deck or pin any opponent, and usually successful. Lately, his constant preoccupation was chess, and once again, he rarely lost. Now, after a number of sessions in which I'd been trying to help him to get to the roots of an unhappiness which all that winning wouldn't eradicate, I found myself stymied. Not in trying to arrive at a diagnosis of that was most ailing him emotionally and spiritually, but in trying to get him to admit that he had once suffered (and so was still suffering) from significant hurts which he'd felt compelled to incorporate as a permanent part of himself. Every suggestion I put forth, every pointer towards key scars and hang-ups was swiftly fended off, and then cleverly rebutted. He nearly had *me* convinced that I didn't really have any idea of what was wrong with him.

Close to desperation that any question I might ask, or hint that I might lay down, would only meet with another crafty counter-move by the master chessman, I sat for a time in silence while I cried out to Heaven with all that was in me for something which would effectively outmaneuver his maneuverings and put him in a "checkmate" that would finally force him to stop playing games, not only with me but with his life.

I got my answer. It seemed to form itself into a question: "Why are you trying so hard to be (the person) that you already are?"

Obviously, he was a prisoner of first, other people's, and then his own, false expectations. The very authority figures he was rebelling against so dramatically, by refusing to wear their kind of clothes and hairlength, or by his unwillingness to obtain the diplomas and degrees they had tied success to, had still won. They'd still been able to sell him on the absolute necessity of competitiveness. They had still managed to convince him that he'd only be who he was meant to be by coming to look upon himself as a radically isolated figure in a hostile world: "It pretends to be friendly and you have to *pretend friendliness back* in order to get the jump on the other guy. You are only a somebody to the extent that you beat out somebody else in the race to get what you want out of life."

And yet, I never saw more clearly than on that day that his bondage to that competition-threaded mask went deeper than his struggles with society's false expectations for him. It went even deeper than that mind so cleverly locked into conscious, and so subtly reflexed into unconscious tricks aimed at keeping me and everybody else (not to mention himself) away from finding out what his inner hurts and hang-ups were. It went right into those scars themselves, the real and imagined blights deforming his spirit. He didn't want me to see how ugly he was deep, deep within himself. He didn't want to know about it, either. Somewhere within, however, he knew, and so felt forced to cover it up. He needed to create for himself a "loveable," "unblemished" surface self, precisely because the core self was, in his eyes, so unloveably and permanently blemished. Surely, the compulsion to mask springs infallibly forth from such a conviction of one's own perceived unloveablness and the fear of imagined rejection on that account.

If we all have known the compulsion to be somebody else, we have also felt the wish that we could be ourselves. Perhaps that feeling was attached to a despairing attitude that such a thing could rarely or never be, but it registered nonetheless. We've wondered whether we could be free of posings, free of having to exert so much energy, just to be sure that the right face is flashed, the right image is struck. By just somehow doing nothing special, could we comfortably be ourselves in such a way that what we appeared to be on the outside accurately mirrored who we were or what we felt like on the inside? Could the inner person and the outer person somehow work together in concert as naturally as a hand moving within a glove? Would it be possible for the surface personality to spontaneously act to reveal who we are and what we most deeply feel on the inside, rather than always feeling forced to conceal it?

Jesus rebuked some of his Scribe and Pharisee opponents for being "hypocrites." The word, as used today, generally refers to the situation wherein an individual pretends to be something other than what he really is, as when enemy pretends to be a friend, or someone with loose morals passes himself off as a pillar of virtue. The word, as Jesus used it, meant something even stronger.

"Hypocrite" has its roots, like that of personality, in the theatre. It could mean, in Greek, simply *an actor* with no disparaging sense connected to it. In the New Testament it connotes the person who goes in for play-acting or theatrical goodness.[4] Jesus singled out for special scorn that variety of hypocrisy in which people fasted, gave alms, and prayed with the intention of impressing men rather than of serving God. Even worse in His eyes were the "false prophets, who come to you in sheep's clothing but inwardly are ravenous wolves." (Mt. 7:15, RSV)

As Jesus clearly saw, the hypocrite ended up being his own victim. He often became taken in by his own performance. He'd trap himself in a self-deluding blindness. A hypocrite is a man putting down a neighbor for a real or imagined "speck" in his eye, while all the time being perversely ignorant of "the plank" in his own. (Lk.6:41-2)

Jesus was so hated by those He called "hypocrites" because He insisted on putting people in touch with their inner selves; in touch with the poverty of their inner selves so that they could be enriched; in touch with the pathology of their inner selves so that they could have it surgically removed; in touch with the weakness of their inner selves to that it could be replaced by strength. But, as He ironically remarked, only the sick need doctors; and folks that play-act health and strength (self diagnosed, out of pride and dishonesty) just end up scorning real help when offered, even when offered as a gift (cf. Lk. 5:31).

Only the people who were not all that heavily into role playing were able to see the bargain and beauty of such an offer: of being able to trade in old for the new, the bad for the good, the unholy for the holy. It wasn't that such sinners had no experience of playing games and wearing masks like "the hypocrites," either. It simply wasn't a habit all that ingrained. *Why not hand over your mask, if you can get a real face in return?*, they must have reasoned.

It surely is no accident that "the disciple whom Jesus loved," namely, the one who really knew how loved he was by his Savior, was likewise the only apostle free enough of fear to show up at Calvary. Indications were that the John of the early days was a "mama's boy," along with his brother James. According to Matthew, with or without their explicit permission, their mother had shown herself to be an aggressive mouthpiece for their selfish ambitions (apparently identical with her own). They were hardly *persons* in their own right, as of yet. They were, rather, scarred examples of motherly domination, pretending to be men standing on their own two feet. Underneath the macho masks, however, could be found frightened little boys terribly apprehensive of making important decisions without mother's OK. (cf. Mt. 20:20-23). In time, Perfect Love was able to cast out that insecurity, however. It can do the same kind of thing for us.

Not so healthy experiences of human love, as we have said, set us up to doubt our inner worth and to fear that we will be rejected, accordingly. We also have intimated that a dominating or possessive human love for another tends to freeze that individual's potentials by ignoring her true talents and manipulating her into the acceptance of a place or a role, or other avenues not really meant for her.

The God of the Bible, on the other hand, is Someone who puts people in touch with their authentic potential. The people He speaks to there — ordinary people like ourselves, who don't know their uniqueness until after they've encountered Him — stand for you and me as well. He tells them that He knew them before they were born. He tells them that they are loved for *who* they are (not for *what* they are). And He tells them that if they allow Him to be their friend and counselor He will lead them into the fulfilling life that He'd eternally envisioned for them.

As someone has said, "God tells us who we are by telling us *who we are to be.*" In practical terms, what this means for each of us is that when we accept Jesus offer of friendship and allow Him to direct and guide us as a matter of course, then His love is poised to free us gradually, gently, but definitively from bondage to these false expectations and artificially-imposed limitations which have denied us at least a partial realization of who we were meant to be. As Adrian Van Kaam (who has written beautifully and incisively on these issues) has observed, we can only discover our originality to the extent that we are truly and constantly in touch with our Origin.[5]

If God has a picture of us not only as we are, but as He would like us to be, this should not strike us as being all that strange. All of us, at certain times in our lives, have pictured ourselves in a better situation, in a more attractive set of circumstances; and resolved inwardly to bring ourselves there. We also have envisioned for ourselves desirable qualities that we presently are without, or possess only to a minor degree — and not just physical qualities, like a trimmer waistline or firmer muscles, either. We've pictured ourselves being morally strong where we've been weak; courageous where we've been timid, controlled where we've been compulsive. Its not wrong then, to possess an ideal or a desired self in addition to the self of the present, the person we are now. This is close to the way that Grace brings us into wholeness. God shares with us His vision of our having come into maturity, our having truly come into our own. But He makes us realistically aware that only with His help can this occur, as He gifts us with the patience and persistence we'll need to stay with this transforming and refining of who we are.

When we accept, as Van Kaam says, that we need to come into the realization of who we are *in relationship to our Divine Origin* then, eventually, we will be able to somehow see ourselves as coming forth in response to God's creative call *as truly original*, along with the rest of humanity, who also come forth as fellow "originals."[6] This will only happen, however, if we are willing to let Him deliver us of false self-statements whereby we, like the troubled man described above, continue to view ourselves as a lonely and an isolated self destined to ever be at odds with every other individual, against whom one will always be pitted competitively, to some extent. The resulting determination to always be offensively-on-the-defensive against an unfriendly world, which is always needing to be manipulated (if I am ever to make myself happy) has got to be let go of and exchanged for something else.

That "something else" derives from the willingness to simultaneously take a new view of ourselves and everyone else. That I accept myself as truly unique, and created by God to *be* someone no one else has been and to *do* something that no one else has done, precisely because it will bear the stamp of that uniqueness.

Secondly, that I take on a willingness to see everyone else as having been given a similar summons: "I will only be the self I was meant to be, to the extent that I am reaching out for God and simultaneously reaching out for my neighbor."

Jesus warned, "Be wise as serpents and innocent as doves," indicating that, at times, we will need to be on guard against deceptiveness and exploitativeness; and that we will not always be able to be as transparently ourselves, as we might wish. The disciple, like his Master, ought to be aware of what is in the heart of man (cf.Jn.2:24); and so, not be naively presumptuous of every person's goodness and sincerity. But at the same time, he will allow himself the graced perspective to "see" Saint Mary Magdalenes hiding within prostitutes; and holymen like Zacchaeus or Matthew imprisoned underneath the shifty masks of wheeler-dealer types, as those Palestinian tax collectors invariably proved themselves to be.

To some degree, we have all allowed ourselves to be mere extensions of the crowds' voice and will — unthinking echoes of public opinion. We have all felt pressured to embrace anonymity at those times when we either have not wanted people to know what we stood for or when we just couldn't stand taking a stand apart from them.

When Jesus commanded His disciples to let their light shine and not to leave it hidden under a bushel, however, He was addressing Himself to just that problem. He is offering us a light so that we might experience ourselves as special to Him and see ourselves, like Peter, as somehow already "rock," when "jellyfish" would appear to be a far more appropriate designation.

But all this building up of me is not just for me, *but for you*. He is intent on making me what I am not yet, but still meant to be, by way of goodness, courage, consistency, compassion, etc., so that these qualities would issue forth from me and somehow uplift, upbuild and enhance you. This cannot happen as long as we secretly choose to be chameleons wedded to convenience; as long as we want to blend with the crowd, whenever standing out (by standing up) would prove to be uncomfortable or difficult.

Jesus was sensitive to people's conceptions and misconceptions of who He was. That's why, among other things, He refused to allow *what people thought he should be* detract in any way from whom His Father told Him he needed to be. He drew His identity from His Jewishness, from his being foster-fathered and mothered by Joseph and Mary, respectively, from being cousined by his cousins and neighbored by his Nazarene neighbors. His deepest sense of who He was, however, He drew from simply being in the presence of a God who called Him "Son," and who encouraged Him to respond in the familiar address of *Abba*, papa, daddy.

His profoundest consciousness of self was derived from simply being with, just attentively relaxing in the Presence of a Father who embraced Him in the Spirit, whenever He was able to go off to be alone with Him. But He also was in His Father's presence when he found Himself standing in the crowded court-yard of the Jerusalem temple or jostled by the throngs who came to hear the famous young rabbi preach, or see the controversial new prophet heal the sick. If, when He was alone with the Father, He was, by faith, enabled to "see" the Father reaching out to embrace Him, then, when He was in the midst of men, by a similar exercise of faith, He was able to "see" that same Father moving there, doing things, unable to cease from His continuing to create, even on the Sabbath. (cf. Jn. 5:10-18)

When Jesus spoke, whenever He did anything, it was always out of that faith which strained to "hear" and "see" as much as it was granted to Him to see and hear of the deeds and works which His Father was doing and saying, there and then. Accordingly, He was able to align Himself with and become fully a part of that creative happening, a happening not only in accordance with the Father's will but also one which directly issued forth from it.

A significant dimension of Jesus' sense of who He was, then, was surely derived from the things He was able to accomplish. He knew that He was called to do *His unique thing,* and was absolutely determined to accomplish it. (Lk. 12:49-50) What He accomplished indeed became, somehow, a significant part of who He was. The Man who reached into so many shattered lives and restored them to wholeness; the Man who did so much saving, somehow became more and more of a Savior with each passing day. And even when the last person on earth has made his final decision to accept or reject that saving, He will still be Savior. It will forever form a part of the fabric of who He is. But this Man who was able to do something uniquely His own, something uniquely unrepeatable, this Man so truly different that He can only be compared with others distantly and superficially, never dreamed of acting alone, acting independently of His Father, acting in any way that would be in ultimate conflict with the best interests of any person on earth. He never feared that the Father's will would "cramp his style." He never perceived the need to do his best as a simultaneous need to better any other human being.

Love has let us all down. And so, we are tempted to see ourselves at the deepest level of who we are as *alone, because we are betrayed* and needing to cling to that aloneness because love will surely betray again. A once apparently sunny, smiling world has come to show itself as wanting to be *over* us (to put us down) and *against* us, in its opposition or indifference to our well-being. An opponent to be struggled with in bloody competition. An adversary to be subdued or vanquished. Almost everyone Jesus knew and trusted let Him down. He refused, nevertheless, to see himself as needing to cling to aloneness, as a defense against future betrayal. No one found himself (and what he stood for) more opposed by seemingly the whole world than He, and yet, He refused to set Himself against it as something needing to be manipulated into submission, by all the competitive craftiness He could muster. *The Father will never betray me. Therefore, I can never view myself as being alone. The Father's love can correct what is wrong with all that humanly opposes me. Therefore, I cannot embitter myself against the world or attempt to force it to be what I want it to be.* What He refused to do, we will have to likewise learn to refuse to do.

Jesus let His Father reveal to Him who He was in the intimacy of mutual self-presence. Jesus let His Father reveal to Him who He was as Son by answering the invitation to enter into what that Father was doing. We, too, will only grow in the knowledge of who we are by constantly seeking Their presence. We will only discover fully who we are meant to be by persistently seeking Their will and choosing to enter into it.

Similarly, if we have spent years approaching life from a platform of isolated aloneness from which we sally forth to independently do for ourselves, then we will not too easily be able to see it as the place where God is constantly doing things and where we are needed to pitch in to help Him. To look for Him there and what He's doing there and our part in that, in a place so rigidly systemized into superficiality, self-seeking, compromise, cynicism and the allowing of evil to parade itself around as good would be impossible without a miraculous and constant instreaming of His grace and faith. But, straining with those new eyes of faith, we will begin to see, and drawing from those new energies igniting from such grace we will begin to do, and we will not be alone. And we will know it.

We need others to tell us who we are. We need others to help us to see what we need to do. We need to hear others call us "son," "brother," "daughter," "sister," "beloved." etc. We need others to call us into places where we're welcomed, places where we're given space to do the things we excel at doing. We need others to help us pass successfully through stages like the ones Erikson speaks of, as we find effective ways of entering into society and enriching it with our unique contribution.

Our identity, however, is only partially formed and remains stunted, the Scriptures show, is we don't simultaneously allow God to tell us who we are; if we don't also allow Him to show us what we are to do. And to the extent that society itself is mired in selfish interests, short-sighted as to the needs of all, in bondage to the superficial and transitory, there will be tension, even extreme tension between the person our peers tell us we ought to be and what we ought to be doing and the person our Lord tells us who we ought to be and what we ought to be doing.

Jesus constantly experienced that tension and unless we similarly experience it we are not truly seeking an authentic coming together of Heaven's contribution to our identity's formation, along with earth's authentic input. Grace is not just given to us to help us to find our right place in the succeeding cycles of life, as society presently conceives life to be. Grace is always poised to transform society by infusing our identities with all the courage and strength needed to oppose anything which robs anyone of life to the full, including ourselves.

The ideal self, just spoken of, is quite different from what some psychologists term the "idealized self." In a way, the idealized self could be called a caricature of the ideal self. It is a false self-picture rooted in feelings of guilt about our inadequacies and the fear of failure. It is the image people artificially construct for themselves when, as children especially, they had been particularly victimized by perfectionist parents or unfairly-demanding authority figures.

To the extent that such unfair pressures are experienced, there will be a tendency to deny one's imperfections and attribute to oneself strengths and virtues one does not really possess. Rather than being challenged forward, then, into increased attainment of new strengths and virtues, such a person statically clings to a false perfection he doesn't possess. He is compelled to project the image of correctness or flawlessness, no matter how painfully he might experience tendencies towards, or feelings of the opposite underneath.

Denial of emotions, then, is often a major factor impoverishing the identity of a person in bondage to the idealized image. Told, for instance that they always had to be strong, they can never allow themselves to cry tears, or admit to being afraid, which would be an admission of weakness. Admonished that they must ever be pure, they may never acknowledge their sexual feelings to themselves and may develop a very cold, anemic manner in relating to others. Programmed into always having to be good, they may end up being unable to experience guilt, which, after all, would mean that they *hadn't* been good, etc.

This is one of the ways that a serious splitting-off of one's emotional life from one's intellectual side happens. Such individuals often have to manufacture artificial emotions on the surface of who they are, since they are too frightened to ever get in touch with what they instinctively feel, deep down. Since, as Philomena Agudo has pointed out, our ability to feel is one of the essential functions of the self, to reject one's feelings is to end up rejecting an important part of who we are, and so, to end up needlessly cut off from ourselves.[7]

It's not enough, then, in all cases, to accept our Lord's deliverance from bondage to society's false expectations of us. To the extent that we have believed those false expectations to be true, they are now a part of ourselves. When they are significant and deep, they may have formed themselves into an idealized self, an ill-fitting mask woven out of the fear of failure and a prideful clinging to a perfection not our own. If so, we will need to accept the strength to let go of this cruel caricature of whom we were meant to be.

People need to be clear not only about their own identities. They need to be clear about who God is, as well. Sometimes that will only come when a person goes alone with Him; and, while focusing on the Father as revealed in and through His Son, lifts up all her doubts about how faithfully loving and gentle God is along with her fears about how all these kindly attributes might be masking a cruelly unrealistic perfectionism.

* * * * *

We need now to reflect briefly on identity as it relates to sexuality. ". . . in the image of God He created him . . ." Genesis says, and lest we tend to think that only Adam was directly in the Divine image, it adds by way of clarification ". . . male and female He created them." (1:27, NIV) Somehow, their being created bodily and emotionally different; somehow, their being able to accept that difference, appreciate that difference and be happy about the difference would help them

214

and all those they stand for, know better who God was. It would not only help them to increase and multiply, and reflect His creativity; it would help them mirror His zest for intimacy as well.

Donald Goergen[8] sees *Genesis*[9], *Song of Songs*, Matthew and Paul as presenting us with four successive stages of inspired understanding of the meaning of sexuality.

Genesis places the sexual in the context of loneliness and fellowship. Because the man and woman are sexual beings, they are able to be more complete. They are freed from loneliness and isolation. The primary focus here is not on propagation but companionship.

The Song of Songs not only acknowledges the sexual but celebrates it. Going further through *Genesis*, it illustrates that sexual affection includes the need for exclusiveness between the couple presented there, so wrapped up in love for each other. The sexual here is more than physical. It embraces both non-verbal and verbal expressions of love, joy in the beloved's presence or pain in his or her absence. The exclusiveness and intensity of this love and its promise lead them to the awareness of the need for fidelity to ensure the permanence of their relationship.

In Matthew's Gospel, Jesus teaches that the man and the woman committed to each other in marriage are no longer two but one. This union is brought about by God Himself. Such sacredness ought to instill a respect in the couple for what God is doing between them. It provides an even deeper reason for clinging to fidelity and rejecting an easy escape through divorce. The new understanding of forgiveness and reconciliation Jesus gives and the power being unleashed to bring it about will even further strengthen His disciples' ability to remain faithful to each other.

St. Paul's teaching builds on Jesus' focus upon the sacred bond. The sexual relationship between husband and wife not only comes from God and is made stronger by His blessing, it is also a sign of Christ's faithful and ongoing love for His bride, the Church. The sexual has not only been placed in the setting of love which endures, it is likewise a sacrament of the Divine faithfulness which lasts into eternity.

215

In his *First Letter to the Corinthians*, however, Paul adds a note of caution. There is danger in that relatively young Christian community, that some might reassume attitudes which would undermine a biblical appreciation of the sexual — attitudes condoning promiscuity, reflecting the cultural viewpoint of times; attitudes which, if left unchecked, could lead to destructive behavior that might even threaten the loss of their newly-embraced life in Christ.

My sexuality is a dimension of my personhood. My primary goal is to become a complete person. Within that category, my goal is to become *this* person, and so enter into the uniqueness of who I am. Part of what constitutes that uniqueness is my being a man or my being a woman and my coming to accept that. To achieve sexual identity, then, is for a man to have a sense of maleness and for a woman to have sense of femaleness.

Healthy sexual identification occurs when a man is able to say and feel that he is a man and a woman is able to say and feel that she is a woman. (By "feel," here, we mean "feel good about.") Such attainment of sexual identity, from the Christian point of view, means that now a man or woman is psychologically prepared to place his or her secure sense of being male or female at the service of loving relationships, and even the exclusive and permanent love-commitment of marriage.

Having briefly surveyed the Scriptures' teaching on sexuality and having also attempted a brief description of sexual identity, we will now present a likewise brief overview of where key healings of sexual identity might be needed and how they might be appropriated.

If only we needed the healing of a distorted understanding about sexuality' significance and purpose derived from a culture as pagan as, if not more pagan than Paul's Corinth, that would be serious enough. Just when we think that we have been exposed to the ultimately erotic, a new ad or commercial shows us otherwise. There seems, today, to be no end to the assaults upon our desires. Healthy control has never been more difficult, because sickly seduction has never been more rampant.

Many of us, however, are simply not in need of deliverance from an eighties-induced grab-bag of attitudes proclaiming that the body is primarily a pleasure machine at the service of self-gratification, whenever convenient. Multitudes of us are only too prone to crumble in the face of such propaganda because, while schooled in the Scriptures or instructed by the Church, we were never given anything close to the digest of the Biblical understanding of sexuality recounted a few pages back.

If we were taught, primarily, to fear sex and were led to believe that what God primarily wanted us to know about it was that sexual sins are always mortal sins; that His main concern was that we not misuse it prior to marriage in masturbation or fornication, and subsequent to marriage in adultery, then we were not taught about sexuality the way the Bible teaches it. The Bible celebrates sexuality as well as cautions about its misuse. The Bible encourages us to see it for the gift of God that it is before warning us that, like any of the other of His gifts, it may be wrongly used for purposes not in accord with the Divine wisdom.

As long as we have not accepted our sexuality as a dimension of ourselves willed by God (and therefore, as something good and even wonderful), we have not broken through to the healthy sexual identity our Creator wants us to have. Many of us were only able to provisionally accept our sexual side, with that acceptance partially undermined by exaggerated fears over falling into sexual sins, or by excessive guilt feelings arising out of present or anticipated, real or imagined moral lapses.

To realize when you are thirty or forty, for instance, that it's good to be a sexual being, that it's wonderful to share the joys of sexual pleasure with your mate, is not automatically to have erased one's earlier fear and guilt-ridden attitudes about its root value. It is possible to enter into a surface appreciation of the goodness of one's sexuality and the rightness of its appropriate expressions and still feel as if it's something you have to do for your partner and yourself, cut off from your love-relationship with God; or that it's something that He, at best, tolerates because of your sexual weakness. For some, the mutual expression of genital affection is almost an activity that has to be performed in defiance of a puritanical deity's displeasure. They see it as something good for themselves, but they can only have it, if like Adam and Eve, they tear it off the forbidden tree and enjoy it together in the hopes of not getting caught. Termites eating away at the floor's foundations, again. Buried doubts, fears, or guilts robbing one of a full acceptance of one's sexual side and therefore, of full enjoyment of mutual marital affection.

As long as those doubts, fears or guilts are there, our sexuality is not fully our own. It remains at least partially walled off from whom we really are, while we, thereby, are cut off from the fullness of who we are. And, as we also intimated earlier, when rooms in that house which is self, are closed off from the rest of the self, they are liable to become a crash pad for demons.

We do not receive our sexuality in its wholeness from the pornographers or the neo-pagan purveyors of the body-as-thrill-mechanism and sex as a vehicle of the casual and promiscuous. We also do not receive it in its wholeness from a Christian tradition infected by a fear—and guilt-ridden caricature of what God really wanted seen and understood. The tradition, by the way, which probably started with the great saint and theologian, Augustine's inability to fully forgive himself for years of debauchery prior to his conversion. That otherwise brilliant thinker taught that the sensual (as in the Song of Songs) is no longer something we celebrate, but merely lust that we must fight against.[10]

We receive our sexuality in its wholeness, then, by receiving it for the gift that it is from the One who gives it. Once we see it for what it is, in the light of scriptural wisdom, we are ready to go before Him in faith, accept it from His hands as good and holy and our own:

"Father, I thank you for creating me. I thank you for creating me a man (or woman). I thank you for my body and all its parts. I thank you that I am able to feel sexual feelings. Help me to see that there's nothing to be ashamed of here, even when they seem inappropriate or are unable to be acted upon . . . If I am a man, help me to be glad about that. If a woman, just as glad about that. I accept your wisdom in designating that I should be one or the other . . . If I have, up until now, thought of my sexuality as something I discovered myself and employ for my own purposes, or solely in accord with my own desires, I do so no more. It is not there to serve my willfulness or my selfishness. It is there so that I who have been gifted with it can give myself to others. It is there for me to use in accordance with your call to love everyone with as much warmth, compassion and sensitivity as I can find. If I am called to marriage, it is there to enable me to bestow myself upon the person chosen to be my spouse; to bring him or her happiness and pleasure, even as he or she brings those same things to me. It is there as part of your Son's promise to help me to live life to the full and help others to do the same . . . If, on the other hand, my sexuality has been tied to self-doubts, self-guilts or self-fears, I now give you the hurts of my upbringing that led me to that, whether it be the silence of parents, the severity of pastors or mistakes spawned by the ignorance and confusion of my puberty. If I need to remember any of these moments of injury, gently bring them to mind and assist me to release to you whatever needs releasing . . . Help me to be a new person sexually, for Your love is able to heal all my hurts and you come to make all things new . . ."

As has been already shown, we are healed not simply because we say the right prayer, echoing the correct sentiments. We are healed because He is the Healer and He wants to heal us. True prayer allows us to be aware of His presence. True faith enables us to know that He is present to heal. In this case, the truth of His word in the Old and New Testaments assures me of who I am meant to be sexually and what I am meant to receive in that dimension of who I am, as His creative love, His recreative grace flows into me and through me. What we need, then, is to let the basic attitudes of a prayer, like the one given above, sink ever more deeply, ever more peacefully within and to root themselves ever more deeply into the soil of our hearts. That healing may happen quickly. It may happen more gradually. In a way, we will only have been saying, "Amen" to the "Be Healed!" that He has always been speaking to us, but that we simply hadn't been aware of until now.

"Macho" men bereft of sensitivity or tenderness; the more recent phenomenon of "macho" women whose aggressiveness similarly eclipses the same qualities; effeminate men or overly charming, slavishly compliant women all point to a confusion of sexual identity. We are not finished, then, with our treatment, necessarily brief and schematic, of healing of sexual identity.

Carl Jung made famous the concepts of "anima" and "animus," the feminine and masculine elements of the inner self. His basic notion is that every person, whether man or woman, possesses an identity formed out of both masculine and feminine components.

We feel that this elementary concept is in basic harmony with the Scriptures which not only inform both men and women that *both* are created in God's image but also reveal a God who possesses traits that we would consider masculine, as well as qualities we tend to think of as feminine. The God who reveals Himself as Father and who is seen as a "mighty warrior" for instance, also declares that even if a mother could forget her child, He could never forget Israel. In like manner, Jesus is unafraid to compare Himself to a "mother hen," etc. (cf. Is. 49:5; Ps. 131:2; Lk. 13:34)

None of us is exclusively masculine or exclusively feminine. To be a man is to have recognized and accepted that I have a man's body and to be comfortable with that. It is also to have noticed what my family, culture, etc. teach me about manhood and to have incorporated that. To be a man is also to respect and value the body of the opposite sex. It is also to respect and value what I perceive to be different about the opposite sex, in emotional and spiritual ways, as well. At that point, I am able to appreciate that, while a man, it is appropriate for me to make my own, in a way appropriate to my sex, qualities that appear to predominate in the opposite sex. To be a man, then, I simply do not come to the stage wherein I appreciate that I would like to embrace a woman's body and even choose a female as a life-companion. It is to want to internalize some of her qualities and make them my own. For instance, as a man, I may overvalue my thinking side and may not be so comfortable with my feeling side. As I come to appreciate the feminine, as a result of having come to value womanhood, however, I may now choose to allow the tender and the personal to moderate my inclinations to be tough-minded

and logical; the intimate and the trustful to soften my tendencies towards the distant and wary, the warm and harmonious
to offset my instincts to be cool and argumentative.[11] Exactly
the same process is able to happen and needs to happen from
the woman's side as she comes to appreciate and chooses to
appropriately internalize so-called masculine qualities.

We have now widened our concept of sexual identity. It
is as Goergen says, a task which enables me to positively accept
that I am both a man and yet feminine, or a woman and
yet masculine.[12] The Jesus who weeps openly, frequently
touches people of both sexes, physically; who is unafraid to
clasp the Beloved Disciple in an embrace against His breast,
is someone like that. The female disciples gathered around the
Cross, full of courage and long-suffering as they boldly ignore
Roman military power and calmly defy the prevailing mood
of the angry crowds, are like that. All know a godly and
appropriate blend of the masculine and the feminine. Yet, Jesus
and John remain men. And the women are clearly women.

But what's the key? What's the proper blend or balance
of the masculine or feminine? God certainly knows, even if
we're not sure. If we ask Him as men to remove our fears
of the feminine, or as women to deliver us of resentments of
the masculine, etc; if we seek His assistance to correct any
imbalances that still remain within us, He cannot fail to answer
such prayers.

Masculine or feminine traits are not necessarily sexual feelings, however. And we still need to talk about that.

Suppose I am a man who is married. Having marriage
relations with my wife on a regular basis is part of my life
and I view it as an attempt on my part to show her that I
really love her. In time, however, she shows increased reluc-
tance to have relations with me and, when I finally confront
her, she amazes me with the accusation that there's no tenderness
in my love-making. That I am too "mechanical" and "matter-
of-fact" about the whole thing. Furthermore, that I never
verbalize my caring, except when in bed.

If her accusation is true, there can be a number of reasons
contributing to my deficiency here. One of them, however,

221

(and it could even be a predominant factor) might be over-identifying with my own sex. We men sometimes over-identify and so, gravitate towards the "macho," when we first experience sexual attractions towards members of our own sex and out of fear or shame repress them. Often, the sweeping of these feelings "under the rug" is done with a force and finality which insures that we never become aware of such attractions again. The result is an overly harsh, generally coming-on-too-strong masculinity that is unable to appreciate the affection-needs of the opposite sex (often deemed by such men to be an *inferior* sex). Individuals of this sort, out of their exaggerated need to appear strong, may find themselves unable to tell their wives that they are needed, that it's good that they are there to lean upon, or even that, "I love you," since to love is to lean and to lean is not to be strong. (Over-identifying with the feminine by the repression of sexual feelings towards one's own sex can work similar damage from the woman's side, in marital relationships as well.)

Sometimes this over-identifying with one's own sex comes from having been deprived of the normal touching which God intended to happen, but didn't, during one's childhood. A boy who was not touched or embraced enough in his youth by his father, for instance, will be prone to so fear male touching later on that he may even find himself awkward in marital love-making. Furthermore, his relations with members of his own sex will tend to be distant and socially superficial. He will not be inclined to enter into deep friendships with males. No man will ever be given access to the secrets of his heart or share a warm or affectionate friendship with him, unless this individual comes to see that he carries such a hurt and searches out healing.

If we have experienced a repetition of symptoms such as the ones described just above, we may need to approach the Healer with guilts or fears about homosexual feelings we've buried or with anxieties about touching arising out of childhood deprivation. (The prayer given a bit earlier ought to provide sufficient example of the ways we might express, in our own words, problems experienced in this area.)

We regret that we are only able to skim, here, a subject which deserves far more extensive treatment from the perspective of inner healing. Our final area of focus will be on the healing of a pathologically homosexual identity. (We use the word "homosexual" here in its root sense, signifying "of the same sex" and apply it to both men and women.) Most providentially, a book has been written which bravely and beautifully brings together sound principles of inner healing, or compassionate understanding of the problem and key insights form contemporary psychotherapy. It is called, *The Broken Image* and is written by Leanne Payne.[13] We recommend it highly.

From what has been already said, it is clear that it is our belief that a person is able to experience both heterosexual and homosexual feelings and not be a homosexual. If it is not already clear, this book further takes the traditional Christian position that genital intercourse, the interacting of the sexual organs of the male and female is what is envisioned by God for a man and woman who have given themselves to one other for life, in the exclusive and faithful partnership of marriage.

We likewise believe that to be normal is to experience the inner freedom to desire and then to embrace that heterosexual relationship, should such be one's vocation in life.

In the chapter on "Healing of Memories" we spoke of how buried recollections of being molested sexually in childhood and buried defenses against that can seriously impair sexual functioning years later. Such experiences, of course, can upset the masculine-feminine balance in a man or a woman in such a way that they are left feeling good only about attractions attaching themselves to one's own sex. Payne's book provides some liberating insights into how healing is appropriated here.

We have also spoken in that chapter on memories about how sometimes the buried traumas that still haunt us are not so much the forgotten remembrance of one of two nasty episodes for example, but rather our amnesia about what *didn't* happen. When what needed to happen didn't happen, or didn't happen very often, the effect of that could be the equivalent of something terrible occurring in one's life.

Love-neglect is, of course, prime example of this. Touch-neglect is, as we just noted, another. Not enough love from mother, not enough love-touch from dad, or vice-versa (or something similar) can upset the inner masculine-feminine balance in the process of formation from birth; in the process of formation long before puberty and the sexual identifications made there, along with the sexual awakenings experienced there.

The upset in the balance ordinarily happens long before adolescence. The male individual experiences himself as a less than loveable boy and the female individual a less than loveable girl. Even *this* then can lead to some primitive conception of self as being defective in one's being male or one's being female. It may even result in a boy's wonderment about whether he'd be accepted more, if he'd been born a girl; or a girl's wonderment as to whether she'd be loved more, had she been born a boy. The wonderment, of course, is able to lead to the wish — the desire to be otherwise than what one is sexually.

We do not mean to suggest that what is presented here is the ordinary course of events leading to the adolescent's experience of himself or herself as a possible homosexual. We have simply presented what we believe to be the kind of neglect-factors that are able to lead to this sort of problem. What we do assert, however, is that the beginnings of such a problem are always tied to self-hate and self-doubt attached to a person's image of who they are; and, therefore, of who they are as boy or girl.

Some kind of imbalance in the child's love relationship to its mother or father leads to an imbalance in that child's internalizing of maleness-femaleness. When it is time for the child, now adolescent, to experience those qualities in a clearly sexual way, the teenage boy feels that his own sex excites him genitally while the opposite provides him with little or no stimulation. Similarly, a teenage girl now finds, members of her own sex stimulating her desires, which apparently do not attach themselves at all to her male counterparts, or only faintly.

If the sexually confused teenager is not provided with appropriate counseling at this time, he or she will be very inclined to make the following self-statement: "Since I am not significantly attracted to members of the opposite sex, I *must be* a homosexual or lesbian. *I now accept myself as such* . . ."

There are two different key elements comprising the homosexual identity, we believe. The first is the damage done in early childhood upsetting the maleness-femaleness balance in a boy or girl, very often brought about through the experience of love-neglect. It is a false perception of one's inner worth as a boy or girl, and always is wedded to self-dislike. The second is the self-inflicted trauma of wrongly declaring oneself to be a homosexual when the male-female imbalance expresses itself in sexual feelings.

To be healed of a homosexual identity, accordingly, at least two things need to happen. Such individuals need to be brought to the realization that they are a victim of nurture rather than nature. They need to be shown how, in the light of their unique childhood experiences, the imbalance established itself. They need to see how their relationship with parent or parents, for instance, while characterized by many good things, was perhaps flawed by certain elements which were able to upset the proper maleness-femaleness balance. They then need to be brought into an understanding of what happens in puberty; of how the identifications made there are *choices*. This would include the understandable, but erroneous choice to look upon oneself as a lifelong homosexual on account of one's experience of persistent and predominately homosexual feelings. The healing, then, comes as a result of realizing not only that one's personal history set him or her up for the imbalance but also from realizing that one has made a destructive decision. It likewise cannot happen, until the individual *retracts* that earlier choice; until he or she rejects it as based in a false perception of whom he or she really is.

Homosexuals likewise need to be delivered of destructive influences from the outside, if they are ever to take the risk of asking for healing. They need, of course, to be freed from the destructive supports of that segment of society which sees them as a "third sex" who ought to be left alone to do their thing. They likewise may need to be freed of internalized anger and shame derived from that side of our culture which views them as hopeless degenerates.

In a parallel sense, with regard to Christianity, they may need to be delivered from an imperious and moralistic summons to change their ways issued by certain smugly, self-righteous "followers" of Jesus who show them nothing of His kindness or compassion. They may also need to be delivered from a superficial and condoning kind of acceptance on the part of another kind of Christian which is often based in a blend of simple despair over the homosexual's ever being able to change and a relatively sophisticated understanding of homosexuality's possibly complex origins.

This writer has had the privilege of counseling with homosexuals and of witnessing their entry into such a healing process. He has also seen them recapture their rightful sexual identity on account of such a therapeutic encounter with the caring Christ. Such a process may well be slower and more painful than either client or counselor could have anticipated. There my be lots of highs and lows to be experienced and lots of see-sawing back and forth, before real victory is fully savored. In the following prayer, we merely hope to summarize certain of the key stages of the healing process. The sentiments of this prayer need to be joined to the spirit of the one given earlier:

"Lord Jesus, you are present to me and as I picture you to myself, I see loving acceptance in your eyes. Let it penetrate to deep and hidden places within me — places where I still hate myself or condemn myself for not being lovable, or even for being less than whole. Let that love of Yours cast out fears that I'm less than a full person, less than a true man or a true woman. Let Your gentleness cast our any false guilts I might experience towards my own sexuality.

"Let Your forgiveness cast our any true guilts I may have, or any self-condemnations I may be nurturing on account of acting out, or following through on, such feelings. Because of such sexual feelings and such increased self-hate or condemnation on account of them, I have chosen mistakenly the identity of a homosexual. I may have also chosen to compensate for guilt by affirming non-guilt to myself. I may even have willed to generate for myself a peace of my own to make up for the absence of Yours. Take that away. I only want Your peace. Help me to choose my true sex with its appropriate balance of the male and female. If a man, I accept my manhood from you. If a woman, I accept my womanhood from you. Help me to know in my heart that it is the Father's will that I be a man (or a woman) in the full sense of the word.

226

"Lord, I want so much to be a sexual person. I'm glad about having sexual desires. On the other hand, help me to see that I may well be tempted to continue willing the permanence of homosexual desires because they're the only kind I've known. Help me to let go of wanting them to predominate. Help me to see *by faith* that I am able to experience desire of the opposite sex. Even strongly. Help me to want that. Keep strengthening my faith, when the old desires come back and seem to say that I'm just going against who I am . . . I accept the body of the opposite sex as good and desirable.

"Take away any resentments I may have of that body because it did not excite me when I first hoped that it would. Finally, remove from me any bitterness that may be in my heart against You, Lord, for having permitted the circumstances in my life that led to this problem. Help me to know that here, where I'm weakest, You can be strongest; that where I've felt most defeated You are about to share Your Easter victory with me. AMEN." [14]

* * * * *

"Martha, Martha, you are anxious and troubled about many things; *one thing is needful* . . ."(Lk. 10:41-2, RSV, italics ours) ". . . And Jesus looking upon him, loved him, and said to him, *"You lack one thing* . . ." (Mk. 10:21, RSV, italics ours) ". . . Therefore do not be anxious saying, 'What shall we eat?' or 'What shall we drink?' or 'What shall we wear?' For the Gentiles seek all these things; and your heavenly Father know that you need them all. *But seek first His kingdom* and His righteousness, and all these things will be yours as well." (Mt. 6:31-33, RSV, italics ours) "No one can serve two masters; for either he will hate the one and love the other, or he will be devoted to one and despise the other. You cannot serve God and mammon." (Mt.7:24 RSV)

In each of these statements, Jesus is showing himself to be aware of, concerned about, and anxious to heal a significant aspect of the fragmentedness of human identity. We are not only people who experience ourselves as mask-personalities and simultaneously as someone else underneath the mask; we are not only people who deny our real feelings, or refuse to own our own hurts, while we manufacture counterfeit feelings or

227

bogus virtues to hide embarrassing realities from ourselves and others.

We are also people with fragmented motives, contradictory intentions and conflicting characteristics. We are sometimes forced to describe ourselves (or others) as "coming apart at the seams," "coming unglued," "coming unhinged," "being at loose ends," "flaking out," "going to pieces," "acting like a scatter-brain," "cracking up" or unable to "get ourselves together," etc. All these non-technical expressions picture quite accurately and describe quite graphically our awareness of being *many* when we ought to be one; *fragmented* when we need to be whole.

To individuals, whose identities are pulling them in different directions at the same time, Jesus offers the same word of counsel: *only one thing is necessary . . . you lack one thing.* There is one thing to pull you together; one thing to give you the proper perspective; one thing to place each of your priorities in the right order; one thing to put an end to one part of you warring with another; one thing is needed so that you can be at one with ourself.

Before we investigate what that "one thing is," let us reflect momentarily upon two other "things" which ape it, two approaches to living which provide a temporary unifying support, or even a permanent integrating base to the qualities which comprise personal identity. (No one, by the way, to this writer's knowledge, has written more clearly, powerfully or pointedly about this aspect of identity than Harry Emerson Fosdick, in his classic, *On Being a Real Person.* We will simply attempt to summarize some of his key insights here and add a few reflections of our own.)

First, the temporary. Fosdick employs the apt image of a sheaf of wheat held together by an outer bond to describe how this kind of identity holds together.[15] The individual wheat stalks stand for a person's separate qualities, traits, motives, etc. as they come together to form the "whole" which is their personal identity. The bond holding them all together symbolizes the fact that the force integrating such a personality comes from the outside. It is held together by external supports — like social status, financial security, business success, etc. If these supports are taken away, however, the apparent integration of the personality crumbles and moves quickly in the direction of dis-integration, just as the once orderly wheat stalks fall into a disordered mess when the band is broken. As Fosdick perceptively comments, the removal of such supports does not so much cause the coming apart of the personality as it simply reveals the hidden disintegration which was there all along.

Secondly, the permanent, or possibly permanent. There is a "wholeness" to this type of identity. The separate elements comprising identity are brought together into a oneness and, this time, *from the inside*. That unifying force is the self-centered will. Examples of this approach want what they want when they want it and are willing to make just about any sacrifice necessary to bring what they want about. From the heart they become absolutely devoted to that goal which organizes and grants a certain connectedness to everything they say and do: the egoistic will to power, prestige, pleasure, etc. Naked willfulness merges with a "single unifying aim"[16] to meld such a person's attributes and drives together into a uniquely selfish style.

But there is yet still another kind of "recognizable singleness"[17] characterizing certain individuals, a unique steadiness and one-directionalness of style, whose lives are organized around a unifying purpose, whose qualities derive like spokes from a central hub. They are not pulled in different directions, split by conflicting motives or torn by various anxieties, for they have learned how to seek *first* God's kingdom and His righteousness.

Although we have, in effect, already described the Kingdom, we haven't labeled it, as such. Seeking God alone and then seeking Him in the midst of the world is seeking the Kingdom and His righteousness. Seeking His presence and trying to discern His will, as our number one priority, each and every day, is seeking the Kingdom *first*. *This* is the one thing necessary, the one thing most of us lack. Many of us even have a place for God and a legitimate concern for His will. Wanting God to be present to us as far as possible every place we are, however, and seeking His will every place we go, is entirely something else again. Especially when having Him around is perceived as a threat to our privacy. Or the seeking His will purely might possibly mean the foregoing or the postponing of some (even good) thing we want or want to do right now.

As implied earlier, we need to be held together from the inside. We need to come from a center. We need to know that we're coming from a center. We need to know that we're coming from a center truly centered upon God and *His* will. Then and only then, will we stop coming across to ourselves and others as what Fosdick pictures as a brush heap,[18] a tangled heap of leaves, twigs and branches, rather than a "tree" which is comprised of the same elements, but organized, growing and drawing its life from within.

We all want to get ourselves together. We constantly experience that want as something which urgently requires our attention. There are, however, only three alternatives to just remaining in pieces; to simply surviving as a bundle of masked, multiple selves, often in conflict with each other. They are: a.)artificially propping ourselves up on the outside; b.)unifying ourselves around narcissistic self-interest and willfulness; c.)letting God get us together (along with our creative cooperation) as we accept His call to seek first the Kingdom and His righteousness along with the gift of His strength to start going about it. William James said of his wife that she'd saved him from his "torn-to-pieces-ness" and gave him back to himself. Each of us ought to be able to say the same of Jesus.[19]

We do, all of us, need a cause. Not to sacrifice our identities to, but to dedicate ourselves to freely, and with all the uniqueness of who we are. That cause, says Jesus, is the Kingdom and the special role each of us is offered to participate in its being built up.

The Kingdom, to some, is an idea. An idea of how Jesus envisioned those things that His Father had already accomplished, along with those things that He some day would. But that's wrong. The Kingdom is God in you *now* — and your knowing it. The Kingdom is God in you and straining to come out of you-and your knowing it. The Kingdom is God finally allowed to come out of you and creating more and more relationship between you and everyone you encounter and your knowing it; and your knowing that more of that kind of thing has to happen tomorrow: that job, wife, kids, salary, vacation are only as right and as real as they're allowed to be drawn into the middle of all that . . . Like Jesus, whatever we say and do is able to bear the stamp of our knowing that we are God's sons or daughters, and that we have been sent to do His will.

It has been said that happiness only happens when a person can find herself always in the state of going somewhere (even if that "somewhere" is inside of us) and when she goes there whole-heartedly and one-directionally.[20] That's what happens when we accept the gift of letting the Kingdom come freely in and go freely out. We are freed to live for God and others in God; and in doing that we experience the truth of the proverb that there's more blessing in giving than in receiving; the truth of the assertion that in His will is our peace; the truth of the paradox that real fulfillment comes only when you don't seek it for yourself, but when you seek to give yourself away. If we can be wholeheartedly devoted to self-interest, then obviously we can be wholehearted; and, therefore, we can be wholehearted for God.

Only one *more* thing is necessary. The author first conceived of a section on healing of identity because in his counseling experience he began to notice how many of his clients were inclined to identify with their psychological scars; how stubbornly they tended to cling to these inner disfigurements as a permanent part of who they were, even though such individuals were not born with them and these scars were not originally a part of their make-up. Although we spoke about this tendency our treatment of "Healing of Memories" and some of the reasons why we might want to hang onto scars, it seems appropriate to include some various examples of how folks commonly justify their clinging to such scars. We are (to a very large degree) what we identify with. When that "what" happens to be our scars, then we are, in effect, *willing their permanence.* We attempt to legitimate that permanence by self-statements which more or less take the form of "I am the kind of person who always . . . ," or "That's just *me*" kind of excuses. Try a few on for size!

"I am the kind of person who must go on doubting, challenging everything, and never fully accept it." *Someone probably "took you in," once or twice. Does that really justify your setting* out on some "quest for truth" which you've already predetermined will never be able to be found?

"I am the kind of person who just has to put up with fits of feeling lazy now and then." *Sometimes laziness or indecision is a cover for not having to expose yourself to the risk of failure by having to do something you once proved unsuccessful at. After all, if you never do it again, you'll never have to suffer criticism for having failed.*

"I am the kind of person who finds that if only I could see what's wrong with me a little more clearly, I'd take steps to change." *This is one of the most common excuses people give to justify not changing. This kind of person often enjoys his self-preoccupation. Sometimes we just have to do. Just move against (with God's help) that feeling of inadequacy. But you can't move and navel-gaze at the same time.*

"I am the kind of person who could never take the risk of being fully honest with himself, or survive a close look at himself." *At least you'll never be lonely. There are so many of you.*

"I am the kind of person who always needs to be 'one up' on everybody." *That's because deep down you feel inferior to everyone else. Ask God to help you to accept yourself for who you are and to see that the only person you really need to compete with is yourself. The only person you need to be better than is the person you were yesterday.*

"I am the kind of person who will rarely, if ever, be happy." *You have a lot of energy, nonetheless. But most of it will be spent on your insuring that his prophecy about your future infallibly comes true. Jesus, the Counselor, speaking to you through prayer, Scripture or others, wants to show you the roots of your despair and negativity. The reasons why they exist and why you want them to remain. The reasons why they don't have to. Ask for the courage to see what you need to see.*

"I am the kind of person who knows that, when put under pressure, I will always give up my belief in favor of the crowd's." *There are some pressures so heavy that, only if God gives us the guts will we be able to withstand them. You gave in often before because you didn't realize that your own guts alone were just not sufficient to fall back on. So start asking for His.*

"I am the kind of person who can't be expected to make deep commitments to anything for any length of time." *But you've made one: a lifelong commitment to never being committed. This kind of person, by the way, is often of the "detached observer" type who makes herself very knowledgeable about the very thing she will never take the risk of committing herself to — like Christianity so that she won't have to give her life to Christ, or psychology so she won't ever have to change who she is. Give God your exaggerated fear of making mistakes, or of being wrong, and hurry up about it.*

"I am the kind of person who will always find himself ridiculed or laughed at." *We all need the attention of love. But when we don't believe that we're loveable we will often settle for any kind of attention. Consciously or not so consciously, then, we might even find ourselves saying or doing things to provoke the ridicule or laughter of others. After all, it is attention.*

"I am the kind of person who must spend large amounts of my day analyzing my thoughts, feelings, and life situations." *You're hooked on self-preoccupation. A person with a sore hangnail thinks about his thumb an awful lot, but then, doesn't any more when it heals. Keep lifting up to God that raw sore of the spirit that drew your attention in on yourself in the first place. Also realize that you enjoy this self-absorption. It's an illicit pleasure. Ask God also to help you to break this addiction.*

"I am the kind of person who can be friendly with people, but doesn't get fulfilled from deeper kinds of relationships." *Most likely, you've wanted to get close to someone and felt rejection, real or imagined. So you make a decision never to let anyone come that close again, so as to protect yourself against ever having to feel such pain again. Ask God for the courage to be vulnerable. Ask Him, to help you let go of your habit of misusing sociability as a substitute for the intimacy your heart is crying out for.*

"I am the kind of person who would never be able to experience God on this earth." *God is Love. If you can experience being loved, then you can experience God. Self-rejection is one of the chief reasons why folks can't feel the love of another.*

God is "Another," too. Ask Him to help you to accept yourself. Everybody was meant to be able to feel Him, to enjoy His loving presence.

"I am the kind of person who generally finds herself in agreement with the majority opinion." *Oh really?! You are the kind of person who doesn't want to take a stand. Ask Jesus to take away your exaggerated fear of criticism. He always got criticized for doing the right thing!*

"I am the kind of person who needs to instinctively resent any unpleasant or opposing circumstance." *Resentment has a bittersweet taste. We start resenting things we are helpless to change or oppose in childhood. We get to like resentment's taste. It's something like acquiring a taste for scotch. We need, then, to admit to ourselves and God how much we enjoy resenting. That's another one of those illicit pleasures.*

"I am the kind of person who rarely happens to be wrong about anything." *That's what you think. You've seen Archie Bunker on T.V. He's afraid to admit that he's wrong even when he knows that he is. He dogmatically asserts the correctness of his point of view, in inverse proportion to how unsure he is about that point of view. As long as you keep laughing at yourself when you laugh at Archie, you'll get better soon.*

"I am the kind of person who rarely feels any emotion." *God didn't decide to leave yours out when you passed by Him on the "assembly line." Probably you weren't allowed to express certain feelings or reactions by overly strict parents, etc. Ask God to help you let go of the fear-and guilt-"lids" sitting on top of emotions that are really and truly still there.*

"I am the kind of person who never changes his mind." *How convenient!*

"I am the kind of person who envisions herself as a bundle of endlessly complicated difficulties." *You've got a lot of company, too. You even exaggerate your actual complicatedness so that no one, not even God, could untangle the mess. That way you can hang onto the distinction of being an incurable. That way you can justify never having to change.*

We could go on an on, of course. Why don't you write a few autobiographical ones of you own?

In a way, we could say that a person's identity always contains his story. We are what we have been through. What we've experienced in our walk through life in some way or other becomes part of the fabric of who we are. Hans Frei says of Jesus' identity that it arose out of the coming together of His "character and circumstances,"[21] as they mutually influenced each other. It is no different for us. We either end up reacting to things; or we learn that we must respond, learning how to handle, rework or rise above the things life hands us, whether they be favorable or unfavorable.

How good of that Father of His that when He raised His Son from death, when He undid the evil doings of Calvary, He saw to it that the Risen Christ would still bear the marks of the Cross. Not hideous scars, but badges of honor; not repulsive disfigurements, but adornments of beauty; not symbols of defeat, but proclamations of triumph.

Those nail holes. They were providentially left there for your sake and mine. So that we could come to look upon those scarring, disfiguring events of our life as being experiences that the very same Father wants to do the very same kind of turn-around thing with.

Chapter 11

Healing of Attitudes and Emotions (I)

To take something apart; to examine those parts, singly; to examine how or whether they are able to interrelate properly—such an approach can leave us considerably enlightened as to the ways that mechanisms function; or the reasons why they sometimes do not. Before the dismantling of an engine, say, it had seemed to be sheer mystery. Now that we have been enabled to grasp its inner workings, however, it is a mystery no more. Still remarkable, perhaps, but no longer something that is totally beyond our grasp.

If only we could similarly dissect ourselves, break *ourselves* down to our more basic functions, we are sometimes inclined to suspect, *then* we'd get to the bottom of things; *then* we'd have definitely solved the mystery—the mystery of who we are; or the mystery of what most repeatedly thwarts us from functioning at our best.

The danger embedded in such an approach, of course, is that we can be left with the impression that we are nothing more than machines. So, if we focus for a while upon our thinking processes, contrast our emotions with one another, or analyze the interaction of our thoughts and feelings, we hope not to do it in the spirit of "tinkering with the parts." We tend to be fragmented enough already, God knows, and never has the pressure been upon us more to perform mechanically or automatically—that is, as if we were mechanisms or automatons.

Even the Church, by the way, has been known to aggravate the problem by traditionally leaving the believer with the impression that God was primarily intent on straightening out two "parts" of him—by replacing unbelief, or messed up religious ideas, with correct doctrines (duly inserted into the "place" where right religious ideas ought to go); and by replacing sinful behavior with behavior of the virtuous variety. This can leave you thinking that God is more interested in what your religious beliefs are, and what your batting average is, vis a vis the Ten Commandments, that He is interested in you, yourself.

About ten years ago, two scripture verses caught this writer's attention:

> May the God of peace himself sanctify you wholly; and may your spirit and soul and body be kept sound and blameless at the coming of our Lord Jesus Christ. (1 Thess. 5:23, RSV)

> For the word of God is living and active sharper than any two-edged sword, piercing to the division of soul and spirit, of joints and marrow, and discerning the thoughts and intentions of the heart. (Heb. 4:12, RSV)

Both made reference to soul and spirit as if they were *not* the same thing. As if they were separate functions, so to speak, of the whole person. To someone schooled in the theological tradition of Thomas Aquinas, a thinker who based much of his theorizing on the philosophical concepts of Aristotle, this was indeed a revelation. Thomas, like Aristotle, looked at mankind out of a dualistic perspective. The human being was an animal that was rational. *Reason* was the spark of the divine in humanity, so to speak, for the Greek sage. For his medieval, philosopher-saint disciple, since *reason* elevated humanity above the animals, it was a person's intellectual nature which enabled her to lay claim to the prerogative of being in the image of God. A person's thinking and willing, the chief functions of her soul, were, therefore, spiritual *functions*. A person's soul *was* her spirit.

Is the person better understood when she is viewed as being simultaneously spirit, soul and body (as the two recently quoted verses suggest)? Or is the Aristotelian-Thomistic body-soul breakdown adequate? This was the practical problem I found confronting me. Before too long, I had come to believe that former view was far more helpful.

The Bible, while inspired by God, we Christians believe, was written by numerous individuals allowing themselves to be His instruments over a nearly two thousand year period.

Some authors were of a comparatively primitive Hebrew cultural background; others of a much more sophisticated Jewish cultural background; still others, as the Old Testament was about to be joined by the New, were somewhat influenced by contacts with Greek or foreign cultures; while, finally, some of the New Testament authors were very much in touch with the contemporary thought-forms and ideas of the Graeco-Roman culture.

This means that when these individuals use terms like body, soul, spirit, or heart, for instance, they may not always and everywhere mean exactly the same thing, or intend it in precisely the same way as certain of the other sacred writers mean it. All we can do here is present a considerably simplified overview, aimed at uncovering a basic common denominator as to what the Old and New Testaments *generally* connote when they refer to human person as body, soul or spirit.

When either Old or New Testament writers speak of body, soul or spirit, they do *not* generally refer to these terms as being *parts* of the whole person. While certain New Testament authors (most probably in touch with the Greek tendency to view soul and body as distinct segments of the overall person) occasionally draw close to doing the same thing, by and large, they soon revert to the more traditional Hebrew practice. This latter approach, when it speaks of "body" is generally referring to the whole person under the aspect of his or her physicalness; when it speaks of "soul" is referring quite likely to the whole person under the aspect of his or her capabilities of self-consciousness, reasoning or willing; when it speaks of "spirit," it is very frequently referring, once again, to the whole person, under the aspect of his or her ability to relate personally to God.

Even the "under the aspect of" qualifier doesn't always hold, especially in the Old Testament. Body, sometimes, is able simply to stand for a single individual, just as soul or spirit may. In this case, they are used interchangeably, as synonyms. By this is certainly implied the relentless Hebrew viewpoint that a person's spirituality is interpenetrated by his rationality, even as that rationality is simultaneously interpenetrated by his bodiliness. They are all one. You can artifically divide them off from one another in your mind if you wish (as the Greeks do); but, in reality, they are inseparable.

Underneath such a way of looking at the human personality (or refusing to look at it) may well lie a profound wisdom. Parts are "things." If we come to see ourselves as no more than the sum total of our parts we are likely to look at ourselves as an arrangement of things, a big "thing," composed of littler things.

But let's go back to the three-fold breakdown, for a few moments, and take a closer look at what spirit, soul, and body generally and ordinarily signify in Scripture.

The Hebrew word for spirit is *ruah*, which also means "wind" or "breath." The Israelites were fascinated by the phenomenon of air which is invisible and intangible — yet able to move, and so exert force. The vitality or energy of the person was his *ruah*, which Genesis had pictured as having been breathed into Adam's mouth by God. *Ruah* eventually came to mean the whole person, as he outwardly expresses his life-force in human behavior — his behavior toward fellow humans, as well as his behavior towards God.

When we currently use the adjective *spirited*, we usually are talking about something that has been accomplished with expression, with vitality, an expression and vitality often expressing the uniqueness of the person who brought about the accomplishment. *Ruah* sometimes carried that sense, particularly in later Old Testament times. It then not only took on that connotation of an almost artistic energy and inspiration, but went beyond this to convey the impression of a person gripped by inner spiritual resolve.

This brings us very close to the New Testament concept of *pneuma*. One of the most starting differences between the Old and New Testament understandings of *ruah* or *pneuma* (its Greek synonym) is that the Old Testament sees every man and woman as being *ruah*. The New Testament, on the other hand, sees *only the converted believer* as being a man or woman of the Spirit. It is almost as if a person were without spirit until being indwelt by God's Spirit at his or her conversion/baptism. Only Christians are empowered with *pneuma*.

A whole new spiritedness is suddenly available to mankind. A whole new way of being empowered, guided, and authorized to live in the awareness of that God, now radically present to love you personally; and to love others personally through you.

The individual, therefore, no longer attempts to hold herself together from the inside, or tries to motivate herself from within. The Holy Spirit now centers the believer and motivate her existence.

Nephesh is the Hebrew word for"soul." When Yahweh breathes into the lifeless body of Adam in Genesis 2 he becomes *nephesh*, a living soul, that is, a living creature. *Nephesh* denotes that which makes a body (whether man or beast) into a living being. It often is used in association with the person as living being, under the specific aspects of one's willing and thinking. When it is translated as "life," however, it refers to the living self together with all of its drives, rather than life as an abstract idea. It can sometimes signify, simply, the person, his or her "self," or be translated by using the personal pronoun. When someone is described as doing something with all his or her soul — reference is made to the fact that the individuals' whole personality is summed up in that act. *Nephesh*, or "soul," in such an instance, focuses upon his or her inner powers pulled together in concert, cooperating harmoniously.

In the New Testament soul, ego or self is a life lived only in and through the body. When Jesus says, accordingly, (in Matthew 10:39) that the person who finds his soul (or life) will lose it, and that he who loses his soul (or life) for His sake will find it, He shows that while there is one kind of life or one kind of soul, this life may be lived in two, radically different ways. One is symbolized by the overly-self-protective individual whose life or soul is so closed in on itself that it is simultaneously closed off both to God and others. The other kind of individual has allowed her Lord to free her from this compulsion to watchguard her life or soul with such egoistic assertiveness. She is thus able to live in such a way that all she says and does is unthreatened by her neighbor's possible needs or God's possible requirements. She finds fulfillment in loving and in being loved by both.

These two different kinds of people whom Jesus contrasts with each other seem to be very close to what Paul calls *anthropos pneumatikos* (the "soulish," "psychological" or "unspiritual" person) in First Corinthians 2:14. These latter types of individuals

241

are filled with soul, or life-force. They are alive particularly in the sense of being empowered and therefore free to think, feel, and will from within. But they choose *not* to know what they could know. Namely, they refuse to see that they are loved by God and called by Him to live according to His purposes. The "soulish" person is unspiritual or bogged down in his psychological life because *he unnecessarily limits himself to what people can know, feel, and choose,* as if God were not around to broaden his horizons or boundaries.

The "spiritual person," on the other hand, because she is in touch with the "place" where she is meant to meet God within herself is also simultaneously in touch with a whole dimension of herself that she otherwise would be forced to live in ignorance of.

"Soul," finally, can take on an extra-special emphasis: life as it is experienced as being inward, insofar as the self-conscious individual moves toward deciding for life or for death; towards choosing to know God, or choosing not to know Him.

Neither soul nor spirit in the Biblical sense are used in the sense of some "part" of man separate from, or superior to his body (another part). A person does not *have* a body. In Genesis, for example, when the man and the woman coming together in matrimony are described as being as "one flesh" or "one body," this union is seen to signify a union of hearts or minds, as well.

Another important concept connected with the Old Testament view of human bodiliness is that it never tries to locate our selfishness, or sinfulness as residing there, or in the body's appetites.

Under Greek influence, some Jewish literature, written in the time between the Testaments viewed the personality with particular regard to its bodiliness, as being especially prone to sin. Some would see St. Paul as going along with, or even extending this tendency, when in *Romans* 7, he speaks of the possibility of falling captive to the sin which dwells in one's (bodily) members, and the need to be delivered from "this body of death." But he is writing here from the traditional Jewish point of view. We live our life before God in and through our bodies. When, from the heart, we ignore God's guidance and grace we often end up acting as if we are little more than a bundle of instincts—a soul-less body. The body reveals itself to be the soul in its outwardness. It demonstrates that soul-life is open to God or closed off from Him.

The emphasis Paul uses, in this instance, when talking of the body or *soma*, he frequently uses when speaking of flesh, or *sarx*. While he sometimes uses *sarx* in the same way we would when we speak of flesh, he very often employs it in a quite specialized way, particularly when he counterposes *sarx* to *pneuma*, "flesh" to "spirit."

When Paul counterposes "flesh" against spirit, he is not talking about one part of the personality in conflict with another. "Flesh" stands for the person of flesh. If a man, he can be called a "man of the world" in the sense that he lives his life as if he were at the controlling center of the universe and not God. He lives as if He were not there or as if His being there didn't matter. No need, then, to lean on Him for love or guidance. His own declaring to himself that he is just "fine" no matter what, and his insistence that rightness or wrongness is always whatever he says it is, fully substitutes for God's affectionate and enlightening support.

The sarx or "flesh," in this context, refers to the whole person, precisely insofar as he or she chooses to live self-centeredly, in denial of his or her creatureliness, in assertion of his or her lack of need for God's grace. Conversely, when Paul speaks of "spirit" in this context, he is talking about the person who wants to be loved by God and led by His Spirit.[1]

This has not always been clearly seen, however, in the course of Christian history. It would seem that Paul has often been misread and misunderstood in these two specific areas we just referred to. At the very least he's been misquoted and wrongly invoked for support by those who were strongly influenced by a Greek or Stoic view of a human nature broken down into parts—a "higher" spiritual part and a "baser," physical part.

In this view, the intellect and will lost their rational control over the physical appetites, as a result of Original Sin. The emotions and passions were viewed, then, as being in a state of rebellion against the rational will. This implied two things:

first, that there was little wrong with humanity's thinking and willing, even though these faculties lacked the "punch" to keep the "lower" nature in line; secondly, that bodily desires and affections were directly tainted by sin. Grace was given to the repentant sinner, in such a view, to restore the control of the mind and the will over the rebellious appetites, to give the (holy) spirit control over the (sinful) body.

The way you got closer to God, then, was by withdrawing all your attention from worldly or bodily things by mortifying (i.e. deadening) anything within you physically or emotionally stimulated by or attracted to them. Thereafter, you could increasingly concentrate on God and the purely "spiritual."

In addition to encouraging a "parts" approach to self-understanding, such an unbalanced spirituality veered away from its Biblical moorings in three other important respects: it failed to provide proper emphasis as to how susceptible is man's thinking and willing to becoming vehicles of a prideful and rebellious spirit; it promoted the view that the physical and bodily aspects of life are evil or sin-tainted, and so, obstacles to union with God; it gave excessive attention to the *importance of rational control* in the development of the spiritual man or woman's personality, even as it encouraged the freezing of any further maturing of one's emotional and physical qualities — a freezing which could only insure that these physical and emotional qualities remain predominantly cut off from true and effective harmony with the rest of the personality.[2]

To conclude our arguments that the New Testament continues on from the Old with a basically positive view of the physical dimension of the human personality, we would simply make the following observation. As R.D.G. Owen points out, Jesus came to renew and redeem not just the soul, but the whole of man, as well as the whole of the world.[3] When the New Heavens and the New Earth are established, the redeemed person will live in a resurrected body. This means that the whole person is destined for everlasting life, and not just a disembodied spirit or soul. It also means that this new spiritual body, for all its fullness and completion, is still somehow continuous with one's original body. They are somehow related, identity-wise, just as the full-grown plant is still one with the seed from which it has sprung, as Paul comments in First Corinthians 15.

It is appropriate to consider briefly one other important example of the biblical vocabulary most intertwined with helping us understand who we are. That word is *heart*. In Hebrew, *leb* or *lebab*; in Greek *kardia*. It most frequently refers to the foundation of human inwardness, in the seat of our spiritual, mental, and emotional powers. Yet not in such a way as to be disconnected from our outer life or character: "it is your own face that you see reflected in the water and it is your own self that you see in your heart." (Prv. 26:19, TEV)

The heart is that "place" where we meet God or choose *not* to meet Him; our innermost center, where our powers of thinking, willing, feeling and choosing join together to answer the One who addresses us, in one way or the other—in the direction of faith in His love, or in the direction of mistrust of the reality of that affection.

At its worst, the heart is the self-deceitful source (Jer. 17:9) of all kinds of malicious activity, whether of word or of deed (Mt. 15:19).

In short, it can be said to be the "center" of the human spirit, for the Holy Spirit of God is said to be sent to dwell there in the heart of the believer (2 Cor. 1:22). Yet, He does not simply come to dwell, but to do. To pour love forth—God's love for the disciple, God's love also for everyone whom that disciple will ever meet(cf.Rom 5:5).

While the Old Testament had certainly viewed the heart as the inner "organ" of love, as well of as the other emotions, (a love which included the individual's love for his God), the New Testament more firmly and finally brings together the notion of heart and love as ideally and properly inseparable.

Heart, in current popular parlance, may be used as symbol for the affections, particularly our romantic ones, along with our compassionate instincts, as well. In that sense, it is close to what the impact of the New Testament understanding leaves us with. First Peter, for instance, hardly denies these romantic and compassionate connotations, when it calls us to be men and women of *heart*, people dedicated to being first of all true

245

to the "inner person of the heart" (3:4), before we are anything else.

But all our love-instincts must be swept up, elevated, radically purified, as they are caught into the constant ebb and flow of His love for us in us and through us. Only then are we "hearted" in the Christian sense, pure-hearted, whole-hearted, God-hearted.[4]

We are not fully ourselves,then until we have experienced our center. We are not fully ourselves until we have come into the experience of having God's love flow into our hearts, of having heard his Spirit give witness to our spirits that we are a *son* or a *daughter* of God Himself. We are not fully ourselves until we know that we've been given a new heart and a new mind. We are not fully ourselves until we know that the inward reality of the spirit is just as real as the outward reality of the visible and tangible. We are not fully ourselves until we have met that Lover within ourselves and have let what He primarily provides us with flow out in and through everything we say and do, as it touches everyone and everything we meet. We are not fully ourselves until we finally realize that we are not only more than body; we are also more than mind, feelings, and inner-or outer-directed motives; until we realize that we are also able to be spirit, alive with His Love, a love so very personal and purposeful. We are not fully ourselves until we've come to realize that He is meant to be the Center of our center, that He's been met somewhere down there at the innermost core of who we are, where he keeps calling us by name, calling us forth to be more and more ourselves, even as He tells us His name and allows us even to call Him, *Abba*, Daddy. We are not fully ourselves until we've met someone within us whose Presence always means a call to reach beyond our currently perceived needs and boundaries, most especially upwards, and away from those interests that are exclusively identical with our own.[5] We are not fully ourselves until we know ourselves not primarily as a bundle of instincts and desires but rather as someone who is first of all most deeply and constantly energized by a pure love and wisdom not one's own — a love and a wisdom powerful enough to embrace and redirect one's instincts and desires into a gentle harmony with those Purposes. [6]

Reasoning and willing may be properly looked upon as spiritual activities, in the Biblical sense of "spiritual." But as Scripture also reminds us, such activities can be just as often "carnal" or "after the flesh," that is, in real opposition to our spiritual nature.(Rom 8:7) We can think and will and feel, as if He weren't there. We can think and will and feel as if He weren't there *loving us*. We can think and will and feel as if He weren't there to love *through* us — always and everywhere.

We need the sword of God's Spirit, God's word personally addressed to us, to enable us to discern the thoughts and intentions of our hearts, the author of Hebrews tells us.(Heb. 4:12; see also Eph. 6:17.) That surely would include the help we need to see at times how heartlessly we are inclined to act and react; how loveless is so much of our planning and choosing, how soulless so many of those activities we dare to call loving and caring.

Rollo May speaks of the goal of any therapy as bringing about a harmonizing of the major elements of the personality, so that the individual increasingly experiences himself or herself as a "thinking-feeling-willing unity."[7] The goal of "salvation-therapy" must go one step further. It must lead us increasingly into that permanent situation where we rejoice in knowing ourselves as a thinking-feeling-willing-enspirited unity, namely, a unity of thought, emotion and motive, unified above all else by the constant awareness that we are loved by God, are in love with Him, and want to love others with Him.

Picture a man in love with his wife. Nothing surpasses being alone with her in moments both lighthearted and relaxed, as well as those intensely passionate. On the way to work, he may recall how special that aloneness with her had been; and, while he'd like nothing better than for those moments to be presently prolonged — in a way, they are. He carries her and what she means to him in his heart. When he works, he does what his job requires of him the best way he knows how. In the past that might have been a matter of self-fulfillment, a matter of simply pitting his talents against the challenges of the moment and experiencing the satisfaction of success, when those resistances were made to be the servants of his purposes.

Now, he does his best for *her*. Somehow, it's an act of love for *her*. Finishing a project, he instantly thinks of her and reaches for the phone: "just thinking about you, honey . . . " They talk about nothing special, but their conversation re-expresses and re-affirms how much they care about one another. He is still somehow living in her presence, though she is at home and he at work . . .

Somehow, last night can be more than a lingering memory. It can be the very fuel energizing the activities of the following day. We can and do carry people we love around in our hearts, when they're no longer physically present. Not only that, but such an awareness can transform the very character of all our actions and reactions. Brighten them with joy. Mellow them with love. Buoy them up with hope.

If last night's encounter with a human lover can constantly color my today, so can last night's romance with the Divine Lover. If I can carry my wife around in my heart, I can carry God around, too. If my thoughts can run back home to her, my thoughts can run "home" to Him as well. If I can do what I do out of love for her, I can do what I do out of love for Him. If I view her as an inseparable "part" of me, I can likewise view Him as an inseparable "part" of me. If I can find the time to phone her a few times a day, I can find the time to "phone" Him just as often. If what I "have going" with her in terms of making me feel good about myself and about life overflows into the lives of others, because I respond to these people out of the positive uplift of such affirmation, EVEN MORE can overflow into my daily personal contacts out of the uplift provided by His affirmation of me.

As far as the man we mentioned is concerned, everything he thinks about and desires is forever intertwined with the way that he feels about his wife. His personality is not only tied *up* with her in a whole new way, once the relationship is established, it is likewise tied *together* in a whole new way. Tied together out of her being allowed into the deepest core of who he is. Now that she's "inside" he doesn't want anything for himself except insofar as it is just as good for her too and is able to be shared with her. Something similar, yet even greater and deeper and more powerful, was meant to come out of welcoming Him into the innermost center of who we are.

Jesus prayed for his disciples that they'd be able to know the same kind of intimacy with His Father that He knew when He went to be alone with Him. He further prayed that they'd also learn how to walk the streets of the world and meet the challenges of the world, in the same way that He did. In the awareness of God's being lovingly present. In the awareness of His being so lovingly and so inspirationally present: *As the branch draws its vitality from the vine, you will be able to abide in, lean into, plug into, gather your strength and purpose from leaning on my Father's love, leaning on my love, which our Spirit is ever ready to bring to you.* (cf. Jn. 15, 16, 17)

It takes time to learn how to be still and know that he is there, and that He is Lord, and that He is Love for us. It also takes time to learn how to "see" Him and "hear" Him in the midst of a noisy, over-busy world. But if we're looking for that to happen and praying for that to happen and longing for that to happen, then we will find more and more that we no longer think as if we left Him at the door of our "prayer-closet." We will be thinking, rather, as if He were there showing us more than we could ever see by ourselves.

No longer will we feel as if we were the final source of our own feelings, we will increasingly find ourselves feeling with the feelings of the Compassionate One. No longer will we choose, as if it all depended upon our own informed decision. We will, instead, be choosing more and more to do the most loving thing — because the Lover is choosing in us and with us.

Chapter 12

Healing of Attitudes and Emotions (II)

> I appeal to you therefore, brethren, by the mercies of God, to present your bodies as a living sacrifice, holy and acceptable to God. Do not be conformed to this world but be transformed by the renewal of your mind, that you may prove what is the will of God, what is good and acceptable and perfect. (Rom. 12:1-2, RSV)

From what we have said in the last chapter, it is clear that from the New Testament point of view, if one becomes aware that she has been given a new heart, a heart to know Him, then that person's thinking and willing will be unable to remain untouched or uninfluenced by such a radical rearrangement of whom she sees herself to be. A new heart means a new mind.

The call to conversion is to allow everything we "see" or "understand" to be redefined in the light of our knowing of, and being known by, Him in love. Three new attitudes, particularly, will increasingly surround, penetrate and enliven our view not only of God but of ourselves, our fellow men and our world. The attitudes of faith, hope and love.

[Author's note: since hope and love ordinarily include an emotional component, we will presently deal only with the relationship of faith to our thought-life. We have already touched on how Love is able to positively affect our thinking. We will deal with hope's influence in a later chapter directly concerned with our emotions.]

It isn't, of course, that we had never approached self, others, or the rest of creation without viewing ourselves or these persons or things in the light of belief-systems; without hope, at times, in an improving state of affairs; or without some kind of affection or compassion. Even agnostics and atheists operate out of unproven assumptions, like, "I'm my own best friend," or "Everything that exists or happens in the universe can be measured or explained, scientifically," etc., namely out of a secular kind of faith.

Faith, as Richard Fowler points out, can be spoken of, in a very general sense, as the way people view themselves against their environment, in the light of the valués they call ultimate.[1] To believe that power, money, or pleasure are the highest goals, against which all striving in the world is to be measured, is not something which can be absolutely proven to be raw "supreme" wisdom. In a way, it's a gamble that there's nothing else, or nothing more important. It's a "faith," then, that there is nothing existent, higher than, or beyond the material.

If, as Paul says in the quote above, that conversion involves a radical changing of one's mind, a fundamental transformation of one's attitudes, it is very important for any follower of Jesus to ask: *"From* what *to* what? from what outworn outlook to what new mind-set; from what former way of looking at things, to what current sense of values?"

Perhaps we could summarize our thoughts about the transformation which needs to happen this way: from a faith in solely human powers and goals, to a faith in God's love and purposes for humankind; from a hope in future solely built out of human ingenuity and planning, to a hope based on what He promised to grant us and He is already freeing us to receive; from a love primarily based on self-seeking and practical convenience to a love which doesn't deny our need for fulfillment but refuses to rest in any fulfillment that isn't able to be shared with others.

We need to be delivered of our "secular" faiths. Contemporary Christianity is rightly accused of being irrelevant and impotent, when it refuses to acknowledge this assertion of Paul's and encourages its believers, in effect, to base their view of life upon an unwise and unhappy amalgam of belief in the credal articles appropriate to one's denomination and half-baked secular assumptions. By assumptions, here, we mean deep-seated convictions about the way things are, like: 1) "You gotta look out for 'old number one,' because no one else will." *Including God?*

2.) "Reality is what you can see, feel and touch." *But what about "the things unseen" that the Book of Hebrews talks about, along with Paul (2 Cor 4:18)? That unseen reality is not just God, His angels and saints in Heaven. It's His being here, right now to lean on and be guided by. True Christian faith calls us to regard this as even more real than the "reality" revealed to us by our senses.*

3.) "We will not be 'together,' or emotionally sound until we become self-reliant or autonomous." *If we rely primarily on ourselves we cannot primarily rely on His love for us. Either we are the primary source of our own personality strength, or He is. Either we are primarily meant to put ourselves together, or He is meant to bring that about. There is such a thing, however, as being really "put-together" because we've let His love be the "glue" that binds us into wholeness and binds us to Him. There is such a thing as being "autonomous" in Him because we have been transformed into truly inner-directed individuals who ever allow themselves to be guided by the love and wisdom He provides from within.*

4.) "I will never be a real person as long as I need to lean on people." *We have not been created as isolated selves but as selves-in-relationship. From God's point of view we are not truly alive, until we have allowed another to love us, until we've admitted our need of their love, repeatedly. From God's point of view we are likewise not fully alive until we have allowed Him to love us; until we've admitted our need of His love, constantly: ". . . may (He) grant to you to be strengthened* with might through his spirit in the inner man, that Christ may dwell in your hearts by faith . . . (that you may be) *rooted and grounded in love . . .* (Eph. 3:16,17, RSV, italics ours).

5.) "The two most important things in life are money and companionship" (overheard by this writer, in a restaurant last week). *As Lawrence Crabb has so persuasively pointed out, if our two most basic God-given needs are rather the needs for security (that I am loveable and loved) and significance (that my being here matters and that I have something important to do while I'm here) and they are not met, then sexual gratification (or self-indulgence) and addiction to power (or*

253

possession) would be the two chief ways of compensating for the absence of that security and significance.[2]

6.) "Only psychotic or highly neurotic individuals are seriously out of contact with reality. Since I am neither, I can safely presume that I am basically and consistently in touch with things as they truly are." *Thomas Merton has, in an insight quite parallel to Dr. Crabb's, described the woundedness which comes to us from the Garden as leaving us extremely inclined to "bad faith" as we attempt to understand ourselves and our world. This bad faith is a stubborn willfulness whereby we are highly disposed to manipulate reality; or extremely inclined to try to make things other than what they are so that they will always be at the service of our desires for power or pleasure . . .* [3]

We tend to be much like the color-blind individual who compliments us on the color of our "metallic brown" auto while the car is actually painted metallic green. A defect in the structuring of her eyes leaves her seeing certain things other than what they really are. Our universal defect, until it is remedied, is the defect of not knowing God's love at the center of who we are. Until our personality is structured upon the awareness of this constant and boundless affection for us, we will see the world "colored" quite differently from what it is. Discolored by the light of our unwholeness and the flickering flames of our misdirected desires.

We mentioned earlier that Jesus saw yet another motive within us inclining us to want to distort reality — the "convenience" of projecting our sins or faults onto others so that we could "correct" and "punish" those "blights" without causing ourselves any personal pain. Our Lord's counsel was direct and pointed in this case. He expects us to assume responsibility for the correction of our vision. He expects us to cooperate with the grace given us all to undistort what we have chosen to see wrongly: ". . . first take the log out of your own eye and then you sill see clearly to take the speck out of your brother's eye." (Mt. 7:5, RSV)

7.) "I will be consistently happy only if I am consistently allowed to have my own way." *God's intent is to heal us of a radical willfulness. He is not, however, trying to eliminate our free will. He is, rather, trying to bring us to the place where we would not think of choosing anything unless it were seen to be in accordance with His perfect purposes for us. We can only do this, however, when we've come to believe that His plans for us are perfect, because His love for us is perfect. Trying to make ourselves our own center when He was meant to be our center cannot help but dispose us towards that pathological twistedness in our thinking and willing, which we just referred to above.*

The contemporary psychologist, Albert Ellis has allowed himself to be influenced by the insights of the Graeco-Roman, Stoic thinker Epictetus, who was, coincidentally, a contemporary of St. Paul's.

Ellis, however, will have none of Epictetus' prayerfulness or belief that our universe is providentially governed from above, even if rather aloofly and unfeelingly. Ellis, in fact, the father of "Rational-Emotive Therapy" even seems to break his own rules and allow the "emotive" to take precedence over the "rational," when he rather passionately insists that we not only need to "accept" the "reality" that there is no God but also that there is no God around anywhere that "gives a damn" about us or "ever will."[4] He manages to fall into the classic trap of insisting that there are no absolutes, even as he "absolutely" proclaims the alleged absolute of God's non-existence. Such an assertion is, of course, an unproveable assumption and unproveable assumptions are precisely what Ellis, following Epictetus, is concerned about uprooting out of our thought-life.

Since he somehow was able to forgive Epictetus for his religious faith and accordingly, accept many of his insights, we will correspondingly forgive Ellis for his hostility to religious faith and now selectively endorse some of his insights. Before we do, however, it ought to be noted that Ellis, after all, might be not all that "far from the Kingdom of God." He sounds a lot like Crabb or Merton, writing about Original Sin, for instance, when he observes that we appear to be "born with" many powerful biological and social tendencies to "think and act foolishly" and to make ourselves "maladjusted."[5]

At the time when the New Testament was being written, non-Christian writers and Christian writers alike were in agreement upon the insistence that we all are very much in need of exercising a careful discipline over our thought-life; that much of the suffering we experience in our emotional life is the result of disordered thinking on our part; that even in the midst of hostile and turbulent circumstances, we are still able to experience a calmness and clear-headedness, if we so choose.

Ellis summarizes what is at the heart of our irrational believing or our illogical thinking when he observes that we tend to react to something experienced as not right for us by viewing it this way: *that it is awful, and therefore shouldn't exist; we will only be able to be happy (again) when the situation has changed.* Our response goes from being normal to unhealthy when we go on to demand that what we would like to happen (or what we think needs to be) *must happen now.* At that point, we not only have a problem, but a problem about *having* a problem, he ironically remarks.[6]

Our erroneous or inadequate belief-system not only leads us to false problem-solving on the outside but confused feelings on the inside. Namely, our ineffective behavior is now matched by distortions affecting our emotional life. It isn't what happens to us that directly affects how we subsequently feel; it is rather *what we think or believe about* what just happened that triggers the feelings. When, accordingly, what we *think* about the happening is distorted, then what we *feel* about it will be distorted as well. Or, as Lawrence Crabb puts it, it isn't the event which controls our feeling, it's *our evaluation* of what happened that controls it.[7] In other words, we cause ourselves a lot of needless emotional suffering and often suffer unnecessary confusion because of our persistence in viewing what happens to us *through the lenses of irrational beliefs*, like the ones listed above.

When we say things like: "She makes me mad!" or "He always makes me feel bad" or "That made me upset" or "They made me feel embarrassed" or "You've ruined my day" (at 10 a.m., no less!) or "This situation makes me worry," we are suffering emotional pain. That pain is undoubtedly related to something that happened to us from the outside. But it was *our perception* of that happening which triggered the flow of self-pitying feelings, or self-frustration feelings, or inadequacy feelings, or desperation feelings, etc.

As we will see shortly in our discussion about the significance of our emotions, it is not inappropriate to feel, or even feel strongly. We were created to. But it is possible to experience disappointment connected with events over which we have no external control, without having these legitimate feelings merging with and subverted by "illegitimate" ones-like feelings of inordinate self-sympathy, self-frustration, bitterness, despair, vengeance, apathy, and so on.

If you make me a promise, for instance, and then deliberately choose to break that promise, it is not necessarily wrong for me to feel "bad" about that. When feeling "bad" in this situation means disappointment over your lack of honesty and faithfulness to maintaining the mutual trust that we need in order to preserve or improve upon the quality of our present relationship with one another, then the feeling is normal and appropriate. But when, in addition to this, I inwardly choose to "mourn" over this misfortune indefinitely — nourishing feelings of vindictiveness against you, or feelings of "what a miserable victim of outrageous misfortune am I," or feelings of "I will probably be betrayed by other friends, too, in the near future," or angry feelings of "I won't ever be able to trust anybody else ever again," or "I must be unloveable, or this would never have happened to me" — then our feelings are *not so normal* and *not so legitimate*.

By choosing to move from a comparatively uncomplicated "feeling bad" in the first instance to the more sophisticated "feeling bad" in the last instance noted just above, I have, in effect, *chosen to make myself feel worse*, considerably worse than I need to. It no longer is simply my instantaneous reaction to our friend's betrayal, but my *considered response* to that betrayal.

This "considered" response may happen very quickly and quite automatically, and so it may not appear at all to us to be anything but impulsive. But this is, most likely, the result of having *developed a habit* of responding to unpleasant and unexpected circumstances in our lives with the rage, self-pity, anxiety, etc. that I've come to deem appropriate to such a misfortune. Over the years, I've learned how to so swiftly pass from "feeling bad" (A) to "feeling bad" (B), you might say, that I can't see the difference anymore. It's all one big inner "blob" of feeling bad. And because, in a way, I would never have initially felt bad without my friend's letting me down, I deduce that I can blame the *whole gamut* of feeling bad (which then ensued) on him. *He* made me feel that way.

But let's go back to "feeling bad" (A). If our relationship is important, and mutual trust is important for that friendship to be maintained, it is appropriate to feel "bad" about the trust's violation. That feeling bad, after all, can be a signal to me that steps need to be taken to repair the trust, or our friendship may end up on the junkpile of broken relationships. It is an appropriate reaction to something not right.

But we often do not simply react. We *over-react*. And we sometimes overreact, primarily on the inside. Noteworthy examples of such overreaction are thoughts like: "since such a condition is inappropriate, it must be corrected this very instant," and the subsequent feelings of anger or frustration when it can't be; or, "since this isn't the first time I've been done in like this, it only goes to prove that I've been rejected on account of my unloveableness" and the resulting feelings of self-put-down or self-pity, etc. Self-rejective thoughts and feelings along with intolerance of anything which stands in the way of my not having my own way right now — such thoughts and feelings tend to merge with the initial and authentic feeling bad. And, of course, all this suffering is completely the other person's fault, we believe.

Rational Emotive Therapy suggests that all of our irrational thinking and unhealthy feeling can be reduced to one or more of these three central "irrationalities": self-rejection, self-frustration at not having one's own way, and blaming all one's suffering on others. We suggested in earlier chapters that Original Sin, the trauma of not knowing that we are loved by God, leaves all of us: 1.) highly inclined to dislike ourselves at the deepest center of who we are; 2.) highly inclined to compensate for this condition of not having Him as our center by attempting to be our own center, a little god at the center of our own little world, who therefore has the "right" to have whatever she wants, whenever she wants it; 3.) highly-inclined to deny our inward poverty and prideful self-assertiveness, even as we attempt to attribute exaggerated variations of these characteristics to others who are blamed for most, if not all, of our difficulties. Ellis essentially confirms, then, what the Scriptures have ever attempted to show us about ourselves, when we are not at one with the One who created us and loves us.

It is at this point, however, that we must part company with Ellis. We will not be able to completely eliminate the twistedness to our thinking and feeling until our hearts have been made right with God, the Gospel emphatically informs us. We may indeed be able to confront and uproot our favorite irrationalities, and, in so doing, eliminate a great deal of our self-caused mental and emotional distress. But even if we could bring ourselves to stop overreacting to reality once and for all, we are still distorting reality, most significantly, so long as we under-react to it. Epictetus, for example, could not watch a beautiful sunset, without reacting with amazement and wonder. He wasn't all that sure who God was, but he knew that he couldn't let such a moment pass by without thanking and praising the Creator for such stunning artistry.[8] If, like Epictetus, we still don't know that the artist is likewise a Lover, then we are even now underreacting — but, we are getting closer to the Kingdom of God. People who assume responsibility for how and what they think and feel, whereas before they hadn't, are likewise one step closer to the Kingdom of God.

But only the fullness of His Love is able to definitively unmess our messed-up thinking and feeling and put us back together the way we belong. The Good News is that while there's a lot of unscrambling that needs to be done to our scrambled-up insides — and our cooperation is utterly necessary if this is to happen — we don't have to do it alone. It isn't even so much that He offers to help us. It's that He allows us to help Him. *He's* the Healer of hearts. *He's* the Healer of minds. He's come to relieve us of the burden of having to be our own therapist, even as He more than assures us that it's quite appropriate for us to stand in the role of therapist's assistant.

At the heart of such a therapy will be: a.) Letting Him love us anew, particularly as we experience situations which leave us inclined to feel rejected. Even if we have actually been rejected by someone, He promises never to reject us and to keep on unconditionally accepting us as loveable and worthwhile in the deepest part of who we are; b.) Letting Him reassure us that we are not only special to Him but that we are likewise called by Him to make a special contribution on this earth that no one else is able to make. Because we are no longer living our own lives as if their significance depended primarily upon our correct choices and our being given the freedom to always implement those decisions, as we turn to Him we will find ourselves increasingly defused of fears. Especially fears that we will not be fulfilled if we aren't given our own way and aren't fully insulated from the frustrations that come from being thwarted. We come to thereby experience that He is living His life through us; and yet, in a way that utterly safeguards the fragility of our never-to-be-repeatedness; c.) Letting him remove "log after log" from our spiritual eyes, even as we allow ourselves to be ever more deeply anointed with the spirit of "there, but for the grace of God, go I," when we are faced with the "specks" of moral and spiritual weakness in others.

> "So get rid of your old self, which made you live as you used to – the old self that was being destroyed by its deceitful desires. Your hearts and your minds must be made completely new, and you must put on the new self, which is created in God's likeness and reveals itself in the true life that is upright and holy." (Eph. 4:22-24, TEV)

The above verses from *Ephesians* may well remind the reader of the passage we quoted a bit earlier from *Romans* 12. Both Scriptures call the believer into the realization that Grace is intent on transforming him, by challenging and uprooting thoughts and attitudes which conform to the "world," (the mentality of those who would reduce reality to so much less than what it truly is). Paul is referring to those who would abbreviate the actual to only that which can be seen or touched and then categorized by the "highest" reality of all, the human mind; or those who would even further insist that whatever exists apart from the mind reaches its highest purpose by serving the aims of human intelligence and the desires that this intelligence deems legitimate. (Such calculation has never left much room for unselfish loving or compassionate sharing, however.) The further refinement of *mind* will finally perfect humankind, according to this philosophy. Human intelligence will finally "figure out" how to eliminate evil and so unhappiness, one of these days, it finally insists. Either that or some metal-and-chip extension of our powers to remember, organize and deduce surely will.

Mind trying to be the whole person. Mind trying to be an end to itself. Mind trying to eliminate the disorders of mind, while all the while the disorder is rooted in a heart whose existence mind either denies or dismisses as a poetic or nearly irrelevant accessory to the business of getting on with getting what life is supposed to get you.

But hearts are good for nothing if not for loving. And so, when they do not work properly, it's always connected to a love problem. Or an "unlove" problem. A heart "unloved" by God because His love is not believed in, and so ignored. A heart "unloved" by fellow humans because their love is similarly doubted or refused. A heart unloved by self because you can only love yourself when you first come to believe in the love that others have for you. A heart too afraid, then, to trustingly reach out in genuine affection for another with any kind of consistency or fidelity.

So much contemporary writing in psychology can tend to leave the reader with the impression that more than anything else she is some kind of cross between a radio-receiver and a computer — something that picks up all kinds of signals and then correctly organizes or interprets such data. Fix whatever is scrambling the signals and interfering with the machine's ability to calculate and, presto, you've got a *whole* human being.

There's another reason why certain contemporary books and therapeutic approaches can leave the prospective seeker-after-wholeness feeling quite dismayed. They will show how to correct your erroneous thinking or nonproductive behavior, but *you* still have to do the correcting. *You* will have to find and develop the will power. *You* will have to shoulder the full responsibility for this undertaking, which, quite likely, is going to be no minor project.

We have already suggested that when more and more of God's love is allowed into a heart less and less inclined to doubt its loveableness, then this is what is going to most profoundly contribute to the undoing of our distorted opinionating, over-reactive emotionalism and selfishly misguided problem-solving. Most of us, after all, have had years of practice in the nurturing or negative opinions, negative feelings, not to mention the unhappiness-producing words and deeds, which invariably externalize such reasoning and emoting. Not having been rooted and grounded in His love, our personalities were at least partially developed in the direction of being rooted and grounded in a mistrust of love's sincerity—His or anybody else's, for that matter. Patterns of self-destructive thinking, feeling and acting developed out of this.

At the very center of who we were, we felt constrained to protect ourselves from, and pit ourselves against, everybody else, to a greater or lesser degree, as Craig Dykstra has so persuasively suggested.[9] To experience real conversion to Christ, he asserts (and we agree) is to simultaneously allow oneself to be freed of this burden to better others in order to banish our feelings of inferiority; or this compulsion to isolate ourselves from, manipulate or even hurt others before they hurt us. The center of the personality has been shifted, then, from one that is compelled to protect itself against others (and even itself) by means of its own energy and devices, to one freed and impelled to reach out in love to others as Our Lord's affection for us overflows its "banks," sweeps us up and out of ourselves in its current, as it targets itself upon others. As the between-the-Testaments apocryphal book, Second Esdras, wisely observed, when " . . .men on earth feel a change of heart" they will then "come to a better mind." (6:26, NEB).

But even if the foundation of our self-centeredness or self-preoccupation has been broken, the automatic or nearly automatic patterns of responding suspiciously, jealously, vindictively, competitively, manipulatively, anxiously, despairingly, self-pityingly, etc., will most likely still tend to hang on, here and there. Even if, as Dykstra says, we now have been given a new point

262

of reference, in and through His love, which is inclined to bring everything else into a sharp, new focus—a focus increasingly free of the old blurs, we will still most likely experience throwbacks to the old ways. Like a projector with auto-focus that annoyingly fades to fuzziness every twentieth slide or so.

So, we will still have to learn how to unlearn. But whereas the experts we've spoken of will insist upon the practiced exertion of will power in some kind of mental calisthenics, the Gospel indeed proves itself once again to be Good News. The New Testament undoubtedly insists that the initiation of a new discipline of one's thought and emotional life is an utter necessity. A discipline of *His* doing, however. Not *our* new control over our thoughts; not *our* new exercise of responsibility for how we feel—but His control and responsibility in us and through us: "For God hath not given us the spirit of fear; but of power, and of love, and of a sound mind." (2 Tim. 1:7, KJV) Or as the Good News Bible puts it, "For the Spirit that God has given us does not make us timid; instead, his Spirit fills us with power, love and self-control."

For the Greeks, a sound mind was a self-controlled mind. The New Testament writers obviously agreed, when they employed the word *sophronismos* to indicate that the Holy Spirit was ready to gift the expectant believer with a control over his or her thinking that would issue forth in sound-mindedness. This passage from 2nd Timothy is best read, I believe in conjunction with Galatians 5:22: "But the Spirit produces love, joy, peace, patience, kindness, goodness, faithfulness, humility and self-control." (TEV)

These qualities listed by the Apostle are the traits of a person who, if they were continually manifest in her makeup, we would have to call a very balanced individual, emotionally and mentally. Happily, they are the qualities or fruits of that Spirit who longs to indwell our spirit. *He produces them* if we give him the soil and the space. The Holy Spirit, the Scriptures tell us, wants to release these powers within us in an ever-increasing intensity and vitality, so that they influence in a healing way our whole personality and thereafter the personalities of all those with whom we come into contact.

We give Him this soil and space, so to speak, by believing afresh that He's there. There to produce these qualities. There to empower us to manifest these traits of personality. There to give us kindness, where we find it difficult to be kind; patience, where we find it impossible to be patient; self-controlled, where we discover ourselves to be nothing else but undisciplined . . .

Someone once handed me a slip of paper with the following words Xeroxed onto it, truly inspired words whose author, to the best of my present knowledge, remains anonymous: "Joy is love singing; peace is love resting; long-suffering is love enduring; gentleness is love's touch; goodness is love's character; faithfulness is love's habit; meekness is love forgetting self; temperance (or self-control) is love holding the reins."[10]

Paul tells us not only here in *Galatians* but in a number of different places that love somehow encompasses and sums up the full spectrum of all that the Spirit bestows. *Romans* 5:5 is one of my favorites: ". . . hope does not disappoint us, because God's love has been poured into our hearts through the Holy Spirit which has been given to us;" (RSV) We are given an endless supply of love, a love which will always give us a reason and the power to respond to whatever we encounter, in a way that could properly be termed, "controlled."

There are two basic ways that we tap into this love. *First*: through daily personal prayer. By putting ourselves in His presence; by allowing ourselves to become freshly aware of His ongoing affection for us, we, in effect, find ourselves formed progressively into reservoirs of this love. Reservoirs whose precious contents cascade constantly and unselfconsciously over our spillways; namely, beyond the boundaries of who we are. (Neglect of this utterly necessary practice will, conversely, leave us with even less than what we need, and with nothing very much left over for others.) *Second*: through learning to remind ourselves that we face nothing alone and that, whenever we are tested, we have Him to lean upon and draw from, primarily, and ourselves only secondarily, and only to the extent that we do this leaning upon and drawing from Him. (This "longer" just-being-in-His-presence kind of prayer and the brief reminding-of-ourselves-that-He-is-still-with-us-and-we-need-to-deal-with-this-problem-together kind of prayer enables us to appropriate the Spirit's priceless gift of self-control.)

This control is not the kind of control that happens when reason coldly and violently refuses to allow emotion to express itself. Nor is it the power (that some people display) of artificially manufacturing surface feelings and facial expressions that tell bystanders they are, say, indifferent when they are really hurt, happy when they are really sad or calm when they are really upset, etc. It is rather the power God gives us to face even the most negative things in a truly positive way. The following Scripture passages are especially helpful in understanding what is meant here:

> Rejoice in the Lord always; again I will say, Rejoice. Let all men know your forbearance. The Lord is at hand. Have no anxiety about anything, but in everything by prayer and supplication with thanksgiving let your requests be made known to God. And the peace of God, which passes all understanding will keep your hearts and your minds in Christ Jesus. Finally, brethren, whatever is true, whatever is honorable, whatever is just, whatever is pure, whatever is lovely, whatever is gracious, if there is any excellence, if there is anything worthy of praise, think about these things. . . . I have learned in whatever state I am, to be content. I know how to be abased, and I know how to abound; in any and all circumstances I have learned the secret of facing plenty and hunger, abundance and want. I can do all things in Him who strengthens me. . . . (Phil. 4:4-8; ll-l3, RSV; see also Rom. 8:28-39)

We can rejoice always because no matter what circumstances sour, or how often, one circumstance refuses to — namely the circumstance that He loves me, that His love is in me, and that He only wants to give me more and more of it; and so, if I have that, in a very real sense I can be said to have everything. This is the "secret" he speaks of further on: *The love is always there, and always there to lean on.*

It is the will of the Spirit who dwells in our spirit to be constantly releasing from within us inexhaustible outstreamings of love — *let them see your unselfishness (or forbearance)*, Paul insists. In the human scheme of things, we tend to rejoice when things seem to be going our way and engage in something of the opposite, when things are not. But the most important thing of all *is* going our way: namely that He loves us right now and is presently getting us ready to unrestrictedly enjoy that love, face-to-face with Him and one another, forever. Therefore, we always have more than enough reason to open up for that Spirit's joy and even more of it than ever before. This joy may have to coexist temporarily with all kinds of disappointment, but it is bestowed in such a way that we are assured of never having to live without it. Our hearts instinctively rejoice whenever they choose to be aware of His loving presence, even when they are burdened with His burdens and groan with His groanings.

"Have no anxiety about anything." "But how?" we ask. Nothing would seem to be more impossible. Impossible, unless we are allowing him to teach us how. *"In everything by prayer and supplication with thanksgiving let . . . (your) requests be made known to God."* A minister-friend once shared with me how, since he'd learned how to ventilate his feelings and frustrations in the presence of a sympathetic group of colleagues, his anxieties had been much reduced. My casually-phrased, but emphatic reply to him was: "That's great; but until you've learned how to ventilate before God, man, you just ain't never known the full joys of ventilation!"

Sometimes we just have to express the depth and intensity of how hurt we are, even when we aren't sure just what is hurting or what we are hurting over. We will speak a little later in more detail about getting in touch with our feelings. Suffice it to say here, however, that letting our hearts spew forth their hurts and our heads spill out their attitudes before One who understands as no other ever can or ever will is, not only allowable, and within the bounds of respect for His dignity, but utterly necessary if we are to grow into the kind of honesty with Him (and ourselves) that will insure our full entry into wholeness. Just take a look at all the lamenting that goes on in the Psalms, if you tend to question that assertion's appropriateness or, its Biblical base.

Paul is saying that, to the extent that we become really prayerful, to that extent we will be delivered from anxiety's power to paralyze us. Yet prayer, it can hardly be denied, for many people does not relieve their anxiety, but only increases it. One reason for this is that folks are only too anxious to have God remove the anxious feeling, without showing them the reasons as to why they are anxious: *"Please take away the bad feeling . . . but don't show me why I feel bad."*

Another reason is that some people's recounting of their problems and needs in prayer amounts to little more than a big worrying session in God's presence. Their hands are lifted up, so to speak, in supplication, towards God. But instead of lifting those hands back to their sides "empty," after having handed over their problems to Him, those "hands" are lowered just as burden-filled as when they were first upraised. Such individuals have not broken through to the renewed realization that "they're His problems, first, now and only mine, second."

"And (then) the peace of God which passes all understanding will keep your hearts and your minds in Christ Jesus." The most instinctive way we are characteristically inclined to think we can get peace is by getting understanding. If we are able to understand what is going on inside us or around us and see somehow that this is ultimately to the good, *then* we can be at peace. In God's scheme of things, however, things will often work quite the opposite. He will not always see fit to show us why He is initiating or even permitting certain things within us or beyond us. If we could only see the whole picture, we'd be at peace. His answer, very often, is: *I see the whole picture and I am insuring that everything is working out for the best, because you love me and trust my love for you. Be at peace that I see everything and have done everything and have promised to work all things together for your good — even the bad things.* (Rom. 8:28)

Our peace is not derived, then, from the satisfaction of having a more than adequate perspective on problems, and then having full control over all possibilities. It is derived from our acceptance of the fact that He has the perspective and He has the control. It comes from accepting His assurance that this is the way things were meant to be: that only God needs to be God.

This is not meant to say that our enjoyment of His peace will not be furthered by being blessed by Him with insights we'd never been shown before. It is simply to assert that sometimes, no matter how hard we try to see, or ask to be shown, no further understanding will be granted us by Him, even as He offers us more peace and assurance than we've ever previously known.

To continue believing that God is; that He's in control, and that He is still someone who loves us, is, we still have to confess, no easy task at times. Personal misfortunes and setbacks can and do periodically stun us with their enormity or intensity: "How could God still be God, and still be love, and still love me, and still allow this to happen; or let this go on as long as its been going on?" There's no doubt that Old Testament prophets and psalmists as well as New Testament apostles and saints thought such thoughts and even dared to think them "aloud" before God in prayer. This means, among other things, that God's greatest and holiest, were nonetheless not supermen or wonder women who just reached inside and pushed some "button" marked "faith," and thereby attained to overwhelming calm or were able to perfectly handle severe adversity, by simply repeating a few favorite inspirational scripture verses to themselves. Their world seemed out of control and they said so. Evil seemed far more powerful than good, and they said so. God seemed to be an indifferent million miles away, and they said so. They fully ventilated to Him, in other words, what they saw and what they felt, boldly and unashamedly and complainingly: "Dear God, we've just got to clear the air here . . . ."

They not only report to us their prayerful protests however, they also tell us what they "heard" in reply, after waiting for His answer. Invariably, the grace they received called them to *trust even more*. They didn't perceive such a call to be "hard rocks," however, because with it came a fresh awareness of "I am with you" and "I am for you." Like Habbakuk, for instance, they found themselves challenged to look beyond what their eyes could see to what only faith could show them: that God *was* there; that He did care and that when He deemed it right, He *would* intervene to turn things around: "The just man will keep on living by his faith, Habbakuk, and that trust in my ongoing concern will also empower you to live before me faith-fully . . ." (cf. Hab. 1, 2:1-4) [11]

Paul put it almost the same way, when he reminded the Corinthians that we are called to walk by faith and not merely by sight alone. (2 Cor. 5:7) Only this faith-vision could enable the believer to "see" that, behind the scenes, God was working all things together for good, *even the bad things.*

Finally, if the Father had already fully turned inside out the greatest evil the world had ever seen, or ever would see, namely, His Son's murder, and this Risen Lord somehow presently dwells within me, then I can trust that Father to similarly reverse all other evils that threaten me or those I love.

There are times, of course, when we will be able to do nothing against the evil opposing us, except to wait on God. There are other times when our turning in supplication to Him will leave us convinced that, armed with His love and grace, we are being summoned to presently move against whatever opposes us. In either case, however, we are meant to be anointed with the peace which only comes from wanting to do His will, buoyed up with the tranquillity that derives from submitting to the rightness of His ways that so often are so far from our ways. (cf. Is. 55:8) One way or another, we will have to make our own the sentiments of the famous A.A. "serenity prayer," drinkers and teetotalers alike:

> "God grant me the serenity to accept the things I cannot change, the courage to change the things I can, and the wisdom to know the difference."

But even if negative conditions and hostile people cannot immediately be changed, at least *our attitudes* can: "Think about these things . . . whatever is true . . . just . . . honorable . . . pure . . . lovely . . . gracious . . ."

When Paul penned those words of "positive-thinking" counsel to the Philippians, he was a prisoner; a victim of unjust persecution on the part of unbelievers and, simultaneously, a victim of considerable jealous opposition on the part of fellow Christians. This apostle of God's love and faith was seemingly surrounded by a sea of hate and mistrust. How could he seriously and sanely insist upon thinking about nothing but the "true," "pure" or "lovely," etc.?

Not by manipulating the positive so as to block out the negative. Not by self-hypnotically repeating to himself sunshine-hued scripture verses, so that they could be employed to totally distract himself from the problems at hand. Not by pretending that everything was fine, even though it wasn't. Not be flashing a smile for "good old Jesus," even when it wasn't in him to smile, etc.

We've already seen how he did it. At least in a general sense — by re-submitting himself to His Lord; by opening up for all the peace Heaven was doling out; by praying a prayer like: "Lord help me to know that even *this*, you can work together for good."

It was, then, out of that freshly-graced frame of mind, out of that "re-faithed" perspective on life and its problems that he was able to begin to see positive slants on the negatives confronting him: "Sure, friends have betrayed me, but God never will . . . Sure, my imprisonment is unjust, but God isn't and even if Paul is in chains, God's word isn't . . . Sure, many have plotted against me, and will probably continue to, but I refuse to believe that life is a plot against my ever being able to be happy."

Instead of copping negative attitudes about negative happenings, he allowed the Holy Spirit to help him find a positive way of looking at undeniably negative realities. Instead of seeing himself as Paul the prisoner of the Romans, etc., he called himself instead, Paul, a prisoner of Jesus Christ.

In some segments of his life, this approach, most likely, was extra difficult. He, like us, undoubtedly, knew certain moments after the experience of misfortune, when he'd be inclined to feel himself entitled to a few minutes or hours of good, old-fashioned resentment, self-pity or despair, etc. There's no way he could have become the furiously obsessed persecutor of Christians prior to his conversion without having had a few screws loose, without being a bit in bondage to some rather negative attitudes. We can be rather certain that no one thought of Saul the Pharisee, as a first-century Jewish version of Norman Vincent Peale.

The Spirit of God must have done quite a job on his thought-life, then. Where, formerly, when things not to his liking occurred, he (like we) had tendencies to "cop" negative attitudes. Not only that, but copping them as a prelude to nursing them. Instantaneous resentments that lengthened themselves into resentment "trips," automatic feelings of being sorry for himself that expanded themselves into transcontinental self-pity "trips," feelings of desperation extended into a generalized despair over life's unfairness.

The Holy Spirit must have shown him those sectors of his make-up that made him most vulnerable to that kind of thing, again and again. Namely the areas where he was most inclined to want to react negatively; where he almost automatically felt entitled to the "joys" of being miserable; where he was most addicted to the bitter (but perversely consoling) liquors of prolonged resenting, mistrusting, worrying, doubting, despairing . . .

Guess what? The Counselor plans to do the same for you and me.

When we were small, we were taught carefully by our elders: "Certain things are poisonous. They're very harmful. Never put them in your mouth . . . See the bottle with the skull and crossbones on the label. Never touch it . . ."

We also may have learned about foods that we're allergic to and so will never eat again. Or how seafood goes bad very quickly in warm weather and can leave you quite sick, if left out to thaw, for too long.

So we formed a code, an internal hygienic code for ourselves. We said to ourselves and we undoubtedly still say: "I will not take poisons into my body, or chemicals whose effects I know nothing about. I won't eat the foods I'm allergic to. I won't eat pink pork or old shrimp . . ."

But as far as something like *mental* hygiene . . . That's another story. All kinds of attitudinal poisons we are gladly willing to take into our minds every day. Perhaps no one ever warned us about that — at least until now. But Paul is warning us in this letter to the Philippians. And Christ through Paul is warning us at this very minute, as His Spirit moves on our hearts, quickening them with the urgency of "*now* is the acceptable time . . ."

When we pray for the mind of Christ, when we ask in faith for the Spirit's gift of self-control in our thought-life, we are simultaneously asking for something specific. Specific knowledge about where our weak spots are, in the realm of negative thinking. We are petitioning simultaneously to be convicted as to how and when *we still want the "right"* to think negatively, and so "feel bad," as long as we deem necessary, when things are not to our liking. We are asking Him, then, to spotlight our pet irrationalities, as well as our tendencies to throw "justifiable" inner and, sometimes, outer tantrums; to expose our inclinations to distort what we see and feel, because life has just been too unfair.

Earlier, we described the woundedness of not knowing yourself as loved by God and called to live out of His love as resulting in a radical willfulness crying out for what we want, whenever we want it. An immediate offshoot of this misconception of who we are is the allied conviction that "I am not truly free unless, I'm free to think whatever I want, whenever I want to and as long as I want to."

I don't know how many clients I have counseled about this gift of God's loving control over our thought-processes who have returned in a condition worse than the one they first walked in with, mouthing the excuse: "I tried it, and it doesn't work!" What they were really saying, however is that they wanted relief from their mental and/or emotional suffering and they wanted the thought-freedom (mentioned just above) at one and the same time.

That "freedom" is really *license* pretending to be freedom, however. Our parents didn't cheat us of the freedom we have to make ourselves ill or poison ourselves to death, by training us to the discipline of a hygiene counteractive to poisons or allergies. They helped us into a freedom for greater health. Similarly, God does not brainwash us into becoming Pollyanna-like automatons, by insisting that we allow him to grace us with a guardedness against indulging the negative. But, so often, like rebellious children who insist upon eating their cake and having it too, we want to have sound minds and we want to be free to feed ourselves upon the bitter yet somehow simultaneously sickly sweet fruits of vengefulness, inordinate self-pity, jealousy, and the like. We want to be healed but we want to be free to indulge toxic attitudes and feelings, at one and the same time.

By calling us to accept His love and the standards of that love, as the guardians of our attitudes and feelings, He is calling us to a new freedom. That freedom is ultimately a free gift from Him. But free gifts have to be picked up by their recipients. Even free gifts have to be taken out of their packages. That is the "price" to be paid, if they are ever to be enjoyed. The "price" of God's gift of self-control is our accepting it in faith. Accepting it in faith as the replacement for something we won't need anymore — namely our childish, unhygienic non-control — our "right" to pore "pornographically" over what is poisonous or negative. It may take us some time to fully unpackage the new gift. Maybe even a whole lifetime to get it fully in operation. He has the right timetable for each for us.

Chapter 13

Healing of Attitudes and Emotions (III)

Emotions and feelings are not simply realities which hinder our thinking, choosing and acting. They also are able to accomplish quite the opposite. In fact, even though they are able to become our "enemies," we are not helped by regarding them with suspicion. Any more than we are, say, by viewing our loved ones as potential adversaries. In either case, such a stance can only set us up for conflicts that might otherwise be quite avoidable.

The word "emotion" is, in today's use of the language, used almost interchangeably with the term "feeling." In the discussion that follows, however, we will attempt to make somewhat of a distinction between the two. In so doing we will be following the lead of Dr. Conrad Baars, a psychiatrist-author, some of whose key reflections on this matter we will now attempt to briefly summarize.[1]

Dr. Baars has made a crucially important contribution to contemporary thought on the role of our emotions by insisting that we stop ignoring the work of our brilliant "forefathers" in this area. In effect, he has had the courage to assert, no one has written more clearly, pointedly or practically on these matters than the medieval theologian, Thomas Aquinas, and his mentor, the ancient Greek Philosopher, Aristotle. These men were both very much concerned with the psychological dimension of humanity. Much of what they wrote has been supplemented and surpassed by breakthroughs in the present and so can hardly, therefore be considered the last word on the matter. Yet, it remains to be seen whether or not their central observations on what constitutes our emotional life have been rendered obsolete.

The words "emotion" and "motor" derive from the same Latin root, *motus*, the past participle of the verb, *movere*, to move. An emotion, therefore, is a movement within the personality, a reaction which causes us to move (outwardly), or to be moved (inwardly). As Baars suggests, emotions may therefore be viewed as "motors" of our psyche, which animate us and move us towards what we see to be good for us and away from what we perceive to be harmful to us.[2] What we are moved towards, or away from may exist either in the world around us, or even within the "inner world" of our thoughts and feelings, by the way.[3]

"Feelings," in this view, would be those sensations we experience above and beyond the eleven to be noted below. Most of the time, however, they are merely combinations of several of the classic eleven, but felt as one.

The primary emotions are six: love, desire and joy, and their correlatives, hate, aversion, and sadness. When we believe something to be good, we feel attracted to it, we find it pleasing (*love*). Because of this attraction and pleasure we may find ourselves wanting to possess it (*desire*). If we are able to gain possession of this object, we experience satisfaction in that possession (*joy*). On the other hand, when we discover something to be as evil, we experience it as repulsive (*hate*). We may further find ourselves inwardly pulling away from it (*aversion*). We may finally discover that we are feeling "bad," because it is still in our sights, or is temporarily eclipsing our view of what is good (*sorrow*).

The above "moved-by" emotions stand directly related to good and evil. They are served by five other emotions which also stand related to good and evil, but not as directly. The latter five relate us to good or evil *under the aspect of difficulty.* These five "moved-to" emotions provide us with extra energy for the things we choose to do, precisely because we have discovered obstacles standing between us and the objects we find desirable.[4] Like the primary emotions, they also pair off into opposites, with one exception, (to be noted shortly).

When we desire something, come up against an obstacle, but finally react with the conviction that we can still achieve our objective, we feel *hope*. But if, on the contrary, we become convinced that this obstacle will prove to be insurmountable, we experience *despair*. Should this obstacle present itself as possibly harmful to us, even as we sense that we can defend ourselves against it and still overcome it, then we find ourselves reacting with *courage.*

On the other hand, if the possible harm posed by this obstacle appears to be inescapable, we ordinarily will experience fear.[5] Finally, when the obstacle is almost sure to harm us or has already done so, that added stimulus or over-drive emotion we call upon to steel ourselves to undo the damage already done, or to prevent further harm from happening, is *anger.*[6] (Its opposite is tranquillity. Since, however, it is not strictly a condition of moving-towards or a being-moved-upon, it is not classified as an emotion.)

When our emotions are looked at this way, as Baars wisely observes, there is strictly no such thing as a so-called "negative" emotion.[7] Even despair, fear, anger, hatred, aversion and sorrow are able to have a positive purpose—to move us away from what is evil or harmful.

Does this mean, then, that our emotions are basically good? In the same sense that our arms and legs are good, the doctor replies, following Aquinas. In themselves, our limbs are essentially God's creation and therefore good. Nevertheless, they are able to be misused, at times, to accomplish evil ends. So too with the emotions. Emotions are movements of the inner person, ordinarily accompanied by certain simultaneous physiological changes. They are "auxiliary" motors meant to support the drive of our personality's main motor, the will, following Baars' imagery.[8]

When we are moved to do something, and our will, under the guidance of reason, follows through to perform what our emotion inclined us towards, then that act is a good or moral act, when reason agrees with what is ultimately best for us, namely God's will. When, on the other hand, emotions incline us to follow through on decisions at variance with what we know to be right, then they are being employed as "accomplices" in actions that are morally harmful.

This points up the necessity of distinguishing carefully between the emotion and *the decision* that may or may not be set in operation by the emotion. For instance, if someone suddenly menaces me with a knife, I will ordinarily find myself experiencing the emotion of hate. That feeling is part of the process whereby I am fueled with the added energy I need to defend myself. If I choose to follow through on this feeling by *willing* every conceivable kind of physical and moral harm upon this adversary, like death or damnation, for instance, then I am *choosing* to hate him. I am choosing to wish evil upon him. This is the *spiritual* act of hate. The defensive emotion, a good in itself, has been transformed in this situation into a choice at variance with my own well-being (as well as my opponent's) and, of course, God's will. It is now a moral evil.

It is possible to come to see all of our emotions as our "friends." Before we are able to do that, nevertheless, some of us may well have to learn to befriend those emotions we had once viewed as enemies to be shunned, or as potentially embarrassing strangers. Just to realize *that* can be extremely important. If this isn't a healing, it's at least the first step towards one.

"Be angry but do not sin . . . ," the *Letter to the Ephesians,* (4:26, RSV) advises. That inspired counsel is more than wisdom on simply how to handle anger. It surely is just as applicable to the other emotions, as well. It says, in effect, don't be afraid to feel what you're feeling, whether it be anger, hate, fear or whatever, in either its psychological or physical manifestations. But do not sin. Don't allow those feelings to become the absolute arbiter of how you come to respond. God's word is able to illumine your intellect. God's grace is able to strengthen your will. That enlightened intellect may need to tell us things beyond what our feelings have told us. That strengthened will may need to restrain, or even counter, what our feelings are prompting us to do.

It may not always be wise to show others what we are feeling. But at the very least *we ought to express inwardly to ourselves our anger*, fears or other emotional reactions. Emotions always need to be expressed, as Baars reminds us.[9]

Life has taught many of us to mistrust or misread our emotions. Parents of Anglo-Saxon background, for instance, may have taught their kids that anger is rarely, if ever, to be manifested in "civilized" society. Parents of Latin lineage, on the other hand, may have taught their kids exactly the opposite:

that any annoyance is worth raising a royal fuss over. Some fathers and mothers rarely, if ever, show open affection for each other or their children; and so, those children grow up, perhaps, learning about their Christian duty to love everybody, or how love is supposed to make the world go round — without ever having *felt* love very much. Without having felt strongly that they were lovable, as a result. Without, therefore, expecting to feel love strongly for others.

Some adults are unable to experience joy on a regular basis because overly strict or overly preoccupied parents wouldn't even let them "raise a holler" or jump up and down, when something good happened to them. As children, they had been unwittingly taught that such external expressions of being happy were unseemly, immature or otherwise unacceptable. Other adults suffer from a similar joylessness, because family hardships exposed them too prematurely to work or other grown-up sized responsibilities at a time when childhood games and amusements should have been the order of the day.

Let's go back, for a moment, to the memory shared in Chapter Seven of the nun who attempted to explain the meaning of the Fourth Commandment to that class of seven or eight year olds to which I belonged. She had ended her discourse with a question: "Now, no one here, of course, would ever do anything so terrible as to hate your father or mother, would you?" "NO SISTER," anxiously responded the thirty, all damp of brow and some, most likely, damp of pants, as we unanimously and piously lied to her right through our teeth.

She hadn't explained to us, of course, the difference between "feeling hate" and "willing evil upon." So we made further progress that day in something that many of us had, undoubtedly, become already quite skillful at: burying our feelings of hate for those parents or others we were supposed to always love; pretending to ourselves that those hate-feelings just weren't there. Similarly, almost all of us have learned how to deny inappropriate hates, and even how to cover them over with synthetically-produced feelings of affection, at some time or other in our lives.

We spoke a bit earlier of a hierarchy in the realm of the emotions, of how the "moved to" emotions serve the "moved by" emotions. But emotions can also impede each other, at our misdirection. The "moved-to" emotions can attempt to dominate the "moved-by" emotions, or even dominate each other. Our most recent example is a good illustration of this: the fear of being a monster (or of going to Hell) was mobilized to sit on top of hate; we kids used it to help us repress the unwanted feelings.

Freud had first spoken of how superego, that pre-conscience conditioning prompting the child (and even some adults) to adhere to the standards of parent and society, is manipulated by many into helping themselves to deny unwanted desires, motives and even emotions. He also asserted that such repression always causes emotional illness in one form or another. Dr. Baars and his associate, Dr. Terruwe, have written at length not to dispute that feelings are often denied by such a process, but only to challenge the assertion they are *always* repressed, as a result of such guilt-conditioning. The two doctors have written extensively and persuasively in demonstration of their contention that much emotional disorder, and its attendant suffering, is the result of one emotion being (wrongfully) allowed to sit on another.[10]

In their opinion, "fear" is the emotion most often pressed into the dubious service of camouflaging the presence of another unwanted emotion. This is the equivalent of burying the emotion "alive." An emotion, as has been said, comes into play in view of achieving a specific purpose. But as long as it is buried, it is unable to do so, and thus remains in some kind of state of tension — an unhealthy tension which always results in suffering of some sort or another. Two "emotional currents" have been released in reference to the same object.[11] But they pull in different directions, wasting the personality's energy, as one emotion conflicts with another in a sort of arm-wrestling fashion. Even if one emotion temporarily wrestles the other into submission, the "pinned" emotion will be inclined to await its moment to make a comeback. It will attempt to rise up and get what it was created to need: reason's guidance.[12]

We gave an example above of how fear can be used to repress hate. It may also be used to repress sexual feelings which, though closely allied to the emotions, are classified separately in the approach of Aristotle — Aquinas. When, for instance, a man is sexually stimulated by an attractive woman, this arousal is usually accompanied by the emotion of desire. But if this man is afraid of women, sexually, or of violating a vow of celibacy (or marriage), he may allow this fear to extend its energy to help him deny that he is experiencing, or that he ever did experience, such desires. Even if such an individual has developed his reflexes of denial in this area to a high degree, however, he may someday find himself in the throes of a compulsion. An irrepressible urge to engage in some kind of promiscuous activity that is in high conflict with what he had previously considered to be his unshakable moral convictions.[13]

When fear is used to dominate desire or another unwanted emotion, that fear often colors much of such an individual's personality with an obvious rigidity. This type of person is often very anxious and doesn't really know what he or she's anxious about. Especially when the ability to make one self unaware of what once that person had at least some awareness of has been relatively perfected.

According to Baars, there seems to be a basic difference between individuals who employ fear to deny other emotions, and those who resort to the "energy" emotions (courage and hope). The former tend to be afraid of the consequences of their unwanted emotions; while the latter are inclined to view their sat-on feelings as "inferior aspects of their humanity."[14]

I came across an opportune example of this kind of thing, it would seem, on the T.V. news, this morning. A reporter was interviewing a man who had just witnessed the gangland execution of a business associate. His recall was apparently perfect; his description of the event was cool, matter-of-fact, precise. The ideal witness for the prosecution, someday, perhaps. Not the slightest sign of any emotion interfering in any way with his perceptions. It was hard to believe that he wasn't simply recounting his remembrances of a gory scene from a "Godfather" type movie he'd attended the night before — and not just now come from being forced to be the spectator of a man's murder. A man that he had known so very well.

Was it fear of appearing to be unmanly sitting on top of the "inferior" or "feminine" feeling of grief (and its frequently attendant display of tears)? Was it hope or courage, manipulated so as to energetically allow him to move right along with that day's demands, without having his judgement or planning impaired by those troublesome and unbusinessmanlike feeling-states? Like zeal for justice, indignation, compassion, or empathy? He was superbly controlled, remarkably unruffled. A regular white-collar Clint Eastwood. Many viewers would undoubtedly find themselves to be in envious awe of such uncommon coolness. In this student of human nature's opinion, however, there is something awfully sick represented by such "cool."

In that engrossing, contemporary cinematic parable, "Ordinary People," a very tense and irritable Conrad Jarrett, decides to visit a psychiatrist. In response to his doctor's query as to what the troubled teenager was hoping to get out of therapy, Conrad replies that he wants more "control."

Conrad's emotions were unpredictably and embarrassingly roller-coasting on him. He found himself angry and irritable when there was little or nothing to be angry or irritable about. Worrying, when there was little or nothing to be worrying about. Despairing, when there was little or nothing to be despairing about. And so, he imagined that *control* would be the answer. Some kind of inner button he could press that would swiftly neutralize the unwanted feelings.

But Dr. Berger knew better. He knew that there was a reason for those irritatingly capricious emotions. In time, he was able to bring Conrad to the point where he acknowledged that he had deeply hidden within himself feelings of guilt and anger as a result of not being able to save his drowning brother, Buck. At that point, he no longer needed "control" over those unwanted feelings he had "buried alive," to borrow Baars" expression. Once he dared to acknowledge the possibility of such a burial, and finally allowed himself to fully feel those feelings, he was free. The intense, and ever-present anxiety disappeared.

Conrad had come from an upper middle-class American family. He had learned from a father and mother who were highly motivated to "get ahead" that the open expression of certain feelings in the market-place or at social gatherings can seriously weaken one's chances of advancement in those theatres of endeavor. Conrad had, for quite some time, been enrolled in the "school" of control—the school that invariably teaches you to mistrust your feelings. When his moment of crisis had come, accordingly, and he desperately needed to experience and evaluate what he was feeling, he was only able to deny those feelings, and pretend the opposite. The fictional Conrad was on his way to becoming, if not a permanently sick, at least chronically afflicted with the same disease so evident in that non-fictional eyewitness to murder we just described.

But if God created us to feel spontaneously; if we were meant by our Designer to freely react from within in a going forth from ourselves to embrace what is good and desirable or flee what is dangerous and undesirable; then to have been schooled to significantly tamper with that inner resonance to goodness or inner dissonance with the absence of goodness can only hurt us. We have been educated to wall ourselves off from feelings judged by our "teachers" to be in conflict with what they see to be socially acceptable, or at variance with their expectations for us. And so, they showed us how to wall one or more parts of ourself off from another part of ourself. The walled-off part was then to be forgotten, as if it had never existed.[15] When deep-seated responses within a person like Conrad start stirring and demand expression, what else is a Conrad likely to do but scramble for the "control button": "I have too many important things to do, too many responsibilities to attend to. Besides it's not manly to cry tears; it's Victorian to feel guilt; it's a sign of weakness to own up to fear . . ."

Instructed not to feel feelings that are expressive of a genuine dimension of who we are; initiated into the skill of manufacturing feelings that are not, it's no surprise that so many of us sincerely suspect that we are nothing more than the sum total of the various parts life expects us to play. It's no accident that so many of us wonder whether, at the center of who we are, we might be nothing.

It's because we fear that at our center lurks restless evil or chaotic nothingness, that we feel constrained to control that evil or shield ourselves from that nothingness. And once we start controlling on the inside, the obsession to control on the outside is sure to follow. The cold efficiency with which we arm ourselves (and, so often, in which we pride ourselves), as we set out to control an uncontrolled world; as we find ourselves constrained to be in control not only of every situation we enter, but *even of every relationship we enter*, as well, is the inevitable by-product of that split-level self-view we were encouraged to adopt. Upstairs sits the cool, controlling intellect (usually in cahoots with a muscle-bound will) making sure that the door to the "cellar" stays securely bolted. For in that cellar roams wild, unhouse-broken animals . . . Obsession with control and even domination is our way of compensating for the suspected uncontrol lurking at our core.

We suggested above that having programmed ourselves to deny certain feelings is only half the problem here. The other side of this culturally-authorized splitting-off of our thinking-life from our feeling-life is that we have often been equally programmed to convincingly broadcast to others, and even to ourselves, that we are feeling feelings that we really aren't feeling. How else can we succeed in the business and social worlds, if we can't manufacture at will joy, hope, affection, compassion, courage, etc. for those important people we need to impress? If we don't flash back to them the facial expression or feeling-tone to our response that they expect to see or hear?

When you do that sort of thing often enough, you can even begin to doubt that there is left within you the ability to experience such things freely and authentically. At the very least, many of us will no longer be able to tell the difference between authentic feelings and the counterfeit ones.

Small wonder, then, that we are witnessing such a widespread breakdown of this contrived and unnatural approach to life, these days, especially as exemplified so often in the so-called, "mid-life crisis." This counselor has run into too many of its tragic victims. The majority of them were perfect examples of what we just described above. Paragons of perfect control: over-developed, head-wise, underdeveloped heart-wise. Often they are pillars of the church, devotees of a religion which is characterized by prideful self-congratulation over how many control-type "virtues" that keep the lid on sinful urges they've managed to amass and develop. That same spartan self-discipline, of course, is also channeled to more worldly ends, as it assures its possessor victory after victory in subduing the adversaries of the market place.

Conrad has now matured into middle age. But only physically. Having downplayed the significance of the feeling side of life for so long, so as to maximize the efficiency of his scheming side, he unexpectedly discovers that he can do so no longer. Having given up all kinds of opportunities to get in touch with, and even develop his potentialities for experiencing life for what it is, in favor of how it can be parlayed into more cash and/or financial security, he now discovers that, at all cost, he must taste the taste of spontaneity, newness, or enter into a heightened awareness of the true the good and the beautiful.

But when he finally releases his finger from the control button, more often than not, it is the button controlling his sexual desires. He decides to rediscover the feeling-dimension of who he is, by attempting to relive his adolescence. A fresh fling with a new girlfriend will surely make up for having fasted from a whole spectrum of emotional experience over all these years. He dimly realizes that sexual play symbolizes and concretizes a certain, spontaneous letting-go; a giving up of controls in the context of the soaring of powerful emotions. Surely, such a full feasting on feelings, a recklessly carefree act of abandon ought to more than compensate him for what he has denied himself for so long . . .

But he hasn't just been artificially separated from many of his feelings, he probably has also been similarly separated from his body. A controlling mind and an iron will now order it to become a pleasure machine, as they often have before. If so, he relates to his body, as Charles Davis observes, as if it were a physical object, alienated from the rest of him.[16] An unfamiliar environment of lovemaking is somehow supposed to make all things miraculously new. He may have rediscovered his genitals and their power to pleasure him, but he is just as feeling-poor as he ever was. He hasn't solved his problem. He's only managed to avoid it once again and probably create a few new ones he didn't even have before.

We have only spoken of one extreme in this area, however. We must not neglect to speak of its "twin," at the other end of the spectrum. If our age is haunted by rampant over-control of its feeling-life on the one hand, it is ironically and simultaneous-ly plagued by widespread under-control on the other. We live in a time, as Alexander Schneiders characterized it, noted for its notorious "anarchy of feeling."[17]

Before we address ourselves to that situation, however, we need to say a little bit more about control. There is a place for it in reference to our emotions and feelings. Or a need, at least, for *guidance*. "Guidance" appears to be a better word than control here, because "control" often seems to carry the connotation, in this day and age, of power being used to check the unruly, ungovernable or rebellious. "Control" almost seems to imply that what needs to be controlled is not good, or is somehow dangerous in itself.

Since, as we have insisted earlier, it is crucial that we accept the feeling side of our humanity as purposefully placed there by a wise and loving Creator, there is no need for that dimension of who we are to be subject to the same kind of control as is applied to rioting crowds or hardened criminals. Our emotions and feelings do, however, need the guidance which the intellect is able to provide them with. They also need to place themselves, to borrow Baars' analogy, once again, as auxiliary motors at the service of our main engine, the decision-making power of the will. In other words, they are not there to supplant our thinking or our willing. They are there to enrich our power to know and strengthen our power to choose.

But, sometimes, we are so focused on those signals which our feelings bring us to that we don't bother using our brain at all. We go totally with what we feel, to the exclusion of any reflection or judgement. At other times, we are moved to do or say things, not because we willed to do or say those things but because we allowed some powerfully reactive feelings to carry us along with them.

A woman is looking for a few acres of land on which to build her new home. She finds a perfectly measured-off plot of flat, dry land. She buys it. A second woman is also looking for a few acres of land, for the same purpose. She is thrilled by the beauty of the plot the agent shows her. She buys it and later discovers that it is half hill of solid rock and half valley of soggy marsh. A third woman is, you guessed it, looking for the same thing. She passes up a plot like the first because it is soil-rich, but scenery poor. She passes up a plot like the second because it is scenery-rich but soil-poor. She finally purchases a piece of acreage because its scenic value is matched by its soil value.

The first woman's choice was the result of too much intellect and too little attention to emotions. The second woman's choice was the result of letting her feelings for the land's beauty overwhelm her need to carefully consider the more practical issues. The third woman's choice was the result of listening to both her intellect and her feelings. Mind, feelings and will came together to act in concert and accomplish the best possible result. Mind and feelings educated each other, so to speak, and the will brought forth the fine fruit of that fortunate dialogue, in the correct choice being realized.

There are, of course, countless ways that our feelings are able to cancel out our thinking or neutralize our willing. All we can do here is attempt to isolate some of the most common varieties of this disruptive anarchy and present them briefly for the reader's consideration.

Emotions or feelings overrule reason and/or will on a regular basis when they are *more* than emotions or feelings. That is, when they have become wedded to a decision to insure their permanence within us. Or, to put it another way, when that which we once relied upon for the moment, is allowed to remain within us as a permanent crutch.

Let's look at *despair*, for a minute. We said above that it is able to serve a good purpose, momentarily, by signaling to us that certain obstacles are presently better circumvented or avoided than met head-on, any further. Suppose, for instance, that I try indefinitely to get someone important, like a parent, to show affection for me, openly and regularly. Then, I fail. It just isn't going to happen. I stop trying. But feeling the pain of this rejection and the disappointment over so much apparently wasted effort, I further decide that any similar attempt to establish a new relationship *with anyone else* will surely meet with equal failure. This mistaken attitude merges with the still-present despair which arose in reaction to the original failed relationship. I choose to allow this attitude, interpenetrated by the emotion, to remain within me as a defense against future hurt. The signal to stop trying to maintain one relationship has now merged with a decision to avoid *all* relationships. Since it may well have been the child who forged that unfortunate emotion-attitude alliance as his defense against future hurt, the adult may not recall such a decision; or even be aware of why, every time an opportunity arises to get close to someone, he finds himself overwhelmed with or immobilized by despair.

Because, to the child, at least, nothing is more important than being loved and experiencing the joy of being found lovable, this kind of despair may well attach itself to life itself, in a feeling-judgement, whereby he attempts to protect himself against further disappointment — by refusing to expect that life will ever bring any real fulfillment or happiness. This refusal to expect good things to happen is frequently viewed by the "instinctively" despairing individual as permanent part of their personality since it has been there for so long (since childhood).

Sometimes despair eventually ends up being self-directed in a rather subtle fashion. Problems are difficulties temporarily experienced as insoluble. Since the answers to the challenges they present are not immediately evident, we experience a frustration in that regard. A frustration which prompts us to search for their solution. On the other hand, this frustration may degenerate into despair, if, after constant effort, we are unable to solve the problem.

Case in point: the child, just mentioned, who unsuccessfully tries to win the affection of his mother or father. Perhaps this is the first major problem that the child experiences *emotionally*. In time, this child may come to realize that he is quite capable of successfully rising to the occasion of all sorts of other challenges. On a very deep level, however, he may find himself reacting to certain kinds of difficulties in relating out of a rigid despair: *situations will never change, because people don't change*, our child (now an adult, perhaps) finds himself thinking and feeling most intensely.

Such individuals often find themselves unable to commit themselves to changes they desire and acknowledge as presently appropriate in their own lives. They are despairing over the possibility of any positive change occurring *in their own relationship with themselves*. It is quite possible, after all, to experience *yourself* as an insoluble problem.

Hostility, (which Ernest Larsen has aptly characterized as the "continual state of defend/attack" or "the felt need to always be in a fighting pose") can develop in a very similar fashion and so manifest itself as a regular "fixture" of certain personalities.[18] If a child is neglected, or even sometimes mistreated on a regular basis, anger may develop as the predominant emotion by which she instinctively attempts to defend herself. She may be angry at not only the offending parent or parents, for example, but even life itself, as a result of not being able to win their love or fend off their unlove. On the other hand, she may be allowed little or no opportunity or outlet to vent her anger. Simultaneously, she may find herself hating the one or ones who so frequently bring her hurt. That hatred may also find little chance to express itself. The personality may be forced, therefore, to develop under such negative circumstances, masking a permanent anger or hatred that generally can't be masked all that well indefinitely. In time, others will see its signs in the face of that unfortunate individual, in her bodily rigidity, or tone of voice, etc. These acquaintances will be sure to keep their distance, as a result. The hostility-afflicted child or adolescent is now able to grasp that her surly way of being with people keeps them backed off. At that point, she may permanently choose to retain her hostility as effective bulwark against future relationships, or, as a powerful tool in the service of manipulating others, the "winning through intimidation" approach to life.

As Dr. Schneiders puts it, if such a person has nothing to do with people, they can do nothing to him or her.[19] Once again, the defects of the original relationships are allowed to spew their poison upon later ones. And, if despair over love can develop into despair over life, so too is hostility against love able to broaden itself out into hostility against life. It may also attach itself to aspects of life against which the hostile individual will regularly rage spitefully. In such instances this raging is very often justified by all kinds of "reasonable" excuses.

(One more note on winning through intimidation. Many Christians I know have prayed to be delivered from an obvious bondage to anger. They hate the embarrassingly childish displays they find themselves giving way to. On the other hand, they love the fact that their anger has enabled them to get their own way, so many times. On the deepest level of who they are, then, they really don't want to let go of the paybacks that their bullying "companion" has won for them. Their prayer, therefore, sadly goes unanswered . . .)

More often than we realize, that persistently heavy black mood, so apparently impossible to shake off, is a self-directed variant of what was just described above. Much depression is the fruit of denied or disguised self-anger, or its extreme, self-rage. Or even camouflaged anger or rage at others; an anger or rage we cannot get ourselves to admit is there.

Much depression over relationships in trouble (or even apathy in regard to their prospective repair) is, for instance, primarily a deep-seated but disguised anger against one's partner. An anger that people would not allow themselves to feel because they deemed it inappropriate.

This self-anger is often connected to a secret grieving over what we sense ourselves to have already lost, like a married partner. Such mourning is also over having lost "part of ourselves," since we had considered that one we once loved, to have been just that.

Depression is often associated with a physical tiredness, which is usually the expression of an emotional tiredness, as well. The rejection we feel deriving from the actual or feared loss tends to drain us of the self-esteem we need to tackle life's challenges. It's just too difficult to handle even the ordinary tasks of daily existence without that buoyancy and enthusiasm which automatically issues forth from properly valuing oneself.

Sometimes, however, depression's tiredness is the result of having unwisely used up the energies of our personality by consistently feeling forced to project to others, and even ourselves, that we are calm, controlled, untroubled, etc., when we aren't: namely, when we are actually quite the opposite.

Imagine being compelled to hold up one heavy mask after another in front of our faces. After a while, our arms would start to feel rubbery and finally we would have to drop them down because of fatigue, revealing our true face. Some forms of depression are nothing else but fatigue of the psyche's "arms."

The emotion of fear is also able to be unfortunately integrated into the personality as a permanent defensive quality that is able to weaken its fabric and flaw its beauty. That buried fear, erected like the above emotions into an enduring buttress against further hurt, is most commonly referred to as anxiety.

If *fear* is the emotion that signals us that something is wrong and that we had better get ready to fight or take flight, anxiety, in this context, is likewise an alarm. An alarm, however, that alerts us to a danger we are hard pressed to identify, or a danger that we are very likely to misidentify.

To feel rejection is to find ourselves infallibly primed for further rejection. To feel the pain of rejection is to simultaneously feel the fear of still more rejection. To suspect that we are unloveable is to invariably fear that we will be shown up to be even more unloveable. To feel that we have failed, for instance, to win our parents' affection is to fear that we are doomed to fail to win the affection of other significant persons, on down the road, as well. And following the same logic we already mentioned, how easy it is, once we fear that we are "failures in love" to fear that we shall also turn out to be "failures in life."

Such fears, we certainly would want to shield from others. Such fears we surely would want to hide even from ourselves. And so, we very often do. Fearful of our (imagined) unloveableness, and so, of future rejection; afraid that we have failed the most important "test" (of winning our parents' affection) and so, afraid that new failures are soon to follow; frightened that there is nothing at our core because there is little or no love lodged there; and so, frightened that there is nothing to hold us firmly together in the face of life's demands and pressures — only to thereupon deny such horrendous fears — many of us often find ourselves feeling terribly anxious. A sense of helplessness in the face of impending doom, powerlessness in the face of immanent danger, insecurity in the face of an enemy that will prove to be too strong.

No matter how practiced or advanced we are in our prayer-lives, we always need to listen afresh for the Father's assurance that we, like Jesus, are a beloved child in whom He delights. He, and only He, is perfect love. Only love that is perfect can cast out this kind of fear and keep it cast out. (1 Jn. 4:18)

Anxiety about having to face our hurts, grow beyond our immaturities, or having to submit to the practical realities of His ways not always neatly coinciding with our ways will somehow coexist within us—next to trust in His ongoing goodness, hope in His faithfulness to his promises. That kind of anxiety, after all, Jesus himself knew and never more frighteningly than in the Garden and on the Cross. God-man He was; but Superman, never.

That Lord surely insists on delivering us from our deep seated, "irrevocable" decisions not to ever feel rejection again—the deadness of heart we wish upon ourselves when we are let down by someone we had trusted or loved. Closing down sectors of one's spirit to prevent further hurt is as a death-wish in His eyes. Life, rather, is riskily reaching out again in hopes that the faithless ones, the unfaithful ones, might turn and be healed, He would have us come to realize.

Abraham Heschel reminds us that those Old Testament saints, the prophets, were individuals who always "felt fiercely," because they were called to make visible and audible not only the words, but the powerful emotions of that God who has felt fiercely first, as well. To be in His presence was always somehow to be privileged to share in feeling what He felt.[20]

When we insisted above that all of us are summoned and empowered to feel His presence, we meant it. We didn't mean that "feeling His presence" is always predominantly an experience of tasting and seeing His goodness. (cf. Ps. 34:8) Sometimes, feeling His presence is tasting His tears and sharing His sadness. People who never "feel" God, after having reached out for Him in faith, as we suggested in an earlier chapter, are very often people whose feeling side is temporarily closed-down in some significant area of their inner person. Their under-emotionality, doubts about their loveableness or cool indifference to love's warmth on the level where they meet fellow humans, clogs the feeling-flow on the plane where they meet God, as well.

Such individuals may even be included among the most devoted and courageous among us, in terms of their consistent service of God and their compassionate service of man. But if they believe that they were never meant to feel His love, this side of Eternity, they are wrong. And His healing can be properly appropriated, so as to prove them wrong. Never will having been proved wrong, be shown to be such a surprisingly delightful experience, as in this particular instance.

To go on to discuss and analyze even more of the predominant feelings affecting our day-to-day living is beyond the scope of this book. Jealousy, loneliness, grief, and boredom, for instance, are just a few of the feelings or moods that likewise powerfully influence the way we look at and respond to the challenges of existence. Another feeling, that almost all of us experience frequently, and which significantly affects the lifestyles of not a few of us is a disturbing sense of personal guilt.

In the eyes of many contemporary authors in the field of psychology, however, — with the notable exception of Dr. Karl (*Whatever Became of Sin?*) Menninger — guilt is the one feeling we need to properly acknowledge, only so that we can summarily reject it as being utterly useless, and invariably injurious.

We will now proceed to disagree with that contention. Before we do, however, we must first address ourselves to the kernel of truth, contained in some of the criticisms leveled by the "anti-guilt" psychologists. There *is* such a thing as a guilt which may rightly be termed unhealthy and even neurotic. This kind of self-condemning feeling needs to be seen for what it is, so that we can clearly distinguish between it and authentic impressions of feeling guilty.

Only just a few weeks before these lines were written I came across another unhappy victim of this not uncommon malady. She was a young woman who had started to attend Bible studies and prayer meetings sponsored by the Christian Community to which this writer belongs. The more she sat in on the meetings, the more upset and anxious she became. Eventually, when she decided that it was time to come to me to discuss her difficulties, she expressed misgivings over not being as good as the majority of the people also attending these meetings (who, of course, just *had* to notice her "superficiality"). She also shared how guilty she was feeling over not being able to adequately respond to the challenges to live the Christian life that the meetings regularly presented her with.

The meetings had been focusing, as usual, on God's goodness and the availability of His love for us; on how that love can gently heal us of the hurts of the past, so that we can increasingly experience increased freedom and strength in the giving over of our selves to be unique channels of this love and healing to others.

What she "heard," however, was something quite the opposite. In her mind, a vengeful, angry "God" was calling her to admit that she was a miserable sinner and to immediately change her wicked ways. Her abiding impression was that she was being constantly summoned to a moral and spiritual level which she could never possibly attain to. A Perfectionist God was demanding of her that she demonstrate an on-the-spot perfection attached to all of her thoughts, words and deeds. Her prayers, accordingly, could never be good enough, or frequent enough. Her charities could never be pure enough or often enough. Her repentances could never be sincere enough, or thorough enough.

Something within her prompted her to automatically and extravagantly distort her image of who God was, not to mention her image of who she was — especially in her relationship to Him. That "guilt-producing" something had little to do with the present, and so was likely to have very much to do with her past, in my estimation. That impression of mine, by the way, was confirmed by her rigid resistance to my suggestion that we might need to rather closely examine her early life and how she had related to her parents during that period.

Something like this had probably happened. Because her mother and father were experiencing significant difficulties in their relationship with one another at the time when she was born, neither of them were able to show her very much affection — the affection God intended for all of us to constantly experience from our earliest days. Instead, then, of feeling joy as a baby over their delight in her, she ended up knowing a lonely emptiness, a mistrustful sense of isolation which developed into fears of unloveableness. This was soon accompanied by the "instinct" to start hating herself. Not getting the attention of love, she started to scramble for attention of any kind. Such attention was bound to often bring irate, disciplinary interventions: the angry over-reactions, most likely, of parents already angry for other reasons. Perfunctory "love" and noisy wrath were, most likely, her two most common experiences of being in the presence of Mom or Dad, along with not being noticed, at all.

Not knowing, then, which of those *three* responses she might draw from these earliest authority figures of her life, she was already programmed, as a small child, for the reactions that would pathologically well up from within her, later on in life, when she decided to chance going into the presence of God, that Authority Figure, par excellence. If she could never be sure, as a child, whether the parent would greet her with anemic acceptance, angry criticism, or chilling indifference, as an adult she could only be similarly anxious that the Divine Parent might lay a nasty put-down on her, instead of extending a gracious welcome.[21]

Or, perhaps, it was just that she started to hate them for being so apparently uncaring or unloving, and then began to feel like an ogre for hating her own mother and father. As we all are inclined to do, she would naturally try to hide from herself, as well as everybody else, these reasons of hers as to why she ought to be rejected and condemned. Later on, feeling guilty for who she was, she would have to find contrived reasons for feeling guilty for what she did.

Sometimes people experience another kind of pseudo-guilt. They do something in violation of their consciences. Then, they inwardly castigate themselves and wilfully generate guilt-feelings, with which to berate themselves. The rationale behind this practice is that, while the individual in question has no real intention of changing his or her ways, he or she wants to maintain the image of a "moral person" because only a moral person would feel this guilty about having authored such a misdeed.[22]

Real guilt feelings, on the other hand, occur spontaneously. They are the result of having considered which values and standards are proper to live by, and then having made them one's own. These convictions about good and evil accompany an act of self-appraisal in the light of such values and standards. I feel tense or anxious or regretful, because, accordingly, I have fallen short of what I have committed myself to; I have not lived up to the qualities of personhood that I have come to see as essential to being authentically human; or in the case of a Christian, essential to being a true follower of Jesus Christ.

When an individual feels uncomfortable because he is violating the ethical principles enjoined by his parents, set forth by society, or insisted upon by his church, he is experiencing a form of guilt based in the fear of not conforming to what others believe to be wrong. All of us have to pass through this stage on the way to adopting a conscience that is truly our own. When, however, I am consistently prayerful because I believe that God has personally called me to be this way; when I am constantly caring because I know that this is the way that I, as a Christian, must live; when I repeatedly forgive those who have wronged me as a result of having come to believe that only in this way can I be true to being in the image of the Crucified One, etc., *then* I have made values central to the *my* values. They are a part of me — a true dimension of who I am.

Should I fail to embody these values in my day to day living, however, I will spontaneously feel uncomfortable with myself, or anxious about myself. This feeling automatically accompanies the awareness that I have not been true to myself. Or, as Vincent Bilotta has put it, that I have in some way betrayed who I am, or who I have committed myself to be.[23]

Even the most balanced of us stands in need of regular dialogue with herself. In need of constant, direct and thorough communication with her attitudes, feelings and motives. There can be no broadly-based and consistent experience of mental and emotional health without it. Whatever within us we refuse to be fully in touch with is sure to secretly, yet surely, control us, misguide us, defeat us. *Don't let the light within you be darkness*, Jesus counseled. (Mk. 6:23, Lk. ll:34) Don't let your awareness of who you are and what you're about within be the "wisdom" of "I'd rather not know."

Probably the biggest reason we'd rather not know is that we are still highly doubtful of our basic loveableness and so, significantly self-rejected. More bad news about the inner me, even more indication of interior blight would simply be impossible to handle. So we build our own tricky defense system, rapid deployment style, to shoot down any self-truths invading our personal "airspace" with a speed and accuracy more efficient than the best anti-missile missile ever invented.

We spoke, in an earlier chapter, about two kinds of prayer, or two different aspects of our coming before God. The first takes care of the reason for our shifty defensiveness: our rejection of self. We keep asking the One who has such infinite affection for us to drain every drop of that poisonous hatred out of us, even as we let Him help us to love ourselves, as He loves us.

The second deals immediately with our preference for walled-offness from self and others. We bring what we believe to be the case about circumstances troubling us, or what we find ourselves feeling negatively about to that Lord who cares so deeply about us, and we ask Him for his light on these matters. Things like convictions concerning certain people's alleged lack of positive qualities; or our own painful feelings of rejection, loneliness, misunderstanding, anger, bitterness, anxiety, etc.: "Why am I so convinced, Lord, that so-and-so is irreformably dishonest, or not worth getting to know? Am I really upset about what I think I'm upset about, or is it something else?"

How often we go to Him, only aware that we are "upset." Even those of us who are bold enough to bring their upsetness before Him are so often only looking for instantaneous relief: "Make me feel better, Lord — right now."

If that kind of prayer doesn't seem to do much good for us, it may well be the result of His wanting to show us more about why we are feeling the way we are feeling, as we suggested earlier, and our not liking that. He may want to show us that we are harboring resentments, feeding springs of self-pity, giving way to envy, burying anger. He may need to show us that our being "upset" is a combination of having rashly judged someone and the accompanying guilt we feel over our phony self-righteousness. Or, that it's a mixture of jealousy and bitterness. Or, any number of things not so respectable or excusable, but conveniently labeled as making us "upset" or "depressed," because those characterizations don't necessarily mean that we've been childish, sinful or stupid — let alone responsible for why we might feel the way we do.

We not only need to make a commitment to daily prayer. We also need to commit ourselves to that kind of prayer wherein we are regularly prepared to ask for and have the Lord shed as much light as He sees fit upon what is murky, twisted or otherwise off-the-beam in what we believe, think or desire.

That light is not the harsh glare of the expose' reporter's flash-camera. That criticism is not the despair-toned lecture of a sentencing judge. That summons to deeper honesty is not the perfectionist nit-picking of an unforgiving and authoritarian parent.

That light is gentle. That light is lovingly hopeful. That light is ever accompanied by a confidence in our ability to be brought into truer, deeper and purer communication with ourselves and with Him.

We said earlier that hope is a basic human emotion, a stirring within us based upon the visible prospect of things getting better. The gift of God's hope is more than that. It's the empowering we get to enthusiastically and optimistically push forward when there is no apparent prospect of things getting better. It can look at all the obstacles and opposition that turns merely human hope into despair and still look forward to victory and turnaround.

Rollo May somewhere describes hope as "joy, borrowed from the future." If faith is, as Hebrews says, "the evidence of things unseen," (11:1) then hope is a rejoicing in the present over what faith assures us is yet to come. But not simply joy over what is yet to come, as promised by our God. It is also a rejoicing over His being here right now. His being lovingly here for us. As well as His already committing Himself to the working all things together for the good right now. We can look forward to a future full of goodness, because He is creating that future right now, and the victory of Calvary-Easter is only the first installment.

Jurgen Moltmann reminds us of a much ignored biblical truth, when he insists that hope is more than a feeling or experience, but *a command*.[24] We need nothing less than God's hope if we are to stand up to all the negatives that life is sure to throw at us. And we can't fulfill that command of His to hope, unless we expect Him to be pumping it into our hearts when we find special reason to be down; unless we expect Him to be pouring it over bruised feelings at such moments, as well as flooding our attitudes and responses with it, as well. Receiving that gift anew, answering that command again and again, we will find ourselves decreasingly anxious about not being able to survive a prayerful truth-session with Him. We will simultaneously discover ourselves to be increasingly anxious to invite Him to stand as constant mediator between what we immediately think and feel and what we most deeply think and feel, on the way to what we ought to think and need to feel.

Armed with this sort of hope and this sort of prayerfulness, the kind of insights provided by books like this will be appropriately brought to mind at the right time and brought to bear, healing-wise, in the right areas of who we are.

Chapter 14

Healed For Each Other

People I know have taken to heart the message of the preceding chapters. No positive suggestions offered to the reader of this book have been left untested—either in the counseling parlor, or the crucible of life. Sometimes suddenly, more often gradually, so many of the clients I have worked with have come to the realization that the healing power of Jesus' love is truly operative in their lives.

Cruel memories no longer haunt the present. Crippling anxieties cease to rob the future of its promise. Overwhelming despairs fail to chain its "victims" to the past. Habits of self-pity become ancient history. Guilts, false and real, no longer impede new beginnings. Chronic mistrust is replaced by the courage to risk love. Nagging doubts of one's own worth are evicted by a confidence that comes from recognizing oneself as a child, beloved of the Father. Compulsiveness yields to self-control. Angry aggression to gentle strength. Masks become faces. Projecting one's weaknesses onto the others is increasingly detected and rejected in favor of an ongoing commitment to self-understanding. Almost automatic impulses to bury the unpleasant are transformed into a calm willingness to face such things in the company of the One who promised to face it with us . . .

That doesn't mean on the other hand, that the way of inner healing proposed here hasn't "failed." What the wise man has observed, concerning Christianity's "failure" in general— that it hasn't been tried and found wanting; it simply hasn't been tried—applies just as surely here. Where long-forgotten or newly-discovered wisdoms as to how we might avail ourselves of the full riches of His grace—present and superabundant, beyond our wildest imaginings—are sadly left untried.

We have made many concessions throughout to wounded humanity's sad affection for grotesque displays of over-complicatedness; its fascination with a sophistication that scorns anything clear or simple. All of this, it seems, is based in misguided compensation for our recurring sense of an inner, naked emptiness, a fear of personal insignificance that we don't know what to do with . . .

How can a citizen of the twentieth century, seemingly in school forever, answer a call to accept God's love as healing, in all simplicity, let alone appreciate simplicity as a hallmark of what that healing is intended to accomplish? Not very easily or enthusiastically, it would seem. The want to have our over-complicatedness affirmed rather than removed has to rank as one of the top reasons why many folks I know don't get healed.

None, of this, however, is to deny the delicateness of the human personality and the many-splendored glory of its ability to reflect and radiate the infinite goodness and greatness of the One in whose image we are created. We are healed (or restored to that image) in order to mirror God's loving kindness according to our own uniqueness and never-to-be repeatedness. We also may need to appropriate this healing in stages, not only, as we grow through the cycles of life, but as we shed the various cocoons of earlier immaturities. The seed must "die" in order to blossom as bud and then as flower. The husks of self-centeredness or self-importance must fall away, if what is true and permanent in us is to come forth mature and endure (cf. Jn. 12:24-26). We are trying to avoid two extremes. The first is the (very often overly-psychologized) sophistication of our current culture, just referred to. The other will be precisely what people embracing such a position will often accuse us of taking: that of a fundamentalist Christianity, comfortable only with the simplistic.

Labels are often dangerous. They frequently achieve the opposite of what is intended. We will try, therefore, to describe what we see fundamentalism to be in its essence: a crippling of the spirit rather than a doctrinal stance. (In so doing, we may even end up reassuring certain individuals who aren't afraid to call themselves fundamentalists and yet who also aren't afraid to grow. This writer is privileged to have known a number of Christians, who while belonging to denominations that overtly claim to be fundamentalist are, nevertheless, free spirits in the

Lord and shining witnesses to the maturing power of His grace within them.)

There is such a thing as an unhealthy affection for the simple, a crutchy need for things to be so absolutely black and white that life is robbed, thereby, of the color God gave it. It is the opposite of the need to over-complicate things. This compulsion to oversimplify, however, still seems to be based in the same basic hurt that spawns pseudo-sophistication — the deep insecurity of not knowing oneself as having worth and value. The sort of fundamentalists we refer to here would seem to feel this insecurity, primarily, as a sense of being out of control. They suspect that they will feel okay if they can simply be put in control — as opposed to having themselves buttressed by a feeling of self-importance, derived from being so darned complicated. They *will* be put in control, they feel, if they can be supplied with the answers or THE ANSWER to the basic meaning or purpose of life. Because they basically sense themselves to be sinking in a hostile sea and close to drowning, they clutch desperately to any passing plank as the solution to their need for saving. And they clutch with the grip of death.

They are indeed grateful for the plank that providentially presents itself. But they are so focused upon it, that should there be other planks around, out of which, perhaps, an entire raft might be fashioned, they are unable to see them. At least as having any value. Surely, such could only be prospective torpedoes that might knock *their* plank, the original plank, from their grasp.

Such people generally believe that they are embracing God and the meaning He has appointed for their lives. In reality they could only be clutching to Him out of fear. And not really to *Him*, either. They are clutching fearfully to old (that is, the earliest) ideas that in all probability, they were violently force-fed about Him, or even clinging sentimentally to memories of a now-old experience of His love or grace. Since, however, sentimentality is a saccharine substitute for real sentiment, even this is most likely the product of fear; the fear of letting go of the old and reaching out for the new.

Faith does bring with it an assurance of things hoped for (Heb.11:1); a certainty about the existence of things we don't see. It is a knowing in the heart that we are loved by God. But, as indicated earlier, it also is a call to leave behind what we're sure of in order to go out and embrace what we're not yet sure of: "By faith Abraham, when called to go to a place he would later receive as his inheritance, obeyed and went, even though he did not know where he was going (Heb. 11:8,NIV). [1]

If Abraham had stayed home playing videotaped reruns of the original vision, he might have been able to entertain himself with thrilling reveries of a once marvelous moment. Those pious and sentimental thrills, however, would have kept him home, not an inch closer to Canaan than the first day of his call. His fear-locked belief in the God who had given him a vision would actually have prevented him from allowing that same God to fulfill the vision.

We can't put God on tape. We must allow him to keep broadcasting his message *live*. The past, no matter how sacred, must never be allowed to eclipse the present. Any blessing God has once bestowed on us must never be thought of as his last and best. No insight into his goodness, no awareness of his forgiveness, no realization of his healing, no matter how real or how powerful ought ever be allowed to establish itself as His full or final revelation of Himself to us. He is always making things new. He is always aching to show us more. He is ever intent on leading us deeper (cf. Acts 26:15-18).

Fear, we have suggested, is why many folks cling detrimentally to the old. Sometimes, because the old was scared into us via an evangelism of intimidation. Sometimes, because we're just afraid of risking the new, of letting go of our grip on the past, like the acrobat who would like to grab onto his partner's hands but just can't because he doesn't want to let go of his trapeze ropes.

A common alternative for me, if I am this kind of a frightened believer, is to then over-spiritualize what I perceive God doing in my heart. It becomes secret and so "mystical" that it has nothing to do with the secular "trivia" of day-in and day-out living. Because I invest so much effort in prayer, bible-reading, church-going, etc., I surely *must* be graced, holy or whatever. The fact that people don't like me and avoid me regularly is probably because I'm so spiritually mature. In such cases, (tragically so very widespread) personality flaws like cold aloofness, arrogant superiority, gossipy fault-finding, and so on, become rationalized into being Christian virtues, somehow. Neurotic traits are deemed to be badges of righteousness rather than recognized as areas that stand in need of healing, or barriers to true relationships.

But Jesus indicated that the work which is begun deep in our hearts, even far below the surface of our full consciousness, is still meant to be seen in the way we speak and the way we act, the way we love and the way we work. The light we are given, we are to radiate outwardly. We are to let it shine so clearly that those we rub shoulders with will be prompted to acknowledge that God's goodness is surely there (cf. Mt. 5:13-15).

The spiritual is to clothe itself in the material. Grace is to become visible in nature. God's word is to take flesh in us. The heavenly is to reveal itself through the earthly by ennobling it. The divine, when it is allowed to genuinely and gradually invade and inhabit the human, can only leave our humanity more and more like Jesus' humanity. A truly healed heart is only able to gravitate towards giving evidence of a healed attitudinal life and emotional life. The new *unity* we have with God will want to express itself in a new closeness to our neighbor. This new affection we have for Him will long to share itself in words and deeds of love, bestowed upon all we encounter.

One final word to our fundamentalist, the individual in bondage to a fear-frozen faith. (According to this definition, by the way, all of us are a least infected with a little bit of the malady.) God Himself may well have given you the very trapeze you now cling to. Now, however, He is the One on that other trapeze you can see swinging toward you. They are *His* loving arms reaching out to you, *His* strong hands ready to grab onto yours. Let go then. He won't miss catching you and He's hardly likely to drop you . . .

The author of this book has not only engaged in quite a bit of counseling over the years; he has also shepherded a Charismatic Christian Community for fourteen years. Its membership has, in effect, heard every word of *Healer of Hearts, Healer of Minds* presented to it in one teaching after another, at their Bible studies and prayer meetings, over those years. A goodly number of these brothers and sisters of mine, however, after giving evidence of genuine conversion to Christ in their lives, and significant inner healing at the beginning of their spiritual walk, have obviously stopped growing. And not only that — they still can't seem to stop projecting *their* problems onto their spouses, children or each other. They often selfishly choose their own will and way, as they refuse to consistently seek first the Kingdom. Now and then a few, even relapse into things like alcohol or drug abuse, greedy over-consumerism or sexual promiscuity, etc. Their prayer lives, while connected to a two or three night-a-week prayer meeting or bible study commitments appear to be oppressed by something heavy, drab and joyless. They have not only lost their first love, but give evidence of neurotic styles of chronic self-pity, snobbish indifference, superficial sociability, along with a generalized lack of passion for the spread of God's kingdom which clouds and darkens what was once bright and promising witness to Christ. Since, on the other hand, they are still neither inclined to buy into secular humanism's slick sophistication or the rigidity of chauvinistic fundamentalism, where does the problem lie?

A number of us can give testimony of having known God's love for us personally. Most of that number would admit to having been driven into His arms because of our pain — and not on account of a long and passionate quest for truth. We finally seek his therapeutic intervention in our lives because it just hurts too much. We therefore give God a chance. At first, we cautiously invite Jesus into the center of our hearts and then, when we discover that He actually took us up on that invitation, we even enthusiastically invite Him to accompany us on our daily rounds ("Are you running with me, Jesus?"). Some even go that important step further and solicit His guidance or Lordship. ("Am I seeking your will and doing your bidding, Jesus?). If so, then we not only know Him as Savior but acknowledge Him practically as Lord. In such instances, the glow of first love, the enthusiasm for this new commitment stirs our feelings and fires our energies. It is a whole new world out there. We've thrown off something burdensome and painful from our past. In gratitude we want to dedicate the new spring in our step, the new lightness in our hearts, the new brightness in our spirits, to Him. How could we ever want to let go of that? Yet sometimes we do. And it still has a lot to do with pain. The pain of further healing. The pain of unselfish giving. Let's take the second kind of pain first.[2]

There comes a time when it seems — quite correctly — as if the Lord is saying something like this to us: "Child, we're not going to presently focus very much on this or that inner scar or personality weakness. Just concentrate on praying for persecuted Russian Christians, every chance you get. Think about *their* pain, *their* discouragement, *their* fears, *their* doubts . . . ," or "Do you see that secretary at the next desk? See how discouraged she is? Make her pain your own. Commit yourself to cheering her up, helping her out. Invite her to lunch at the first opportunity. Lay yourself open to the possibility of her sharing her burdens with you. Pray a lot for her, too!"

> "Is not this the kind of fasting I have chosen: to loose the chains of injustice and untie the cords of the yoke, to set the oppressed free and break every yoke? Is it not to share your food with the hungry and to provide the poor wanderer with shelter when you see the naked to clothe him and not to turn away from your own flesh and blood? Then your light will break forth like the dawn and your righteousness will go before you and the glory of the LORD will be your rear guard. Then you will call and the LORD will answer; you will cry for help, and He will say: "Here I am." (Is.58-6-9,NIV; see up to V. 14)

Our healing will come from unselfishly giving to others. At least some of our further healing will only ensue if we find ourselves compassionately reaching out to those about us in *their* pain. If we do this, we will not, of course, have as much time as we used to have to concentrate on our own problems and work on our own healings. Little or no time for self-examination. Little or no time for prayerful self-analysis. Little or no time to seek further wisdom as to why we feel so down, weak, or powerless in this or that situation affecting our inner or outer lives, or both.

307

This summons from the Lord to come out of ourselves and put somebody else's pain or need first, or even somebody else's healing first is the perfect antidote to a deadly tendency we all carry deep within us: The tendency to manipulate prayer for inner healing into an excuse for self-preoccupation. The tendency to so prolong a necessary quest for self-understanding, that it transforms itself into a narcissistic quest for scab-picking or scar-gazing; The tendency to transform degeneratively the necessary practice of a dialogue with the inner self in His presence into the destructive practice of self-pity-drenched sympathizing with one's woundedness (or even a self-congratulatory enthusing over one's healedness) as we talk *at* a present God we really won't listen to; the tendency to turn Jesus into a (quack) psychoanalyst who can only heal us by inches, through years and years of prolonged therapy; or rather, into one who cannot really heal us, but who is certainly willing to reassure us about how victimized we've been by life, mother or whomever. A fake Jesus, in other words, who helps us carry a "cross" the real Jesus wanted to rid us of.

A common reaction to such a summons to concern ourselves with somebody else's problems is not always out-and-out refusal, but a seemingly logical insistence upon a bit of procrastination: "I can see the Lord is healing me so that I can be freed up enough to spend some of my energies helping others. But I don't think that time has come yet. I've still got too much woundedness or weakness holding me back, even though, thanks be to God, I can see the light at the end of the tunnel . . ."

He does not wait until we are fully healed, totally sanctified or completely put together before He deems us fit to go out into the world on His behalf. Like the seventy-two who get sent out to preach and heal only one third of the way or so through the course on discipleship, we, too, are given missions by the Master at a moment that almost certainly seems premature to us. Just when we feel we're getting the knack of receiving His love and accepting His healing, He commands "Go out and love! Go out and heal! Your internship is at hand."

Oh, yes. He'll call us back to his bosom; back to sit at the Teacher's feet. But not until we've gone out and produced. Then, before we know it, the new wisdom we receive and the new sense of being all the more beloved will lead to new sharings of these things with others, new attempts at loving the unloved and the apparently unloveable.

Thank God for the saints and mystics. Every now and then, however, instead of inspiring us to follow in their holy footsteps they effectively end up scaring us away. Perhaps because they "won their haloes" (in good faith, of course) more by dint of their exercise of the will-power which they thought God required of them, than the grace He wanted to empower them with. Grace is there to make it easier. His love is there for us to love with, precisely because human love is just not resilient enough. His Spirit is willing to produce marvelous fruits of love, joy, peace, patience, self-control faithfulness, gentleness, and the like precisely because human nature's power to generate virtue tends to degenerate into traits characterized by the harsh, demanding and brittle, not to mention, the self-righteous and perfectionistic.

Maybe some of our hallowed fathers and mothers in-the-faith died as martyrs, as their Savior did; but that doesn't mean that Jesus ever wanted them to live out a martyrdom of non-fulfillment. The best of the saints, like Francis, knew the experience of perfect joy. But even Francis overdid the self-sacrificial thing and ended up apologizing to "Brother Ass," the body he'd been far too demanding of.

Jesus came to show us how to love *this life* to the full (cf. Jn.10:10). How to be sacrificial, and yet happy. How to be unselfish without neglecting our legitimate personal needs. How to be other-centered without giving up things like the enjoyment of friendship, nature's beauty and even a good glass of wine.

We can follow in Jesus' steps because He loved life, loved this planet and loved to share in life's joys, along with its other inhabitants. While He knew crosses on the way to the Cross, throughout His life; while He gave and gave of Himself even to the point of exhaustion at times, it was only in response to the overabundance of hurt He encountered. Not because He loved suffering or hated rest and recreation.

So many of us, I'm afraid, fear the fullness of the Christlike life because we fear the pain of a harsh misery-filled, totally sacrificial life, selfless to the point of non-fulfillment. If so, we fear a caricature of Jesus and a caricature of His lifestyle.

Yes, it hurts to give, it hurts to love, it hurts to keep on giving and loving. But not the way we think, when we let His love and His compassion well up in us and overflow into kindly words and caring deeds. We come to learn the secret of leaning more perfectly on the One who dwells within us. We allow Him to do His thing in us and through us. His energy doesn't peter out, His caring doesn't thin out, His goodness doesn't run out. Even though, of course, we'll find ourselves needing to rest, needing to refresh ourselves, needing to enjoy life's blessings anew, needing even to just be alone with the One who loves us, as if we were the only person in the world. If so, then we will find ourselves increasingly freed of the fear of pain, the pain of being like Christ, the pain of loving like Christ. We'll know that any discomfort we endure will be more than outweighed by the joy and fulfillment of becoming the person we were always intended to become: *this* unique reflection of the Son of God, appointed to radiate a portion of His presence, compassion and healing to *this* part of the world at *this* point in history.

The second major reason, I believe, that impedes plateaued brothers and sisters of mine, that prevents their Savior from finishing the good work He obviously started in them (cf. Phil.1:6) is fear of the pain of further healing. I also believe that this fear is often just another word for laziness.

For a long time, I'm afraid, I had misjudged Alcoholics Anonymous. One member after another shared with me how A.A. had miraculously gotten them off the bottle — once and for all. They were healed. All else was just maintenance. They could never go back to booze, of course. But with the advantages of the membership's mutual support, they'd be able to resume normal living and maintain their sobriety.

How sadly superficial, I thought. But, after all, at least the destructiveness of alcoholic abuse had been checked. That itself was no small accomplishment. Then, one day, I reluctantly consented to read *Twelve Steps and Twelve Traditions*.[3] I was overjoyed to discover that the A.A.'ers I'd hitherto encountered had misrepresented the program. That marvelous book (outlining the official position of the program) counselled, in effect, that once you'd dealt with the pain-killer, you then had to begin dealing with the pain. The problem, or problems, that literally drove you to drink in the first place. That latter goal was even more important than the elimination of one's addiction, it insisted.

The Christian who views the healing of the problem that originally catapulted him or her into the arms of Christ as THE PROBLEM is generally just as mistaken as the reformed alcoholic who believes that all he or she needs is deliverance from the compulsion to drink. The problem goes a lot deeper in either situation. And in either case, considerably more healing is still needed, no matter how glorious one's beginnings in the new life of grace or sobriety might have been.

Love has let us all down (human love, that is). But love has let as all down a little differently. We are bruised, therefore, in different "parts" of our inner anatomy. So, we each carry our woundedness a little differently. Just as we also tend to shield those wounds a little differently and fend off possible future blows with different styles of feints, blocks, jabs or holds.

We've had a lifetime to discover all sorts of ingenious ways to bury our traumas, deaden our sensitivities to their painfulness and develop scads of compensations that cover them up, and even proclaim, at times, the opposite of what we are most afraid or ashamed of.

The original problem was unfortunate; the self-doctoring (or cover-up quackery) even more unfortunate. Even if skilled therapists were able to uncover and help us with some of them,, only the patient genius of God Himself would be able to find them all, let alone have the boldness to suggest that we might want to pray to be fully free of them. Allow me to now present a little overview of the healing process I sometimes find myself forced to present to clients at the moment when I sense that they might be digging in their heels. I realize its imperfection. I also know that it may run the risk of bastardizing the mysterious, sovereign and uniquely different approaches that His healing may need to take in certain people's lives:

"You may have come to believe that God has worked a major healing of personality in your life and so indeed He has.

For you, it represents something terribly important and He knows that. He rejoices with you. From His point of view, however, the healing you have received is minor-compared to deeper healings He is presently prepared to bring about in your life. Because these things are generally less obvious, more inclined to be hidden beneath the surface of your life or consciousness, you might not deem them to be important; or you might regard them as not awfully significant; you might not even be able to acknowledge their existence. Don't let that upset you. If you prayerfully lay yourself open for the *next* healing, He will begin to reveal to you what you need to know about it in all gentleness and hope. (He is ever the Lord of: 'only one thing is necessary').

"Do you remember how quick and relatively painless the original operation was, once you turned to Him? And how glad you felt when it was over? For all the value it had in itself, it also was there to help you grow in faith. To increase your trust in His skill, in His will to heal and in His determination to cause the least amount of pain He can. Because this new healing goes deeper and is concerned with problems so very rooted in your inner self, you may find yourself instinctively resisting and even overwhelmed with fear. Recommit yourself to Him and once again entrust yourself into the hands of One who loves you and who has already brought you much healing. If He was so skillful and sensitive in the minor procedures, will He suddenly be sloppy and harsh in the major? . . ."

We have an unlimited capacity to grow. While we Christians could hardly accept as virtues some of the traits or "strengths" endorsed by certain human potential or developmental psychologists, we certainly need to re-examine a basic premise of theirs that life is either growth or stagnation. As it unfolds before me, it presents problems which either of themselves, or because of weaknesses they make me aware of within myself, will cause me discomfort. The ache of exertion, or just plain old pain. If I choose to face that discomfort, ache or pain, work with it and honestly attempt to overcome its cause, I will grow. If I deny it, evade dealing with it, or seek refuge in the most available pleasures or comforts as an avoidance technique, I will fail to grow and may even bond myself to the immature and superficial.

A stirring up of human courage, a commitment to spartan self-discipline, and a muscular display of will power seem to be at the heart of most recommended antidotes to non-growth. Some people think that a Christian version of this just includes a dash of prayer and the initiation of other new spiritual disciplines, in addition to the above. No wonder they are scared off. Even though some of my spiritual charges have been told otherwise, a hundred times over — they just can't quite shake the impression that any further growth will demand of them more asceticism, greater athleticism of spirit, than all the sweating and straining required of a candidate for the Olympics.

It isn't, of course, that Grace abolishes the exercise of will power, the determination of free choice. It's somewhat rather like the difference between rowing a boat across an expanse of water or sailing across. We lift our little sails (our want to be receptive and guided) and the Spirit of God fills them with His breath of love which is ever, nonetheless, a mighty wind.

And so it all begins, maintains itself and even climaxes with the first of the beatitudes. *Poverty of spirit,* a sense of one's inner impotence apart from His Spirit, an awareness that apart from the Father's love for us and the Son's hope in us we can do nothing. "Let us begin again, for up 'till now we have done nothing," was the way St. Francis put it, and the attitude he lived by — daily.

What a grace to start each day a fresh, just as humbly, just as unsure of our virtue as the day we first came to Him, just simply surrendered to whatever He might ask. What wisdom to have come to the realization that we need Him no less (now that the original problem is on the mend) and may well need His further healing intervention for our more serious ailments; that we are ever to be "beggars before His Spirit."[4]

But the first beatitude is not only the threshold to conversion, a new life in His Spirit and the key to our wholeness. It is also the doorway to those special characteristics, those Christ-like qualities that so succinctly summarize who we are called to be, become, and keep on becoming ever authentically in Him: *an openness to mourn and grieve* over what is not right in our world that will not leave us comforted until we have prayed and worked to make things right; *a gentleness of spirit* that doesn't aggressively insist upon its own way but firmly asserts itself in favor of God's loving will ever being accomplished; *a heart that hungers and thirsts,* and keeps on hungering and thirsting, for righteousness — not for the sake of promoting our own homemade holiness or displaying our virtue — but rather out of a yearning for God's own life to always be springing up within us, so that it can then be constantly channeled beyond us; a righteousness of living in God's heart and from His heart, namely, an insistence upon the establishment of a "true justice of heart" which can only be faintly suggested by the best of human legislation and even the Ten Commandments themselves, as Eberhard Arnold notes [5]; *a longing to become ever more filled with compassion,* therefore, so that out of a new-found freedom from our own personal pain, from our guilts and from self-hatreds we can, in this new spiritedness that comes from Him, find ourselves unafraid to enter into a sharing in the pain of His Heart; a sharing in the world's suffering, a heartfelt solidarity with those who need our prayers, need our love, need us to brother them and sister them, in Christ; *a willingness to have that heart of ours rendered ever more pure in His sight* — purified of splintered and selfish motives and drawn ever more surely into that wholeheartedness that seeks His face; that singleheartedness that seeks His will; that tenderheartedness that seeks out the next problem we are to plead for prayerfully, or the next person we are to minister to in His name; *the want to be there as His peacemakers,* coming to believe that if God was in Christ reconciling the world to Himself in all its affection for power and violence, than Christ is similarly in us to continue that work of reconciliation between man and our fellow man and man and God; that God who cannot stop forgiving and empowering us to forgive, by not counting people's sins against them (cf. 2Cor.5:16-12); finally, *by strengthening us to patiently and lovingly withstand all opposition* to this "craziness," this "insane" way of responding to the world's ills and life's problems; by making us folks who can handle the real insanity of such an inconceivable affection's being ignored; such an unimaginable compassion being dismissed as irrelevant and turned away, along with ourselves, it's emissaries, now and again.

This last of the beatitudes is no afterthought, by the way, and it should not frighten us. It, too, like the others contains a call to be blessed in the present and blessed mightily. It is an invitation to know that salvation is not just God delivering us from the pain of our guilt, along with these fears that our being here doesn't matter. Salvation, when all is said and done, is also God being there with us in the midst of our pain, the pain which for one reason or another cannot all be taken away right now, but which we no longer have to suffer alone.

The God who rescued the Hebrews from their slavery in Egypt and silenced their enemies, also revealed Himself to be a saving God by comforting their descendants centuries later, as they languished in exile. *I am still with you and I am still for you*, He declared, in effect, even before He came to promise a further deliverance.[6] Jesus revealed the same thing to us and more, in and through the Cross. He showed us His Father's wounded heart. A heart tortured by humanity's rejection of Him, now embodied and shown forth to all in the rejection endured by His Son.

Jesus gave us a glimpse into the vulnerability, the wound-a-bility of His Eternal Father's love, as well as that of His own. That Father and Son felt (and still feel rejection) just as much as we do — far, far more, of course. They hate and dread that pain of pains, somehow, just as we do. Only they don't close down. They don't close off. They don't numb their hearts' ability to feel grief, or allow them to degenerate into scar-tissue. They just keep on hoping in the one who rejects them. They just keep on believing the best of the one who spurns their love. They just keep on loving, as they extend invitation after invitation to that individual who continues to think that it is a joke. Jesus even now still offers His cross-prayer and it still meets with acceptance: "Father, forgive them, they don't know what they're doing."[7] (cf. Lk.23:34; Heb.7:25; 1Jn.1:9)

When you or I attempt to do things like that because of them; when you or I refuse to harden against those who reject our love and our attempts to reconcile; when you or I say to the one who betrayed us so cruelly: "it is as if you never did it," and, somehow. are enabled to mean that, then, *that too* is Redemption. That too, is Salvation. That, too, is the Kingdom of God continuing to create new worlds out of chaos; resurrected relationships out of former alienations; fresh loves out of old hates; compassion out of indifference; suffering with and for others, out of those things which once had to be endured in solitude.

Yes, Salvation means that all the pain will be abolished some-day and that all the death we give Him will be turned into eternal life. All things, He promises, He will work together for good — even the bad things. But in the meantime, He is grieved over our griefs, pained over our pain, and wants us to know that He suffers with us, as well as for us. Because servants of His show us that, by the way they live and the way they are there for us in our pain, we are enabled to know that it is true.

The Holy Spirit is called a down-payment on our Salvation, a foretaste of what is to come. So also might those who let Him make the beatitudes of Jesus, the hallmarks of their relating and accomplishing. They show us visibly that Salvation is still with us and that someday it will surely come in all its fullness.

Of all the varied and powerful descriptions of Salvation we are given in Scripture, the image of healing is surely one of the most touching. Liberation from slavery, comfort in our exile, being brought home, God's refusal to accept our refusal in the vulnerability of His love are also profoundly beautiful and awesomely encouraging word-pictures. There are others, also, but we cannot touch on them all here. None of them can ever exhaust the richness of Salvation's significance. Each of them unfolds another incredible aspect of what we are offered in and through that Saving Lord who is Himself our Salvation (cf. 1 Cor. 1:30).

By now it should also be clear that we never intended to equate that healing which removes people's childhood scars, traumatic memories, defense mechanisms; which leads people out of immaturity into maturity, from stagnancy to growth, with what happens to us as a result the free gift of His saving grace. Psychotherapy, then, is not a simple synonym for Salvation. Many of these therapeutic happenings can and do occur without a client's ever consciously turning to God. (I don't believe, however, that productive therapy can ever happen without the presence of that Unseen Healer working behind the scenes. In such an instance, however, getting un-hung up from hang-ups, or experiences of release and healing may well serve as a prelude to conversion — a conversion that eventually happens (or never comes about, for reasons of stubbornness, etc.)

We have, in effect, argued here that such breakthroughs into mental and emotional health most certainly ought to issue forth as a result of one's conversion to Christ, ought to be included as part of that ongoing process, namely, that lifelong turning towards God and His will and away from selfishness and willfulness. Otherwise, our personality scars and character flaws will end up weaving themselves into that bushel basket which filters out, and even blacks out the light whose brightness and warmth we've been explicitly given to reflect outwards into a world so desperately in need to it (cf. Mt. 5:15).

There are also people, perhaps even people you've known, remarkably free of inner trauma, refreshingly non-defensive, disarmingly outgoing, amazingly clear-headed in perspective or consistently polite, who, nonetheless, are unaware that God loves them. Whatever therapy life has provided them with or whatever benefits they've derived from a relatively trauma-free childhood, etc., has still not brought them Salvation. Blessed as they are with emotional and mental balance, they may end up thinking that they thereby would be untrue to that balance of theirs by leaning on the Lover. Health of body and mind (not to mention health of pocketbook) can conspire to leave many of us complacently indifferent to our need to know His love and our need to love others out of that love. Such blessings hide from us our lostness; they can rob us of our awareness of not only other people's poverty but even our own. Namely, our poverty of grace and what it frees us to be and do.

Then, too, there are Christians who have accepted Jesus's reconciling love from the Cross and are grateful for that, as well as giving similar evidence of the qualities just noted above. Are they to be thought of as being "saved," as well as being healed of heart and mind? Not if they're too well adjusted to *this* society.

I'm not making any judgement, now, about whether or not they're presently eligible for Heaven. I'm rather referring to being saved, in the full sense of the word. In the sense that Jesus surely intended it to be experienced in the here and now. Salvation as not only being healed *of* something but being healed *for* something. Salvation as not just my being loved by God but as your being loved by God through me. Salvation not just as my being reconciled to God, but Christ in me reconciling you to Himself, as well as to me. Salvation as my being freed from personal pain so that I am now free to share in your personal pain. Salvation, then, as a state of ongoing *maladjustment* to the kingdom of this world, insofar as it is mired in dishonesty, powerism, selfish consumerism, neglect of the poor and exploitation of the weak, or indifference to His healing presence, even as I cry out to Him for, and work with Him for, the coming of the kingdom of Heaven. For, if such evils can be resisted, exorcised and even begun to be undone, step-by-step, then Heaven's kingdom is already breaking in upon us and the world is given a faint glimpse of what is fully to come.

This chapter has loosely wrapped itself around a burden this writer has for his little flock, a Christian Community that doesn't always make it. Isn't always consistent or thoroughly Christian. Isn't always true community. This focus, as we've suggested, is not rooted in a despair over those people's weaknesses or prompted by a vengefulness over their periodic stubbornness. They are brothers and sisters I know and love; and without giving them credit for it when I described just above the beautiful Christian ideal of people incarnating the spirit of the Sermon of the Mount, I can honestly say that I have been awed and overjoyed to see them wonderfully, frequently, and even to some degree of unison, provide precisely that witness.

And yet, switching to the vocabulary of the psychological world, I am sometimes forced to say, on the other hand, that their knittedness seems to be in danger of coming undone by neurosis; their unity at times, in danger of corrosive deterioration on account of denial and projection, most especially. Human beings that they are, when they fail to look to Him; when they fail to focus on His call to a constant commitment on ongoing healing; more often than not, they end up trying to reform in others the very flaws and foibles they are blind to in themselves.

Jesus, just in case we take our call to individually let the light, His light in us, shine forth into the kingdom of darkness as His final word to us on the matter, suddenly switches images on us in the Sermon on the Mount: A *city* on a hill cannot be hidden. A *city* of *lights* is required, if the world's darkness is to be effectively countered. A *community allowing itself to be illumined, as community*; a community wanting to shine forth as a collectivity is Jesus' master plan for casting out the powers of darkness, and the establishing of the new order of love's kingdom.[8]

The new personhood we are called to exemplify cannot happen unless we are also committed to being a part of a new peoplehood. The new unity of a personality freed of fragmentation is, in Jesus eye's, a tragic waste if it isn't harnessed to a new determination to counteract the world's bent on fragmentation. The new healedness of heart and mind is ultimately wasted if it isn't harnessed in the service of *society's* being healed. Our individually being brought into the environment of His affection and compassion runs the risk of souring into the obscenely selfish if we don't allow ourselves to become impassioned with a fierce desire to see everybody else equally blessed, as well.

Many of us seem to be convinced that Heaven will be something like a movie theatre. As we sit there in the Pearly Gate Palace, we will get to watch God in technicolor, 3-D, and sensesurround. We will undoubtedly be so mesmerized by such an overwhelming vision, such an astounding experience that, just as when we used to watch the old flicks down on earth, we will forget that anyone is behind us or in front of us or beside us, to left or to right. The huge figures on the huge screen will capture our full attention.

But is that really the way it will be? Prayer meetings in which all folding chairs are arranged concentrically; or churches-in-the-round give us, I'm convinced, a far more accurate symbol of what is to come. When true prayer happens in such places, at times we will find ourselves almost totally focused on Him; but, then, just as appropriately, we will find ourselves focused on one another. Sometimes, on how much we need each other. Sometimes, on how much we are all getting blessed together. Sometimes, on how He almost seems to fill the spaces between us. Sometimes, on how much we fear each other, especially coming closer to each other. Sometimes, on how much we need to forgive each other. Sometimes, on how *we've* let our commitment to one another slacken or become diluted.

Even though we know that any of these negative elements will be fully turned inside out in the life to come; already we sense the call to let Him show us the beginning of that. To put it a little differently. He will in no way come between what is between us, when what is between us is His love. And, conversely, what is properly between us – our respect for and rejoicing in one another's unique sonship and daughterhood will in no way distract us from the enjoyment of His presence, either here or hereafter.

The other side of our resistance to this desire to be built into His temple, stone by stone, or knitted into His body, joint to ligament, member to member, might come from another false impression. The same world which bombards us with the "need" for exaggerated individualism, also unblinkingly calls us to embrace what is nearly its opposite-stifling conformity: "All you individuals out there doing your own thing – come now and be herded into the pastures of majority opinion, where we all dress ourselves in the fashions of the times . . ."

The prospect of artificial uniformity and its plastic, superficial way of living; or memories of how society, or even church, taught us the "virtue" of lockstep, and discipline of not ever allowing ourselves to listen for, let alone march to, the beat of a different drummer. So many of us, so need to be healed of that hurt, that relentless pressure to conform, whereby we sadly betray our uniqueness or write off the relevancy of our specialness. Along with the unique and special gifts we have to give and contributions we have to make.

Wisdom for living in the world as He would have us live; wisdom for kingdom living needs to be above all else to be a wisdom of true relating, or "the rules of relationship" as Richard Rohr says.[9] In addition to what has already been said about making the Lord's vulnerability our own, I will end by leaving you with a few favorite insights that in their own way sum up what we need to know about growing in intimacy and relatedness.

The first is a piece of wisdom from John of the Cross which I'd never seen until recently, but now many contemporary writers are quoting. It goes something like this: "Where you find no love, plant love, then love will be there . . ." That quote becomes extra special to me, because I know that it can only be the fruit of one who realized growth painfully by entering into the risk of relationship.

John's biographers tell us that while novice-master of the Carmelites, he was once noticed to be verging on ecstasy, while contemplating what appeared to be an ordinary rock which he held in his hand. One of his novices ventured to question him later about what he had experienced while gazing upon the rock. He admitted to having somehow seen the presence of God radiating out of that stone, the God who holds all things in existence. He added further, whether out of either blunt irony or biting humor, I do not know something along the lines of: "And furthermore, rocks don't hassle you, the way people do . . ."[10]

At some point in time, this saintly man had moved from the "easy" love of God in nature, to the more difficult love of God in people. Instead of turning away, when we can only see their hatred or walled-off-ness, we have to call on His help to bridge the gulf between us in love. By faith we have to see that somewhere down there, underneath all the hurt, is hidden a candle wick, which the lamp of His love can ignite through us. Through our persistent prayer and relentless reaching out. Or, rather, *His* pleading and caring through us.

> Put on then, as God's chosen ones, holy and beloved, compassion, kindness, lowliness, meekness, and patience, forbearing one another, and, if one has a complaint against another, forgiving each other; as the Lord has forgiven you, you must also forgive. And above all 'these put on love, which binds everything together in perfect harmony. And let the peace of Christ rule in your hearts, to which you were called in the one body. And be thankful. Let the word of Christ dwell in you richly, as you teach and admonish one another in all wisdom. . . (Col. 3:12-16, RSV)

We are empowered, Paul tells us, to instruct and admonish those who have hurt us or are pulling away from us out of nothing less than "wisdom make perfect" as other translations render verse 16.

How do we avail ourselves of "perfect" wisdom? Doesn't only God possess perfect wisdom? He also is the only one to possess perfect love, but John in like manner informs us that we are able to recognize ourselves as its recipients as we increasingly trust in its power to free us of all our fears (1 Jn. 4:17-18). We are also able to open our hearts to be shown what we need to be shown, precisely when we experience our frustration at being really or apparently put off by someone we love. Only He really knows fully the heart of the one who is bringing us pain. Only He knows how to most effectively reach that heart and free it to love aright and afresh.

The tragedy of so many deteriorating relationships is that people keep postponing confrontation when they sense that they are being wronged and then when they can hear the pain no longer, they erupt into a tirade of criticism which is rarely constructive, edged with so much bitterness prone to self-righteousness and almost certain to widen the gulf rather than close it.

But what else can we do but confront out of our hurt, criticize from our pain? If we are Christians, we can confront from *redeemed hurt*, criticize constructively out of a sense that Jesus is gracing us to speak the truth in love. If we might only slightly paraphrase what Paul said to the Colossians: "When you experience the pain of rejection, bring it to prayer, bring it to Christ. Let Him comfort you with a fresh knowing that even if the whole world has rejected you, He hasn't. Let Him bless you with a fresh compassion for those you believed to have taken advantage of you; a new awareness of the fact that you also haven't always been wholehearted and faithful in your loving, and that, therefore, you have also been guilty of similar lapses. Claim His peace and don't stop claiming it until you've got it. Pray Jesus' Calvary prayer for them: "Father, forgive them, they didn't know what they were doing." Pray, finally, for a sense of His timing and then confront humbly, forgivingly, peacefully, and out of all the love you can find.

When we do that, we are beginning to learn about wisdom made perfect. The destructive put-down criticism the world resorts to under such circumstances is, perhaps, all the wisdom it has access to. But how tragic when Jesus' disciples, who ought to know better, act as if the path to reconciliation and the power of it were unavailable to them.

The final piece of wisdom I'd like to share is simply a bit more on the wisdom of forgiveness. A few years back something within me kept calling me to pray during the election of the new pope. I was not able to immediately accept this prompting as the Spirit's call. At that point in my life, I'd been suffering from quite a bit of disillusionment with institutional Christianity. Perhaps only newly-sparked attempts at forming community, charismatic or otherwise, would afford me the fellowship of true brotherhood and sisterhood in Christ. That narrow view of mine was born out of some hurts I'd sustained as a result of what I deemed to be the not-very-inspired response of churchly authority to what I saw as my own areas of personal giftedness.

I thought I had thoroughly forgiven those whom I believed to have wronged me. After all, I prayed for them every day. But I now found myself resisting this call to pray for the cardinals in conclave. So vigorously, in fact, that I was led to suspect that there must still be further pockets of resentment, well-buried , somewhere deep within me. It had only disguised itself as a kind of generalized disdain for what I judged to be the top-heavy over-structuredness and often arbitrary authoritarianism of contemporary Catholicism. By and large, it was still *people* that I had it in for, I now came to see.

So I began my repentance by following that inspired summons to pray that they'd pick the best man to be the new pope. Each day I prayed for hours. At a certain moment, I felt that the burden was somehow no longer there. Maybe they'd elected a new pope. So I turned on the TV. Sure enough, there he was, Albino Luciani, John Paul, the First. The man who'd soon be remembered as the September Pope, the shepherd of the whole church that was only given one month to show his stuff.

At first, all I felt was annoyance: "Who's that?!" I scrutinized his obviously Italian features, but couldn't identify him. Obviously, not one of the front runners: "Just what we need. More narrowmindedness from some out-of-touch backwater . . ."— The bitterness hadn't all disappeared during my prayer marathon, apparently.

But something within called me up short. *Look at the man*, that inner stirring seemed to say. I did, and I saw a smile, the smile of love. I knew that he was loving me. I knew that it was Jesus in him loving me.

Accept him as your brother, I was somehow instructed. It wasn't very hard. That bitterness now drained out of me. The despair of Jesus' ever being able to ever work within a Catholicism not always very Christian left me. A holy man had somehow become the Holy Father, for real. Once again, I felt like I was growing. Once again, I'd known the touch of the Healer.

NOTES

Introduction

1. Bernard J. Tyrrell, S.J., *Christotherapy II* (Ramsey, New Jersey: Paulist Press, 1982), P.70.

2. See Bernard J. Tyrrell, S.J., *Christotherapy: Healing Through Enlightenment* (New York: Seabury Press, 1975); *Christotherapy II.* also John A. Loftus, S.J., *The Integration of Psychology and Religion: An Uneasy Alliance* (Whitinsville, Massachusetts: Affirmation Books, 1982); John M. Mc Donagh, *Christian Psychology: Toward a New Synthesis* (New York: Crossroad Publishing Co., 1982).

3. Abraham J. Heschel, *God in Search of Man: A Philosophy of Judaism* (New York: Farnar Straus and Giroux, 1955).

4. Walter J. Brueggemann, *In Man We Trust: The Neglected Side of Biblical Faith* (Atlanta; John Knox Press, 1972, p.25. See also pp. 18, 24 on the meaning of Biblical wisdom.

5. J. B. Phillips, *Making Men Whole* (London: Collins Fontana Books, 1955), p.75.

Chapter One

1. "Man and "Woman" are literal translations of the Hebrew names, Adam and Eve.

2. See Victor E. Frankl, *The Unconscious God* (New York: Simon and Schuster, 1975); Carl G. Jung, *Modern Man in Search of a Soul* (New York: Harcourt, Brace, Jovanovich, 1933); Gerard May, M.D., *Will and Spirit* (San Francisco: Harper and Row, 1982); Rainer Funk, *Erich Fromm: The Courage to be Human* (New York: Continuum Publishing Co., 1982); Abraham Maslow, *Religious, Values and Peak-Experiences* (New York: Viking Press, 1970).

3. Earl Jabay, *The God Players* (Grand Rapids, Zondervan House, 1969), p. 67.

Chapter Two

1. Robert Short, *The Gospel According to Peanuts* (Richmond: John Knox Press, 1964), p. 43.

2. See Joseph Pieper, *About Love* (Chicago, Franciscan Herald Press, 1974). Pieper's recounting of some of the key insights of Thomas Aquinas on love are most clear and extremely valuable.

3. John Powell, *Unconditional Love* (Niles, Illinois: Argus Communications, 1978), p. 66.

4. Conrad Baars, M.D., *Born Only Once* (Chicago, Franciscan Herald Press, 1975), p. 99.

5. Carl Jung, *Modern Man in Search of a Soul* (New York: Harvest/H.B.J. Books, 1933) p. 235.

Chapter Three

1. Robert H. Bonthius, *Christian Paths to Self-Acceptance* (New York: King's Crown Press, 1948), p. 178.

2. Martin Buber, *The Way of Man* (Secaucus, New Jersey: Citadel Press, 1966), p. 12.

3. Keith Miller, *The Becomers* (Waco, Texas: Word Books, 1977), p. 40.

4. Eugene Kennedy, *The Pain of Being Human* (Garden City, N.Y.: Doubleday Image Books, 1974), p. 93.

5. Rollo May, *The Art of Counseling* (Nashville: Abingdon, 1939), p. 45.

6. Miller, Chapters 8, 9 and 10.

7. Lawrence Crabb, *Basic Principles of Biblical Counseling* (Grand Rapids: Zondervan House, 1977) and *Effective Biblical Counseling* (Grand Rapids: Zondervan House, 1975).

8. Eric Berne, *Games People Play* (New York: Grove Press, 1964) and Thomas Harris, *I'm O.K. — You're O.K.* (New York: Harper and Row, 1969).

9. William Coleman, *Those Pharisees* (New York: Hawthorne Books, 1977).

Chapter Four

1. There is a sense, of course, in which it is correct. Namely, when the saying is simply seen as a summons to work and pray with all of one's heart. The problem is that it rarely seems to be understood this way.

2. J.B. Phillips, *Making Men Whole*, p. 41.

3. J.B. Phillips, *Your God is Too Small* (New York: Macmillan, 1961) and Morton T. Kelsey, *Myth, History, and Faith: The Remythologizing of Christianity* (Ramsey, New Jersey: Paulist Press, 1974), Chapter One.

4. Abraham J. Heschel, *The Prophets* (New York: Harper Torchbooks, 1969), 2 vols.

5. Wayne Dyer, *Your Erroneous Zones* (New York: Avon Books, 1976), chapter 10.

6. Lawrence F. Carew, *The Indwelling Intercessor* (Danbury, Connecticut: Community of the Cross Publications, 1978), p. 63.

7. E. Stanley Jones, *Victory Through Surrender* (Nashville: Abingdon, 1966), p. 77.

8. Erich Fromm, *To Have or To Be?* (New York: Harper and Row, 1976), p. 42.

9. The author is an inveterate listener to the many taped Bible teachings and retreats presented by this gifted speaker. I regret that I am unable to give precise references to insights of Father Rohr's (recalled from memory) which I occasionally refer to throughout the book. Most of his talks are available on cassette from St. Anthony Messenger Press, Cincinnati, Ohio; Christian Media, Ogden, Utah; and NCR Cassettes, Kansas City, Missouri.

Chapter Five

1. Andrew Murray, *The Two Covenants* (Fort Washington, Pennsylvania: Christian Literature Crusade, N.D.), pp. 3-59.

2. Abrahem J. Heschel, *Between God and Man: An Interpretation of Judaism*, ed. Fritz A. Rothschild, (New York: The Free Press, 1959), P.201.

3. Paul Tournier, *The Naming of Persons* (New York: Harper and Row, 1975), pp. 99-100. Also see Tournier, *The Meaning of Persons* (London: SCM Press, 1957), chapter 3.

4. Abraham J. Heschel, *The Sabbath* (New York: Farrar, Straus and Giroux, 1951), p. 14.

5. Martin Buber, *I and Thou*, trans. Walter Kaufmann (New York: Charles Scribners Sons, 1970), p. 158.

Chapter Six

1. John Sanford, *The Kingdom Within* (Philadelphia: J.B. Lippincott Co., 1970), pp. 77-79.

2. Sanford, pp. 147,151.

3. For a far more thorough and truly inspiring treatment of this passage from a point of view that integrates the spiritual and psychological, see Adrian Van Kaam, *The Woman at the Well* (Denville, New Jersey; Dimension Books, 1976).

4. See note 10, Chapter Four.

Chapter Seven

1. Ruth Carter Stapleton, *The Gift of Inner Healing* (Waco, Texas: Word Books, 1976); *The Experience of Inner Healing* (Waco, Texas: Word Books 1977) and Dennis and Matthew Linn, SJ., *Healing Life's Hurts: Healing Memories Through Five Stages of Forgiveness* (Ramsey, New Jersey: Paulist Press, 1978).

2. Mother Elise Euverard, C.H.S., "Children's Concepts of God as Related to Other Authority Figures," Diss. Columbia Teachers' College, 1955.

3. Sanford, pp. 184-7.

4. Linns, Chapter 6.

Chapter Eight

1. Thomas Kane, *The Healing Touch of Affirmation* (Whitinsville, Massachusetts: Affirmation Books, 1976), p. 23.

2. Bernard Bush, "I Have Called You by Name." in *Intimacy: Issues of Emotional Living in an Age of Stress for Clergy and Religious*, ed. Anna Polcino, M.D. (Whitinsville, Massachusetts: Affirmation Books, 1978), p. 41.

3. Powell, p. 66.

4. Conrad Baars, M.D., *Affirming Living and Healing*, Ogden Utah: Christian Media, 1979. (cassette lecture).

5. William Kilpatrick, *Identity and Intimacy* (New York: Delta Books, 1975). Kilpatrick has since resumed the practice of Christianity. His change of attitude is described in *Psychological Seduction: The*

Failure of Modern Psychology (Nashville: Thomas Nelson, 1983). Also see "Professions of Faith: Peter John Kreeft and William Kirk Kilpatrick" by Dana Narramore in Boston College Magazine, Fall 1984, p. 14.

6. Kilpatrick, *Identity*, p. 24.

7. Erik Erikson, *Identity and the Life Cycle* (New York: International Universities Press, Inc., 1959).

8. Kilpatrick, *Identity*, p. 9.

9. Rollo May, *Man's Search For Himself* (New York: Delta Books, 1953), pp. 160-1.

10. Kilpatrick, *Identity*, pp. 24-28.

11. Kilpatrick, *Identity*, p. 32.

12. Kilpatrick, *Identity*, p. 24.

Chapter Nine

1. Robert Jay Lifton has carefully documented numerous cases of brainwash victims in *Thought Reform and the Psychology of Totalism: A Study of Brainwashing in China* (New York: Norton, 1963).

2. Erich Fromm, *Escape From Freedom* (New York: Avon Books, 1965), pp. 177-178.

3. Eric Hoffer, *The True Believer* (New York: Harper and Row Perennial Library, 1966), p. 37.

4. Hoffer, pp. 94-5.

5. Hoffer, p. 76.

6. Thomas Merton, *Seeds of Contemplation* (New York: Dell, 1953), pp. 18-24.

7. H. Wheeler Robinson, *Corporate Personality in Ancient Israel* (Philadelphia: Fortress Press, 1980), p. 52.

8. Robinson, p. 53.

9. Harry Emerson Fosdick, *On Being a Real Person* (New York: Harper and Row, 1943), p. 102.

Chapter Ten

1. Fosdick, p. 108.

2. Tournier, *The Meaning of Persons*, p. 22, Chapters 2 and three.

3. May, *Man's Search*, p. 15.

4. William Barclay, *New Testament Words* (Philadelphia: Westminster Press, 1974), p. 142.

5. Adrian Van Kaam, *On Being Yourself: Reflections on Spirituality and Originality* (Denville, New Jersey: Dimension Books, 1972), Chapter 11. Also see Van Kaam, *In Search of Spiritual Identity* (Denville, New Jersey: Dimension Books, 1975), p. 183.

6. Van Kaam, *On Being*, p. 93.

7. Philomena Agudo, "Intimacy with the Self vs. Self-Alienation" in *Intimacy: Issues of Emotional Living in an Age of Stress for Clergy and Religious*, ed. Anna Polcino, M.D. (Whitinsville, Massacuusetts: Affirmation Books, 1978), Chapter one.

8. Donald Goergen, *The Sexual Celibate* (Garden City, New York: Doubleday Image Books, 1979), pp. 24-28.

9. In particular reference to what many Scripture scholars refer to as the "theology of the Yahwist."

10. Goergen, pp. 48-55.

11. The masculine—feminine contrast of adjectives used here are employed in a slightly different context by W. Harold Grant, Magdala Thompson and Thomas E. Clarke in *From Image to Likeness* (Ramsey New Jersey: Paulist Press, 1983), p. 109.

12. Goergen, p. 81-90.

13. Leanne Payne, *The Broken Image: Restoring Personal Wholeness Through Healing Prayer* (Westchester, Illinois: Cornerstone Books, 1981).

14. For a psychiatric evaluation of homosexuality, viewing it as a pathology in need of healing, we recommend along with Payne: Ruth T. Barnhouse, M.D., *Homosexuality: A Symbolic Confusion* (New York: Seabury Press, 1979).

15. Fosdick, p. 28.

16. Fosdick, pp. 41,47.

17. Fosdick, p. 42.

18. Fosdick, p. 26.

19. Fosdick, p. 48.

20. Fosdick, p. 32.

21. Hans W. Frei, *The Identity of Jesus Christ: The Hermeneutical Bases of Dogmatic Theology* (Philadelphia: Fortress Press, 1975), p. 160.

Chapter Eleven

1. The treatment here of the meaning of the New Testament Greek words for "body," "soul," "spirit," "flesh" and "heart" is based upon, but does not slavishly follow, definitions given in *The Theological Dictionary of New Testament Theology*, ed. Gerhard Kittel (Grand Rapids: Eerdmans, 1964) and *The New International Dictionary of New Testament Theology*, ed. Colin Brown (Grand Rapids: Zondervan, 1975). Also see, *Theological Woodbook of the Old Testament*, ed. R. Laird Harris (Chicago: Moody, 1980).

2. Charles Davis, *Body as Spirit: The Nature of Religious Feeling* (New York: Seabury Press, 1976), pp. 48-54.

3. R.D.G Owen, *Body and Soul: A Study on the Christian View of Man* (Philadelphia: Westminster Press, 1956), p. 59. Also see pp. 216-17.

4. "Heart," as Conrad Baars, M.D. has astutely suggested (in the light of the categories of Thomistic thought), is what happens when our intuitive or contemplative "mind" (our ability to know "things" beyond the reaches of reason or senses, most particularly "things" of God) unites itself with those emotions which automatically react to what is good or attractive (love, desire and joy). The resulting interplay of this special kind of knowing and those specific feelings result in "heart." Baars, *Feeling and Healing Your Emotions* (Plainfield, New Jersey: Logos International, 1979), p. 32.

5. Abraham J. Heschel, *God in Search of Man*, p. 397.

6. Everett Shostrom and Dan Montgomery, *Healing Love* (Nashville: Abingdon, 1978), p. 128.

7. May, *Man's Search*, p. 53.

Chapter Twelve

1. Richard Fowler, *Stages of Faith: The Psychology of Human Development and the Quest for Meaning* (San Francisco: Harper and Row, 1981), p. 4.

2. Crabb, *Basic Principles* and *Effective Biblical*

3. Thomas Merton, *Zen and the Birds of Appetite* (New York: New Directions, 1968), p. 83.

4. Albert Ellis, *Humanistic Psychotherapy* (New York: McGraw Hill, 1973), p. 16.

5. Ellis, pp. 32-3.

6. Ellis, p. 38.

7. Crabb, *Basic Principles*, p. 80.

8. Epictetus, *The Discourses As Reported by Arran, The Manual and Fragments*, trans., W.A. Oldfather, 2 vols. (Cambridge, Massachusetts: Harvard University Press, 1928), Vol I, p. 113.

9. Craig Dykstra, *Vision and Character: A Christian Educator's Alternative to Kohlberg* (Ramsey New Jersey: Paulist Press, 1981), pp. 118-119.

10. If anyone is able to inform the author of this quotation's source, he would be happy to give credit in any further editions of this work.

11. See Donald Gowan's simple but powerful commentary, *The Triumph of Faith in Habbakuk* (Atlanta: John Knox Press, 1976).

Chapter Thirteen

1. Conrad Baars, M.D., *Feeling and Healing; Psychic Wholeness and Healing* [with Anna Terruwe, M.D.] (Staten Island: Alba House, 1981).

2. Baars, *Born Only Once*, p. 86.

3. Baars, *Feeling and Healing*, p. 12.

4. Baars, *Feeling and Healing*, pp. 15-19.

5. Baars, Terruwe, *Psychic Wholeness*, p. 13.

6. Baars, *Feeling and Healing*, p. 19.

7. Baars, *Feeling and Healing*, pp. 5; 35-36.

8. Baars, *Feeling and Healing*, pp. 19-21.

9. Baars, *Feeling and Healing*, pp. 35-6, 102.

10. Baars, *Psychic Wholeness* and *Feeling and Healing*.

11. Baars, Terruwe, *Psychic Wholeness*, p. 37.

12. Baars, *Feeling and Healing*, p. 125.

13. Baars, *Feeling and Healing*, p. 125.

14. Baars, Terruwe, *Psychic Wholeness*, p. 99.

15. Davis, p. 71.

16. Davis, p. 43.

17. Alexander Schneiders, *Anarchy of Feeling* (New York: Sheed and Ward, 1963).

18. Ernest Larsen, *How to Understand and Overcome Depression* (Ligouri, Missouri: Ligouri Publications, 1977), p. 46.

19. Schneiders, p. 169.

20. Heschel, *The Prophets*, Vol. I, Chapter I, esp. p. 5.

21. *Guilt: Issues of Emotional Living in an Age of Stress for Clergy and Religious*, ed. Kathleen E. Kelly (Whitinsville, Massachusetts: Affirmation Books, 1980) Chapters 1 and 2, esp., p. 39.

22. Joseph L. Hert, "Guilt Feelings: What Do They Accomplish?" in *Guilt*, ed. Kelley, pp. 128,129.

23. Vincent Bilotta, III, "Guilty For Betraying Who I Am" in *Guilt*, ed. Kelley, p. 101.

24. Jurgen Moltmann, *Experiences of God* (Philadelphia: Fortress Press, 1980), p. 19.

Chapter Fourteen

1. This description of faith is Richard Rohr's, (See Chapter 4, note 1).

2. A brilliant treatment of how the fear of the pain of facing up to one's personal hurts operates in such a way as to rob people of healings they might otherwise receive may be found in psychiatrist M. Scott Peck's *The Road Less Travelled* (New York: Simon and Schuster, 1978).

3. *Twelve Steps and Twelve Traditions* (New York: Alcoholics Anonymous World Services, Inc., 1953).

4. Eberhard Arnold, *Salt and Light: Talks and Writings on the Sermon on the Mount* (Rifton, New York: The Plough Publishing House, 1962), p. 7.

5. Arnold, pp. 8,18.

6. God's being "with us" and "for us" is seen by Walter Brueggemann to be a simple but repetitive theme of both the Old and New Testaments in *The Bible Makes Sense* (Winona, Minnesota: St. Mary's College Press, 1978).

7. This is not meant to contradict the traditional Christian position that, sooner or later, we all are required to make a final and irrevocable decision to accept or reject that invitation.

8. Joseph Donders, *The Peace of Jesus: Reflections on the Gospel for the A-cycle*, (Maryknoll, New York: Orbis Books, 1983), pp. 64-67.

9. See Chapter Four, note 10.

10. This story is recounted from memory of a biography of John read many years ago. I have taken the liberty of employing American slang in my paraphrase of the saint's remark.